EL
NORTE

EL NORTE

THE CUISINE OF NORTHERN MEXICO

James W. Peyton

RED CRANE   RED CRANE BOOKS   SANTA FE

New Edition

Printed in the United States of America

Photographs: Michael O'Shaughnessy

Illustrations: Andrea Peyton

Food Stylist: James W. Peyton

Cover and book design: Jos. Trautwein

Library of Congress Cataloging-in-Publication Data
Peyton, James W.
　　　El norte : the cuisine of northern Mexico / James W. Peyton. — New ed.
　　　　　p.　cm.
　　　Includes index.
　　　ISBN 1–878610–58–9
　　　1. Cookery, Mexican.　I. Title.
TX716.M4P492　1995　　　　　　　　95-14930
641.5972´1—dc20　　　　　　　　　CIP

Red Crane Books
2008 Rosina St., Suite B
Santa Fe, New Mexico 87505

DEDICATION

*It is only fitting that this book be dedicated to the
people of northern Mexico, who have provided so much joy.
We have a great deal more to learn from them
about living than just their recipes.*

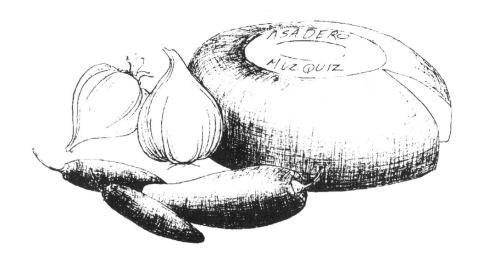

Contents

STATES OF
NORTHERN MEXICO

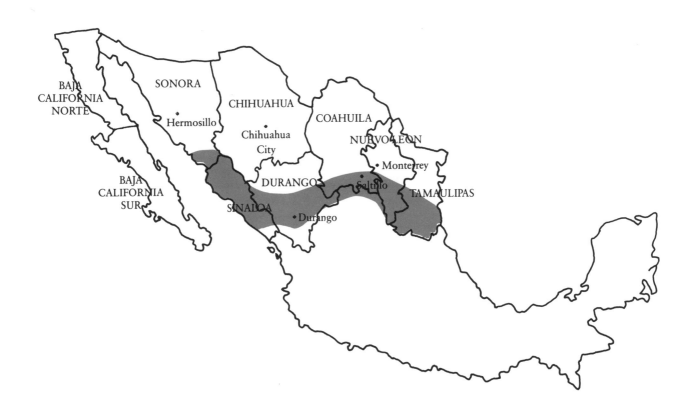

NORTH – *Upper blank area*
TRANSITIONAL – *Shaded area*
SOUTH – *Lower blank area*

Preface

Northern Mexico is ranch country. There the good land is grazing land, and cowboys and horses work a space that goes purple at the edge. Most of the cooking is still done over an open fire.

It is the pervasiveness of the campfire, I believe, which gives the cooking of this region its uniqueness and adds to the food a subtle flavor of the wild.

This love of wood fires is common from backcountry to hacienda, where the cooking for traditional weekend fiestas is always done on the ground outdoors. Meals are prepared over wood fires in the villages, where few homes are without a patio and a wood-burning oven. In the cities, too, most restaurants prepare mesquite-smoked meat over grills.

What in the United States is generally thought of as "Mexican food" is really *antojitos mexicanos*, or snacks—such as tacos, enchiladas, and tamales. Several excellent cookbooks have also introduced us to the more elaborate dishes of southern Mexico.

But the cuisine of northern Mexico, too, is beginning to find a following north of the border. Recently, the popularity of such mesquite-grilled dishes as *fajitas* has spread from the Southwest. In fact, there are probably few cities in this country where *fajitas* are not featured now on restaurant menus. This book celebrates the cuisine of the north, the "other" Mexico. On these pages the reader will find a comprehensive array of dishes from a style of cooking which favors broiling and beef and flour tortillas, and a perhaps unexpected variety of seafood entrées and simple but elegant home-style dishes. Familiarity with the many subtleties of this cuisine, some of which found their way to the open range through immigrant sheepherders from the Basque region of Spain, is sure to enhance the pleasures of your table.

One of the happy surprises for the reader is that this fare, for all its variety and distinction, is amazingly easy to prepare, using ingredients that are readily available. Surely this simplicity is born of the campfire tradition, of dwindling daylight that calls for shortcuts, and saddlebags that admit no more than the most essential ingredients and tools.

The recipes of this book are the foods of the open fire, a flavor of burning mesquite that blends with the evening breeze: the cuisine of *el norte.*

ACKNOWLEDGMENTS

One of the things you learn from writing a book requiring research over an extended period is that you should keep a detailed record of all those who help. After more than sixteen years of work on this project, it is impossible to remember all those who provided assistance, much less find the space to thank them. Many were cooks in restaurants, and many more supplied food at private gatherings. So, I have decided to confine my expressions of gratitude to those whose contributions were critical. I hope the countless others who shared their cooking and helped in so many ways will realize how much I appreciate their efforts. My sincere thanks to them and to the following:

My wife Andrea, whose love, support, and patience have been complete and unselfish. My mother, who instilled in me a love of travel and adventure, a "double-edged sword." Andy Martin and Charles Busch, who were there during the early research and helped with the writing. Ray Salcido for his olives, salsa, fabulous memories, and so much else that helped. Truman Smith, who shared his home and friendships, and without whom my understanding of Mexico would not have been possible. All the fine people at Red Crane Books and especially Carol Caruthers and Ann Mason. Also, Joe Trautwein for his fine contribution in the design of this book, and Winnie Culp for her help. José Ortega, a true scholar, who provided both encouragement and help with the Spanish. Ralph Howell, a fine photographer and teacher. David Cohen, owner of the marvelous Old Mexico Grill, in Santa Fe, New Mexico, for his encouragement and review of the manuscript. David Dewitt of The Whole Chile Pepper Magazine *for his suggestions and help in clearing up some of the more confusing issues in the section on chiles. Rogelio Chavarría, whose hospitality and friendship would make anyone feel a part of northern Mexico. Elena Hannan, who, among other things, went to a great deal of trouble to deliver a tortilladora. Margo Given for her typing in the early days. Johnny Rodríguez, whose knowledge of Chihuahua helped enormously. Juan Elguezabel for showing me how to make asadero cheese. Polo Elguezabel for the information about making Machaca and the tour of the "Kickapoo" dried beef factory. Rudy and Pat Lira and Margarita Abril of Tania's Flour Tortillas and Mexican Food in Tucson, Arizona, for spending a morning revealing the secrets of Sonoran-style tortillas. And a special thanks for those whose help on the second edition was invaluable: Cornelia Muzquiz, for the recipes and encouragement, Louise Hannan, who graciously opened her home and friendship to me, and Graciela and Luis Jaime, owners of Saltillo's magnificent La Canasta restaurant, for sharing their recipes and incredible generosity.*

Introduction

When you cross the border into northern Mexico, the sweet smoky tang of meat cooking over mesquite, mingled with the pungency of garlic, onions, and chiles, instantly invites the senses. Whether prepared in sunbaked adobe ovens, over campfires, or in elaborate commercial kitchens, this distinctive cuisine recently has begun to inspire the more venturesome chefs of the United States.

That cooking reflects culture is nowhere more evident than in Mexico. Before the arrival of the conquistadors, the Indians in the north lived on a limited diet of corn, beans, squash, and game flavored with chiles. With the Spanish came a greater variety of foods, including pork, beef, lamb, wheat, sugar, cheese, garlic, vinegar, and limes. The combined resources of both cultures created the cuisines of Mexico as we know them today. In the south, where cooking evolved from ancient Indian recipes modified by the Spanish, the ingredients were those of the traditional small farm economy, and much of the cooking was done in clay ovens and stovetop *cazuelas*. The cooking of northern Mexico, on the other hand, was developed by and for the *vaqueros*, sheepherders, landowners, banished intellectuals, and smugglers who settled the frontier.

The people of northern Mexico brought recipes from their many places of origin and adapted them to the available ingredients. Over the years the recipes merged, as did the people, creating a distinctive cooking tradition. Newcomers were drawn to northern Mexico because of the adventure and opportunities offered by the frontier. Sheepherders from the Basque area of Spain brought their cooking techniques, garlic, and olive oil, and immigrants from southern Mexico brought their corn-based dishes and tortillas. *Vaqueros* from both sides of the border created the outdoor broiling techniques so well suited to beef dishes and the nomadic nature of ranch life. As time went on, talented chefs adapted local ingredients to recipes learned elsewhere: garlic soup and garlic sauce from Spain, shish kebab from the Middle East; from Italy a dish called *Milanesa* (p. 130), breaded and fried veal or tenderloin; and *antojitos* from the south of Mexico. Each dish, altered to suit the northern taste and ingredients, became unique in the process.

Southern Mexico is renowned for its complex sauces which complement the usually oven-baked, boiled or sautéed or braised chicken, pork, seafood, and corn-based dishes, commonly served with corn tortillas. The northern cuisine, however, is based on beef, lamb, and *cabrito* (kid) cooked over mesquite wood or charcoal and served with flour tortillas as often as corn. *Fajitas*, charbroiled strips of skirt steak, a dish currently enjoying great popularity in the United States, is probably the best-known example of the cooking of northern Mexico.

While meats are the staple in northern Mexico, seafood also plays an important role in the cuisine. Elegant waiters hurrying by with plates of broiled black bass brought in daily from Boquillas Reservoir are a common sight in Ciudad Juárez's fine restaurants. In Guaymas you will find huge platters of broiled and fried shrimp. The fishing village of Puerto Nuevo, located between Tijuana and Ensenada, specializes in a unique lobster dish served with beans, rice, hot sauce, and huge, paper-thin flour tortillas.

However, it is not only ingredients and cooking methods that distinguish northern cooking but also the distinctive combinations of foods and the sauces with which the food is served. A Steak *Tampiqueña* (the ultimate Mexican combination plate) served at the México Típico restaurant in Nuevo Laredo best illustrates this. In addition to charbroiled strips of tenderloin, the plate includes a chicken enchilada in *mole* sauce, a crisp chicken taco, refried beans, Mexican rice, *rajas* (strips of fried *poblano* chile and onion), fried potatoes, guacamole, and a garnish of sliced onion, tomatoes, lettuce, and *tostadas*. (It is a large plate!) Unlike Mexican-American cooking, where everything on the plate is heated in the oven and drenched with chile sauce, each item here is separately prepared and keeps its distinctive character. The proliferation of northern-style *taquerías* and steak houses along the border indicates that we will have increasing opportunities to enjoy this type of cooking.

The original migration of Mexicans to the United States, mostly from the north, brought about the development of what is loosely called Mexican-American cooking. Coming from the lower economic levels in Mexico, these newcomers chiefly brought recipes for the less costly dishes of their region. This is why most Mexican-American menus are limited to *antojitos mexicanos*, which represent only one (although an important) element of the northern cuisine. Later, economic problems in Mexico and more recently NAFTA led to an influx to the United States of more prosperous Mexicans. This, and the growing popularity of such early imports as *fajitas*, is creating an increased awareness of the northern cuisine in its entirety. This trend itself is manifested in the immensely popular culinary wave of "southwestern" cooking, much of which is based upon Mexican ingredients and mesquite broiling.

Any discussion of influences on northern Mexican cooking requires mention of New Mexico. Following the Spanish conquest, for all practical purposes New Mexico remained part of Mexico for more than two hundred years, and New Mexican cuisine evolved, as did that of the Mexican interior, from the combination of Spanish and local Indian cooking traditions. The area's major trade route, the Camino Real, ran between Chihuahua City and Santa Fe. In fact, for a short period beginning in 1824, New Mexico united with the states of Durango and Chihuahua to form the "Internal State of the North." Unlike other areas in the southwestern United States, where so-called Mexican-American food is common, the cooking of New Mexico was not brought across the border by immigrants: the border itself was moved south, leaving the cuisine intact. The influence of the distinctive New Mexican cuisine on that of present-day northern Mexico is evident in the use there of green chiles and green and red chile sauces.

An additional interesting aspect of northern Mexican cooking is its intraregional variety. Because of the region's vastness, settlements were isolated. This caused recipes to be developed more or less independently. Because of this the cuisine is much less codified than that of the more densely populated south. Names of dishes and their recipes often vary, not just from state to state, but from village to village. This is illustrated by the differences in the names of chiles. A *chile de árbol* in one place may be known as a *chile japonés*, or by several other names, over the next mountain. So there are subcuisines within the overall northern cuisine. For example, the state of Sonora produces huge, paper-thin flour tortillas that are not found elsewhere. In and around Monterrey *cabrito al pastor* is very common, but less so in other areas.

El Norte: The Cuisine of Northern Mexico is the product of twenty years of research and the encouragement of many friends on both sides of the border. The recipes were collected exclusively from Mexican cooks in restaurants, food stalls, private homes, and ranches and are, as with all Mexican cooking, flexible to variation. So, for example, if a recipe is too piquant, take out the veins of the chiles to keep the flavor but lose some of the heat. Where appropriate, common variations are provided. The chapter "Basic Ingredients" offers suitable substitutions for those which you might prefer not to use, or which might not be readily available in your area.

Basic Ingredients

AVOCADOS

Guacamole, made with avocados, is served with almost every meal in northern Mexico. The two popular California avocados, the haas and the fuerte, are superior. The haas, which has a rough, dark skin is preferred to the fuerte, which has a smooth green skin. Do not use the large, smooth-skinned Florida avocados, which either are too sweet or too watery and tasteless.

BEANS

Where beans are called for in this book, the reference is to pinto beans. As far as I can determine, soaking beans will not affect their flavor, although soaking does reduce the cooking time. From my observation, Mexicans rarely soak their beans. However, it has been demonstrated that soaking beans reduces their gas-producing properties.

CHEESE

In Mexico most cheese is made by small, local operations. Even brands that are widely distributed within a region may be made in a home kitchen or garage. Northern Mexico has some of the most interesting cheeses found anywhere. From the *añejo* or *queso cotija* of Sonora to the *queso Chihuahua* or *Menenito* made by the Mennonites, they are excellent and sometimes unique.

The cheeses used most often in the recipes in this book are *asadero* and *queso Chihuahua*. *Asadero* is made by combining sour and fresh milk and consists of long braids woven together. As you might suppose, it has a slightly, but not unpleasantly, sour flavor. *Queso Chihuahua*, or *queso Menenito*, is made by the Mennonite community outside of Cuauhtemoc. The Mennonites are a strict religious sect from northern Europe that immigrated first to Canada and then to Mexico in the 1930s and 1940s. One group acquired the 5,000-acre ranch, about two hours southwest of Chihuahua City, that used to belong to William Randolph Hearst. I pass this way nearly every year and have watched them create what is one of the most advanced and profitable farm operations in Mexico (excluding marijuana).

I have spent considerable time watching cheese being made in Mexico and have made it at home, but I would not recommend this for most people. The difficulty of finding unpasteurized milk, cheese presses, suitable utensils, and rennet makes it impracticable. In addition, the dangers inherent in using unpasteurized milk, and the fact that dry and liquid rennet react differently under different conditions, compound the problem. However, for those who are interested despite the difficulties, I have provided a general description of the process for making two types of Mexican cheese.

Fortunately, some acceptable *asadero* and Chihuahua cheeses are now being made in this country. But beware of any that have the word *processed* on the label.

If you cannot find a decent domestic *asadero* or Chihuahua cheese, either mozzarella, provolone, or farmer cheese (or a combination of all these) make reasonable substitutes. My favorite substitute is a mixture of equal parts of mozzarella and provolone. For dishes requiring yellow cheese, such as some of the enchiladas and nachos, use a good mild cheddar. Other substitutions will be found in the individual recipes.

Queso añejo, or *cotija*, is a flavorful cheese that crumbles easily. (When it is impregnated with chile powder, it is called *queso enchilado*.) It is very difficult to melt and is used principally as a garnish for tacos, enchiladas, and refried beans. A good substitute is feta cheese.

Making Mexican Cheese

The difficulties of making cheese are not too great if you are willing to take the time to find the right equipment and ingredients and to follow a process of trial and error. But using unpasteurized milk can be dangerous. I have had no luck in trying to make cheese with supermarket milk. A few years ago many people became seriously ill, and I believe there was at least one death, from eating a domestic Mexican-style cheese made of spoiled ingredients. The fact that *asadero* cheese uses day-old milk increases such risks.

Following is a list of types of Mexican cheeses along with general guidelines for making two varieties—*queso asadero* and *queso cotija*—for those who have a real interest and the knowledge and resources required for cheese-making. For further information, consult books dealing exclusively with this process, some of which provide sources for ingredients.

Queso Asadero

Nothing matches the flavor and texture of *asadero* for making enchiladas, *Chile con queso* (p. 56), and *Queso flameado* (p. 55). It also is excellent for sandwiches and pizza.

Asadero is made with equal portions of fresh milk and milk that has been left at room temperature for one day. The amount of rennet to be added is based only on the amount of fresh milk used. This cheese is not pressed but cooked and made into strips that are then braided into balls of 1 to 2 pounds (450 to 900 grams).

Mix the sour milk with the fresh milk; then heat the mixture to room temperature. Next add the rennet, cover with a cloth, and let the milk rest for ½ to 1 hour, or until coagulated.

Next, cut the curd as finely as possible and allow the whey to rise for about 10 minutes. Strain off the whey and add salt. Wrap the cut curds in cheesecloth and allow to drain for 3 to 4 hours.

Then place the drained curds in a double boiler over medium heat and begin to stir. Mexican cheese-makers often use their hands and will increase the heat until it is as hot as is comfortable to the touch. The cheese is ready to be braided when you can stretch out strips an inch (2.54 centimeters) in diameter and 2 to 3 feet (.61 to .91 meters) in length. Braid the strips into balls about the size of a small grapefruit and allow to cool.

Queso Cotija

This cheese is often called *queso añejo* ("aged cheese") in the south. It crumbles easily and is difficult to melt. It is used primarily as a garnish for *antojitos* and beans and is somewhat similar in flavor to a mild feta cheese.

To make this cheese, heat fresh milk to room temperature and add rennet. Allow the mixture to rest until coagulated; then cut the curds as finely as possible. Put the curds in cheesecloth and allow them to drain overnight.

Remove the curds from the cheesecloth, add salt, and knead into a ball for 2 to 3 minutes. Place the cheese in molds and press with very heavy weights for two days.

Remove the weights, brush the cheese with oil, and allow to age at room temperature for three days, wiping and reoiling the cheese each day. Refrigerate.

Queso Fresco

Queso fresco is a semisoft, white cheese that is also now being made domestically. Monterey Jack is the only commonly found American cheese that can be used as a substitute.

Queso Manchego

This is a white, moderately soft cheese with lots of flavor. It can be used as a stuffing for *chiles rellenos* or for almost any other purpose. A good substitute is to mix Monterey Jack cheese and Gouda cheese together in equal portions.

Queso Panela

Queso panela is a dry, medium-flavored cheese much like feta cheese in texture, although feta cheese has a much stronger flavor. Nevertheless, feta cheese can be used as a substitute in very small amounts.

CHILES

Chiles rank with tortillas as the most important ingredient in Mexican cooking, regardless of the region. Hardly a meal passes where chiles, in one form or another, are not served. One conjecture regarding the use of chiles in Mexican cooking holds that the traditional Indian diet of corn and beans, while reasonably nutritious, was pretty boring. The Indians, so the hypothesis goes, used chiles to infuse some excitement into their meals.

Chiles are currently the subject of a great deal of research as well as popular folklore, and it is often difficult to know where one ends and the other begins. We know for certain that they contain high amounts of vitamins C and A. They also may be helpful in the prevention of heart disease and stomach disorders. It is probable that ingestion of chiles (or rather the element capsaicin that creates their heat) causes endorphins to be released in the brain. The effect is said to be similar to that of a mild dose of morphine, relieving pain and creating a general feeling of well-being. The theory is that when the body begins to feel the chiles' heat the brain says, "uh-oh, danger" and releases the endorphins. This may explain the fact that people who are accustomed to a regular diet of Mexican food experience serious cravings or symptoms of withdrawal when unable to partake of it for any length of time. Are we really getting high on chiles? Another theory, based on some research, is that consumption of chiles helps burn calories at an increased rate, thereby enhancing weight loss.

One of the most common misconceptions in the culinary world is that chiles derive much of their heat from their seeds. According to Dave Dewitt and Nancy Gerlach in *The Whole Chile Pepper Book*, "the seeds are *not* a source of heat as commonly believed." They go on to explain that this misconception is because the seeds are located near the placenta, the location of the glands that produce capsaicin, the real source of heat. I always remove the seeds because I find them bitter and unpleasant in texture.

The neophyte will encounter a bewildering array of chiles from which to choose. Many cookbooks list varieties of chiles of which the casual reader may never have heard and will never see except in Mexico or as a devoted patron of Hispanic food stores. To further frustrate the novice, most chiles are known by different names in their fresh and dried forms. Additional confusion is added by the tendency of different regions, and even different villages, to call the same chile by different names. Variations in growing conditions also produce different degrees of heat and flavor in each type. Happily for us, in northern Mexican cooking the majority of dishes utilize only a few varieties of chile. Even more fortunately, they are the ones that are commonly found in supermarkets in the western United States and in Hispanic groceries in other parts of the country.

"Which chile is hottest and by how much?" is a question that is often asked. Until recently the system commonly used for judging the heat of chiles was one originated by a pharmacist named Scoville early in the century. It requires five expert tasters, who sample mixtures made of different types of chiles and rate the heat content of each in incremental units of 100. Three of the five must agree on the results. The measurements, expressed in "Scoville Units," range from 0 for a bell pepper to more than 250,000 for the *habanero*, the hottest pepper of all. Because of the differences in conditions of cultivation, the same variety of chile may receive widely varying Scoville ratings. For example, the *piquín* chile ranges from 44,000 units to more than 70,000 units. As you can see, the system is less than exact, and the results can be confusing. To remedy this the staff of *The Chile Pepper Magazine* (Albuquerque, New Mexico), an excellent publication for aficionados of picante foods, has developed a simplified heat index scale. The scale, based upon the Scoville system, rates chiles from 1 to 10, with 1 being mildest and 10 hottest. The rates are verified by high pressure liquefied chromatography (HPLC) testing, which measures capsaicin in chiles in parts per million. These heat scale ratings will be provided in the following descriptions of individual chiles.

Chiles, as mentioned earlier, come in two forms: fresh and dried.

Fresh Chiles

Fresh chiles are used in the preparation of sauces and to flavor beef, chicken, pork, and fish dishes. In *salsas crudas* (uncooked sauces), the chiles are chopped or diced and mixed with the other ingredients, such as onions and tomatoes. Fresh chiles are often broiled first for cooked sauces, complementing the wonderful smoky flavor typical of so many northern dishes.

To broil fresh chiles, place them on a grill over a wood or charcoal fire and cook, turning them often, until the skins are well charred.

This also can be done in an oven broiler by placing the chiles on a metal cookie sheet about 3 to 6 inches (7.6 to 15 centimeters) from the heating element and proceeding as above.

Some dishes, such as *chiles rellenos*, call for chiles to be skinned. Many cookbooks suggest that skinning is facilitated by broiling or roasting the chiles over a gas flame, then placing them in a polyethylene bag to "sweat" for 20 minutes before peeling. Another good method is to fry them in deep oil at 350 to 375 degrees F (177 to 190 degrees C) for 30 to 40 seconds, or until the skins have turned completely white (as they separate from the chiles). After frying, place them in a plastic bag for about 10 to 20 minutes, after which they can be easily peeled. This method also preserves the firmness of the chiles.

Jalapeño

The *jalapeño* is probably the most familiar chile to most Americans and is slightly less piquant than the *serrano*, at 5 on the heat scale. It is sold fresh and pickled in most parts of this country. Never use the pickled *jalapeño* as a substitute for the fresh version. A *serrano* may be used instead.

Poblano

The *poblano* chile is named for the area around Puebla and is one of the oldest chiles indigenous to Mexico. It is also called *chile para rellenar*, or chile for stuffing, as it is used to make *chiles rellenos*. The *poblano* chile is large, often 5 inches (12.7 centimeters) long and 3 inches (7.6 centimeters) in diameter, and has an attractive dark green color. The *poblano* has a heat scale rating of 3 to 4. The Anaheim chile, or green chile, is a good substitute.

Serrano

Although the *jalapeño* is much better known, the *serrano* may well be the favorite chile throughout the north. It is about 1½ to 2½ inches (3.8 to 6.4 centimeters) long and ¼ to ⅓ inch (.6 to .9 centimeter) in diameter. Ranging between 6 and 7 on the heat scale, this is

one of the hottest of the fresh chiles used in our recipes. As is true in all cases, using a different chile will produce a different but equally tasty result. In this case, *jalapeños* are the best substitute.

Chile Verde, Californio, Anaheim, or New Mexico

This chile is usually called *chile verde*, or green chile. It was originally developed in New Mexico and California and is as long as the *poblano* but narrower and lighter in color. It is usually the mildest of the fresh chiles, being rated at 2 on the heat scale, but it is sometimes hotter. This chile, like the *jalapeño* and *serrano*, is widely available in western American supermarkets in both fresh and canned forms. Use it fresh whenever possible. The *poblano* chile may be substituted for the Anaheim.

Dried Chiles

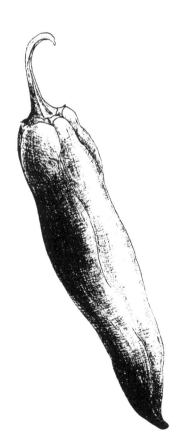

Dried chiles are usually used to make sauces. Many recipes call for the chiles to be toasted and/or softened.

To toast dried chiles, first warm a *comal* or heavy iron skillet over low heat. Then cook the chiles, turning them constantly until they are softened and fragrant. Take care to avoid burning.

To soften dried chiles, place them in a bowl and cover them with very hot or boiling water and let them sit for at least 10 minutes. If they are very dry, 20 to 30 minutes will be required.

To seed dry chiles, slit them down one side with a sharp pointed knife and remove the seeds, stems, and as many of the veins as possible.

Ancho

The *ancho* chile is the dried *poblano* chile. This chile rates 3 to 4 on the heat scale. It is usually about 3 to 4½ inches (7.6 to 11.4 centimeters) long and 2 to 3 inches (5 to 7.6 centimeters) wide. If this chile is not obtainable, substitute either a dried New Mexico or Anaheim chile, or use 1 tablespoon (6.5 grams) of mild chile powder for each chile called for in the recipe. However, since chile powder often contains ground cumin, oregano, salt, and, in most cases, the seeds too, the result will be slightly more bitter and less rounded.

De Árbol

The *de árbol* chile is longer, thinner, and has a smoother texture than the wrinkled *japonés* chile. Because of its long, thin shape, it is often called *pico de pájaro* (bird's beak). The *de árbol* chile rates a 7 on the heat scale. Substitute ¼ teaspoon of cayenne for each *de árbol* chile.

Chipotle

The *chipotle* chile is the *jalapeño* which has been dried and smoked. It is available in dried form or canned with *adobo* sauce. For a short-cut *adobo* sauce, mix 6 pickled *jalapeños* with ⅓ cup (71 milliliters) tomato sauce and 1 teaspoon (5 milliliters) of liquid smoke.

Japonés

The *japonés* chile is often described as a dried *serrano* chile. In fact, it both looks and tastes like a dried *serrano*. However, experts contend it is not the dried *serrano* but a small cayenne variety, although some believe it to be a *piquín* variety. It takes its name from the fact that it is widely grown in Japan and other parts of the Orient. It is very hot and is used extensively in oriental recipes and Indian curries and is therefore widely available in oriental as well as Hispanic food stores. For the recipes in this book that call for *japonés* or *de árbol* chile, use the *de árbol*, if available. It has a smoother texture and flavor. The *japonés* chile is mentioned principally because it is a good substitute and easy to find. Although not officially rated, the *japonés* chile probably rates a 6 to 7 on the heat scale. As a substitute, use ¼ teaspoon cayenne pepper for each *japonés* chile.

Pasilla

The *pasilla* chile is somewhat similar to the *ancho* except that it is thinner, longer, and nearly black in color. In fact, *anchos* are often

called *pasillas*, especially in Baja California. The *pasilla* has the same heat rating as the *ancho*, 3 to 4 on the heat scale.

Piquín and Tepín

Piquín and *tepín* chiles are essentially the same, although they have different shapes. The *piquín* chile is very small, usually less than ¼ inch (.65 centimeter) long, and shaped like a tiny football. The *tepín* chile, often called *chiltepín* (its original name in the Nahuatl language), is about the same size but round. Because of their size, these chiles are not seeded before use. These chiles make ornamental, as well as useful, houseplants. Both these chiles grow wild in many parts of northern Mexico, where villagers gather them by the basketful to be dried or pickled for future use. In fact, they are so abundant in the wild and so easy to grow at home that, compared with other varieties, very little is planted commercially. The *piquín* is the hottest chile used in the recipes that follow, and, as with all chiles, extreme caution must be exercised in handling them. The *piquín* and *tepín* are rated at a formidable 8 to 9 on the heat scale.

Guajillo

About 3 to 4 inches (7.6 to 10.2 centimeters) in length and ¾ to 1 inch (1.9 to 2.5 centimeters) in width, the *guajillo* is a dried chile with a smooth skin. It resembles a small, dried New Mexico or Anaheim chile and is about medium on the heat scale.

CILANTRO

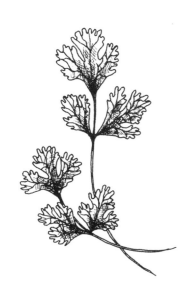

The English word for this parsley-like plant is *coriander.* In the Southwest, where it is found in most supermarkets, it is almost always called by its Spanish name. It combines well with chiles and is used in many northern Mexican sauces. Cilantro is also an ingredient in many other ethnic cuisines, including East Indian, African, Southeast Asian, and Chinese. In fact, it is often called Chinese parsley. However, do not let this terminology mislead you: parsley is no substitute for cilantro, nor is there one. While parsley provides a subtle flavor and a garnish effect, coriander has a distinctive flavor for which there is no substitute. Ground coriander, which is made from the seeds and is often used in southern Mexico and other parts of the world, is also no substitute for fresh. Cilantro is easily grown in a greenhouse or garden. It does well in cool to moderate temperatures and grows very quickly.

COOKING OIL

Unless you must, do not economize on cooking oil. In deep-frying, a cheap oil will break down much sooner than a good one. There is nothing worse for cooking than an inferior olive oil. Use good quality regular or extra virgin olive oil whenever possible; or select a good peanut, soy, canola, or safflower oil.

CORN HUSKS

Corn husks are used for wrapping tamales and can be purchased in supermarkets in the Southwest and in Hispanic groceries elsewhere. You can also dry your own husks or, in a pinch, use a thin parchment paper or white cloth, such as an old pillowcase.

CREAM

In northern Mexico cream is often used as a topping for enchiladas and tacos. Their cream is thick and fresh, resembling the crème fraîche of France. As with cheese, some domestic companies are making an authentic "*crema mexicana,*" as one is labeled. If you cannot find this kind of cream, sour cream can be substituted, but it is better still to make your own cream. To do this, mix 1 tablespoon (15 milliliters) of buttermilk with 1 cup (225 milliliters) whipping cream; let the mixture stand at room temperature for 5 to 6 hours, then refrigerate.

CUMIN

Cumin, *comino* in Spanish, is an herb used in many northern recipes, usually in combination with oregano. Use only the whole cumin, as the ground is much blander.

GARLIC OIL

Garlic oil is used for basting meats before, during, and after broiling; in the dressing for Caesar Salad; and for other dishes when a touch of garlic is desired.

To make garlic oil, peel 10 cloves of garlic and bruise them slightly by pressing them with the flat edge of a cook's knife or cleaver. Place the garlic cloves in a medium-sized bottle or jar (a salad dressing cruet is perfect) and add 1 cup (225 milliliters) of a good cooking or olive oil. Refrigerate the container immediately or the oil will lose its freshness. Please note that some experts advise that garlic oil can spoil after more than 3 days, even if refrigerated.

LARD

Our commercial lards are much blander than those used in Mexico. To render your own lard, place 2 cups (312 grams) of chopped pork fat in a heatproof saucepan in a 300-degree F (148-degree C) oven and cook for about 1 hour, turning every 10 minutes.

In parts of the north, beef suet is used instead of lard. The flavor is excellent and is particularly interesting when used to make flour tortillas. Render the beef suet or fat according to the above directions for rendering lard.

With today's emphasis on diet and health, people prefer not to use saturated fats such as lard. The same quantity of vegetable shortening (as indicated for lard) can be substituted when making flour tortillas, *empanadas*, and tamales, and good cooking oil when making other items.

LIMES

When a Mexican uses the Spanish word *limón*, he is referring to a lime. Lemons are virtually nonexistent in Mexico, and there is no word in Spanish which distinguishes the two. Mexican limes, similar to key limes, are small and very tart. The large, seedless Persian limes may be substituted, but they are sweeter. Lemons can, of course, be used, but the taste imparted will be altogether different. In any case, never use frozen or reconstituted lemon or lime juice.

OREGANO

Whole oregano should be used rather than ground. This flavorful herb should be used in moderation as it has a very strong flavor. It is closely related to marjoram and in many places is known as wild marjoram. For a really authentic taste, you can easily grow Mexican oregano and use it fresh. The plant itself is beautiful and easy to cultivate.

PILONCILLO

This is the dark brown, hard cone made of unrefined sugar that you find in Hispanic grocery stores and the ethnic section of southwestern supermarkets. Brown sugar makes an acceptable substitute.

PUMPKIN SEEDS

For recipes which include pumpkin seeds, do not use the commercially roasted seeds. Buy them raw from a health food store and roast them yourself.

SESAME SEEDS

Sesame seeds are usually toasted for Mexican recipes. To toast the seeds, place them in an ungreased skillet over low heat and stir them constantly until they are nicely browned. Care should be taken, as they burn easily.

SOUR ORANGE JUICE

Although orange juice is not used as much in cooking in the north of Mexico as in the south, it is an ingredient in the recipes for *Carnitas de jugo* (p. 148), *Cochinita píbil del norte* (p. 148), and *Pollo en pipián verde* (p. 169). Mexicans usually use the juice of the sour, or Seville, orange for cooking. If you are unable to obtain sour oranges, add 2 tablespoons (28 milliliters) of lime juice to 6 ounces (170 milliliters) of fresh orange juice for a substitute. (Never use frozen concentrated juice, as it is too syrupy.)

TOMATILLOS

Tomatillos, often called *tomates verdes* or *fresadillas*, look like small green tomatoes. However, they are actually a relative of the goose-

berry. *Tomatillos*, which turn slightly yellow when ripe, are almost always used in their unripe stage, when they are a lovely, bright green color. They are now often sold fresh in the southwestern United States and can be found canned for use in sauces, or in prepared sauces, in other parts of the country. The widely distributed La Victoria and Herdez brands offer good *tomatillo* sauces, although the Herdez is too salty for my taste. However, canned or bottled *tomatillos* in any form are a poor substitute for fresh.

Tomatillos are easily grown at home and make an attractive plant. Because they are used in their unripe form, *tomatillos* must be simmered for 10 to 15 minutes before being incorporated into recipes. Put them in cold water and bring them slowly to a boil to prevent the skins from splitting.

VINEGAR

Northern Mexicans regularly use four types of vinegar: wine, white, apple, and cane. Cane is the favorite for most uses, particularly in making sauces. Since our commercial vinegars are much stronger than Mexican varieties, they should be diluted with 1 part water to 1 part vinegar. A mild rice vinegar makes a good substitute for cane vinegar.

NOTE: Metric conversions have been provided for all liquid and dry ingredients except those measuring less than 1 teaspoon.

Kitchen Equipment

BEAN MASHER

This device consists of a circle of steel with holes drilled in it, about ¼ inch (.6 centimeter) thick and about 4 inches (10.2 centimeters) in diameter. A handle is attached to the center. It is used to mash cooked beans in the preparation of refried beans. A heavy slotted cooking spoon also may be used for this purpose.

BLENDER

Blenders, or *licuadoras*, are ubiquitous in northern Mexico. They can be great labor savers, but their limitations must be well understood. They are most useful for making sauces from dried chiles, grinding the ingredients quickly and producing excellent smooth-textured sauces. They should, however, never be used for making sauces from fresh chiles and tomatoes. The result is normally a frothy mess. Fresh sauces should always be made in a *molcajete*.

COMAL

A *comal* is a long iron Mexican griddle that is made to fit over two stove burners. It is used primarily in the north for making and warming tortillas. A heavy iron skillet is an excellent substitute.

COOKWARE

For Mexican cooking, considering cost and quality, nothing beats good old iron skillets and Dutch ovens. They are durable, heavy enough to be used over an open fire, and heat evenly. Equip yourself with small, medium, and large iron skillets, as well as a medium-sized Dutch oven.

FOOD DEHYDRATOR

Unless you live in a warm, very dry place, an electric dehydrator with a fan is indispensable for making *Carne seca*, or *Machaca* (p. 140), northern Mexico's famous beef jerky. Once you try it you will probably discover a great many other uses that appeal to you such as drying fruits and vegetables. In San Antonio's humidity it is usually the only way I can get chiles dry before mold forms and spoils them.

FOOD MILL

This piece of equipment is extremely useful for straining blended chile purée when making chile sauces.

FOOD PROCESSOR

For many types of cooking, a food processor, if properly used, can be a servant in the kitchen. I find it most useful for grating cheese, making tortilla dough, and grinding meat. It is also good for chopping large quantities of vegetables, although I think chopping by hand produces a better, more uniform result. As an alternative to making a fresh chile-tomato sauce from scratch, a food processor will do a much better job than a blender.

FOOD SCALE

An accurate kitchen scale is useful in many ways. When making large quantities of chile sauce, it is helpful to measure chiles by weight rather than number because their sizes can vary so dramatically. Also, when making items such as tamales, it is much more accurate to weigh ingredients than to measure them.

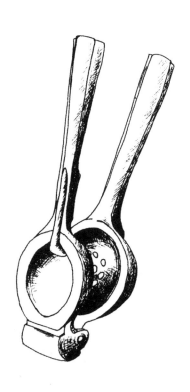

LIME JUICER

When making drinks that contain lime juice, Mexicans always squeeze the juice fresh. They have a juicer that, while simple, is the most efficient I have ever seen for squeezing small quantities. You place a cut lime in the receptacle and squeeze the hinged handles, and with very little effort the majority of the juice is extracted. The only problem is that these items are made with uncoated aluminum, which is believed to be potentially dangerous to the health, especially when combined with acidic foods. This may be why the Mexican juicers are not sold in this country.

MOLCAJETE

This is perhaps the most useful piece of equipment in the Mexican kitchen. A *molcajete* is a mortar and pestle, Mexican style. Made of black stone, the rough surface is ideal for grinding spices and is almost the only utensil that will allow you to mash chiles, onions, tomatoes, and other ingredients into a sauce of the proper consistency. The most practical size of *molcajete* for home use is approximately 8 inches (20.3 centimeters) in diameter. In Mexican homes table sauces are often served in the *molcajete* in which they are made, providing an efficient and attractive presentation. While they are difficult to find in some parts of the country, a search of Hispanic food stores will usually be rewarded. The Japanese rough mortar and pestle is a good substitute, but if neither is available an ordinary smooth mortar and pestle will do.

POTTERY

Nothing tastes better than beans and stews cooked in Mexican pottery and nothing looks better than *antojitos* served on hand-painted Mexican plates. However, I have a beautiful collection of Mexican pottery that I almost never use, because Mexican artisans still use lead-based finishes on pottery, and health officials contend this can be very dangerous. So I use American-made pottery instead, which is not as authentic but safer. When preparing oven-baked dishes like enchiladas, be sure to use well-fired pottery to avoid breakage. I have found Francoma ware from Oklahoma to be both well made and attractive.

TORTILLA CHEF

This is a small appliance made by Vitantonio Cookware which resembles an electric waffle iron; it takes much of the labor and need for experience out of making homemade tortillas.

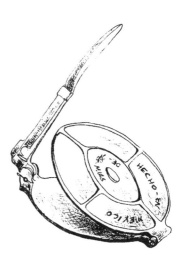

TORTILLA PRESS

A tortilla press is a must if you live in an area where freshly made corn tortillas are not readily available. Even if they are, you will find that, as with many other foods, the homemade variety has both better flavor and texture. Tortilla presses can be purchased or ordered at specialty food and cookware stores.

TORTILLADORA

This is an ingenious hand-cranked machine that is used to make corn tortillas in small restaurants. In appearance and operation it resembles a simple pasta maker but requires a bit more experience to use in that the texture of the dough and the adjustment of the machine must be just right. Nevertheless, once mastered it is capable of forming a lot of tortillas with relatively little effort.

Recipes

Drinks

◆◈◆

Bebidas

There is a saying in northern Mexico, *"No hay sábados sin sol ni domingos sin borrachos."* ("There are no Saturdays without sun nor Sundays without drunks.") In spite of a popular misconception, Mexicans are very hardworking and particularly so in the north, where they are as tough and rugged as the land itself. However, they also believe that there must be a time set aside to relax and to blow off steam. Saturday is frequently chosen for this purpose. The results are often all too plain on Sunday, as partygoers return home for the traditional day of winding down with the family before the workweek begins.

In their choice of drinks, the average northerner is somewhat more sophisticated than his counterpart in the south. It is not uncommon to see such exotic drinks as Planter's Punch and Singapore Slings on the menus of northern restaurants. This is mostly due to the fact that during Prohibition gringos came by the thousands to the free and easy Mexican border towns. Places like Tijuana, Cuidad Juárez, and Nuevo Laredo built elegant establishments, and fortunes, catering to North American tastes, and the influence remains.

Although drinks of all types are consumed in Mexico, I have found the following to be, by far, the most popular in northern Mexico.

1 lime
  Salt
1 shot (28 milliliters)
  tequila
1 shot (28 milliliters)
  lime juice
1 shot (28 milliliters)
  triple sec

Margarita

The Margarita is the favorite drink of Americans when they go to Mexican-American restaurants. When traveling in Mexico, they are surprised to discover that it is difficult to find a bartender who can make this drink, except in tourist-oriented establishments. The reason is that Mexicans rarely drink Margaritas.

Rub the rim of a martini glass or specially designed Margarita glass with a half lime; then dip the dampened rim into salt to coat it.

Pour the tequila, lime juice, and triple sec over ice in a bar mixer, cover, and shake for 20 to 30 seconds. Strain the mixture into the salted glass or serve on the rocks; or blend with the ice to make a frozen Margarita. Garnish with a lime wedge. Serves 1.

NOTE: In Baja California bartenders sometimes substitute *damiana*, a liqueur made from the local *damiana* plant (which is also used to make tea) for some or all of the triple sec.

1 shot (28 milliliters)
  tequila
1 shot (28 milliliters)
  lime juice
1 shot (28 milliliters)
  Simple Syrup (p. 35)

Tequila Sour

This drink is far more popular among Mexicans than the Margarita.

Pour the ingredients over ice in a bar mixer, cover, and shake for 20 to 30 seconds; strain into a sour glass or serve on the rocks. Garnish with an orange slice and cherry. Serves 1.

Tequila Sunrise

Fill a 12-ounce (240-milliliter) tumbler with ice and add the tequila. Fill the glass with freshly squeezed orange juice and top with a dash or two of grenadine. Serve with a straw or stir the drink to blend the grenadine. Serves 1.

1 shot (28 milliliters)
  tequila
Orange juice
Grenadine

1-2-3

This is probably the most popular way to drink tequila in Mexico. Use the best tequila available or suffer the consequences.

Place a small amount of salt on the soft fleshy part of your left hand (if you are right-handed) between the thumb and forefinger. Lick the salt and drink the shot of tequila (which is held in your other hand). Finally, bite into the lime half. Then hold on!

There is some dispute over the best order in which to take the tequila, salt, and lime. Experiment and adopt your favorite. There are six different combinations, so don't try them all at one sitting! Serves 1.

Salt
1 shot (28 milliliters)
  tequila
½ small lime

Tom Collins

Fill a tall bar glass with ice, gin, syrup, and lime juice. Add club soda and stir. Serves 1.

1 shot (28 milliliters)
  gin
1 shot (28 milliliters)
  Simple Syrup (p. 35)
1 shot (28 milliliters)
  lime juice
Club soda

Rum Collins

This drink is the same as a Tom Collins (p. 27), except that it is made with light rum rather than gin.

Ramos Gin Fizz

1 tablespoon (12 grams) powdered sugar

Juice of 1 lemon or lime

White of 1 egg

10 drops orange flower water

1 ounce (28 milliliters) gin

2 ounces (56 milliliters) milk

This is the original recipe from the famous Cadillac Bar in Nuevo Laredo.

Shake all ingredients over ice in a cocktail shaker for 30 seconds. Strain and serve. Serves 1.

Don Chuy

1 shot (28 milliliters) vodka

1 shot (28 milliliters) lime juice

Clamato juice

Worcestershire sauce

Tabasco sauce

Club soda

I have named this drink for the colorful character who first made it for me at a carne asada *(cookout) on the Sabinas River in northern Coahuila. It is an excellent alternative to a Bloody Mary.*

Pour the vodka over ice into a 12-ounce (240-milliliter) tumbler. Add the lime juice; then nearly fill the glass with clamato juice. Add about 3 dashes of both Worcestershire and Tabasco, top with club soda, then stir. Serves 1.

Sangrita

Sangrita *is most often used as a chaser with tequila or mixed with it to make a* Vampiro. *In Mexico* Sangrita *is sold in bottles, but this fresh, homemade version is far better. While most recipes for* Sangrita *that I have had call for tomato juice, some do not. Because the results are quite different, I have made the tomato juice optional.*

If you decide to try *Sangrita* without tomato juice, mix all the ingredients together except the tomato juice and use just 2 teaspoons (12.4 grams) salt. If you use tomato juice, add a total of 3 teaspoons (18.6 grams) salt to the mixture. Makes 2 to 3 cups (450 to 675 milliliters).

2 cups (450 milliliters) freshly squeezed orange juice

3 tablespoons (42 milliliters) grenadine

Heaping ¼ teaspoon chile powder or cayenne pepper, or to taste

1 cup (225 milliliters) tomato juice (optional)

2–3 teaspoons (12.4 to 18.6 grams) salt

Vampiro

This drink is very popular in the states of Coahuila and Nuevo León.

Pour tequila into a tall glass over ice cubes and add *Sangrita*. Add club soda, if desired. Garnish with a lime wedge. Serves 1.

1½ ounces (42 milliliters) tequila (p. TK)

Sangrita (see above)

Club soda (optional)

Lime wedge

Beer

Mexican beers, like European beers, and indeed like beers in almost all parts of the world except the United States, are distinctive, each one brewed to have its own special character. Most Mexican beer is brewed in the industrial city of Monterrey, which is also the home of *Cabrito al pastor* (they make a wonderful combination). However, some excellent beers are brewed in other parts of the country, including Chihuahua and Yucatán. Many Mexican beers are now exported, so you can try them all to determine your favorite. You might begin with the following: Bohemia, Corona, Tecate, Dos Equis, Carta Blanca, Chihuahua, and Negra Modelo. And don't forget Noche Buena, made by descendants of German brewers only at Christmas time.

Coca-Cola

Coca-Cola is the traditional *refresco* of northern Mexico. One sees Cokes everywhere. In fact, in Mexican homes in which I have taken meals, a liter of Coke is usually placed on the dining room table, much as we would a pitcher of water. It is interesting to note that Mexican Coke is noticeably sweeter than that in the United States, and many aficionados who live close to the border regularly bring it back by the case.

Rum and Coke

In addition to being a major producer of rum, Mexico is also a major consumer of this product. Rum mixed with Coca-Cola is the favorite rum drink in all of Mexico. It is called a Cuba Libre when ¼ lime, squeezed—or more to taste—is added.

1 shot (28 milliliters)
   dark rum
   Coca-Cola
¼ lime wedge, or to
   taste (optional)

Pour the rum over ice cubes into an 8-ounce (225-milliliter) bar glass, fill with Coke, and stir briefly. Squeeze the lime and add to the glass, if desired. Serves 1.

Brandy

In addition to tequila and rum, Mexico produces a large amount of brandy. The local brandies, while not equal to their European counterparts, are acceptable and economical alternatives. Brandy is often drunk straight, after dinner, but it is also popular at parties. At a carne asada (picnic or barbecue), people typically will begin by drinking beer, then switch to brandy, usually mixed with Coca-Cola or club soda, or a mixture of both. The most popular brandy is Presidente, which is available in this country. Viejo Vengel is also a good choice.

2 **cups (450 milliliters)
port wine**
²/₃ **cup (166 milliliters)
fresh orange juice
Juice of 1 lime**
3 **ounces (83 milliliters)
brandy**
1 **orange, sliced
Club soda**

Sangría

*There are many versions of this wine punch, which originated in
Spain. This recipe was given to me by a friend in Monterrey.*

Mix all ingredients in a pitcher and chill for several hours. Serve in
tall glasses over ice. Fill the glasses about ¾ full, add club soda, and
stir briefly. Serves 2.

Lemonade

*For a good portion of the year, northern Mexico is very hot and dry,
and nothing is more refreshing than an ice-cold lemonade. "Lemonade" is actually a misnomer since the drink sold by Mexican
street vendors from 5- to 8- gallon (18- to 28.8- liter) jugs is always
made with lime juice. Mexicans almost always sweeten it with a
sugar syrup instead of the plain sugar we use, which gives their
drinks a distinctive flavor.*

For 1 glass of lemonade, place 3 tablespoons (42 milliliters) lime juice
in a 12-ounce (240-milliliter) glass filled with ice. Add 2 to 3 tablespoons (28 to 42 milliliters) Simple Syrup (see p. 35) or sweeten to
taste. Fill the glass with water and stir.

To make 1 quart (900 milliliters) of lemonade, mix ²/₃ cup (166 milliliters) lime juice, ²/₃ cup (166 milliliters) Simple Syrup, and 2²/₃ cups
(616 milliliters) water in a pitcher. Place in the refrigerator to cool.
Serves 1.

Horchata

Horchata *is an extremely refreshing soft drink, popular through-out Mexico. It is variously made with dried melon seeds, rice, nuts, and fruit, often in different combinations. This simplified north-ern version is my favorite and a wonderful antidote to the area's dry, hot summers. It makes a great fruit punch, to which you may add a little gin or rum. This is a good example of the type of recipe that can be modified to suit your taste. Use more or less sugar, lime juice, and vanilla, or add some almonds or cooked rice to the mix-ture before blending.*

1 ripe cantaloupe, 2–3 pounds (900–1,350 grams)
¼ cup (56 milliliters) lime juice
2 tablespoons (24 grams) sugar
½ teaspoon vanilla
2–3 cups water (450–675 milliliters)

Cut the cantaloupe in half and scoop out as much as possible of the flesh and seeds. There should be about 2½ cups (560 milliliters). Place in the jar of a blender. Add the other ingredients and 2 to 3 cups (450 to 675 milliliters) water and blend for 2 minutes. Strain and refriger-ate or serve over ice. Makes 4 cups (900 milliliters).

Café de olla

COFFEE FROM THE POT

This is the traditional way to prepare coffee in Mexico and the way it is still served in Mexico's finest restaurants, where it more than holds its own against espressos and the like. Café de olla *should be made with the conical pieces of raw sugar called* piloncillo, *but you can substitute brown sugar.*

1 quart (900 milliliters) water
6 ounces (168 grams) *piloncillo* or 7 tablespoons (98 grams) brown sugar
1 3-inch (7.6- centimeter) stick cinnamon
1 ounce (28 grams) Mexican or bittersweet chocolate (optional)
⅔ cup (44 grams) medium-coarse ground coffee

Place the water, *piloncillo* or brown sugar, and cinnamon in a pot over medium heat. Heat until the *piloncillo* or brown sugar is melted; then turn the heat to high. Bring the water to a boil and continue boiling for 1 minute. If you are using the chocolate, add it at this time.

Remove the pot from the burner and make sure the chocolate is completely melted. As soon as the water is still, pour in the coffee and cover the pot. Do not stir the coffee at this time. After 5 minutes remove the cover and very gently stir the coffee *just* until it sinks to the bottom of the pot. Pour the coffee into cups through a very fine strainer and serve. Makes 4½ cups (1,012.5 milliliters).

Café filtrado con leche

FILTERED COFFEE WITH MILK

This coffee-making technique involves filtering cold water through ground coffee to produce a concentrate which is then mixed with boiling water or milk. It is very popular in Mexico and throughout Latin America, where restaurants often keep a small carafe of the concentrate on their tables alongside the salt and pepper. Although there are a large number of devotees to this method in the United States, it has never achieved the popularity that it has south of the border. This is surprising since the concentrate keeps for nearly three weeks in the refrigerator, is great for travel, and is said to reduce the acids in coffee without affecting the flavor. A widely available device called the Toddy Maker is excellent for making this type of coffee.

Follow the Toddy Maker directions to make the concentrate and an ordinary cup of coffee. To make a Mexican favorite, place 2 tablespoons (28 grams) of concentrate in a coffee cup, add 6 tablespoons (83 milliliters) boiling milk, and about 2 teaspoons (8 grams) sugar if you like it sweet. Serves 1.

Simple Syrup

Mix the sugar and water; then heat, stirring the liquid until it just begins to simmer. Cool and store in a glass or heavy plastic container (a pancake syrup dispenser is a good choice). Refrigerate if the syrup will not be used within a day or two.

1 cup (225 milliliters) water
½ cup (100 grams) sugar

Northern Mexican ingredients are beautiful before as well as after preparation.

Northern Mexican sauces such as (clockwise beginning at the top) *Salsa cruda de Chihuahua, Salsa borracha III, Salsa de chile ancho, Salsa de aguacate* and *Salsa corriente* are a colorful and delicious addition to any meal.

Items like *chimichangas* and soup are often made with
Carne seca, especially in Sonora and Nuevo León.

A rich *Arroz verde* with stuffed chiles is one of northern Mexico's most elegant dishes.

The *parillada,* a selection of broiled meats with side dishes, is often the center piece at northern Mexican celebrations.

Steak *Tampiqueña* is the ultimate Mexican combination plate.

Camarones adobados is one of the best and simplest
ways to prepare Baja California's delicious shrimp.

Fish and shrimp in garlic sauce is popular wherever
seafood is found in Mexico.

Antojitos mexicanos like *flautas, gorditas, Flautas del norte* and *Tacos alambres* are popular for snacks and light meals.

More like enchiladas than tacos, *Tacos potosinos* are a specialty of San Luis Potosí.

While not well known in the United States, sandwiches like the *Torta especial* are very popular in Mexico.

Northern Mexico is famous for its *dulces*, sweets and candies which are often served with *Café de olla.*

Sauces

❖❖❖

Salsas

Salsas, tortillas, and beans are the mainstays of Mexican cooking. A bowl of some kind of hot sauce, or perhaps several, is always on the dining table. During years of traveling in Mexico, I have encountered the many excellent variations included here. The secret of a successful sauce is always to use fresh ingredients.

Warning: exercise extreme care when handling chiles. They can cause severe burns. The use of rubber gloves is recommended. Wash your hands thoroughly and never touch your eyes or other sensitive areas after handling chiles.

Almost all of the following sauces may be eaten with *tostadas* as a snack or appetizer. It might be fun to make a bowl of each and have a tasting party to become familiar with them and select your favorites. However, be sure to warn your friends about some of the hotter selections, such as *Salsa de chile piquín.*

Salsa jalapeño cocido

COOKED JALAPEÑO SAUCE

1 tablespoon (15 milliliters cooking oil

2–3 medium *jalapeños*, minced

$^1/_3$ medium onion, finely chopped

1 medium garlic clove, minced

2 medium tomatoes, peeled and chopped

2 teaspoons (7 milliliters) vinegar

$^1/_2$ teaspoon salt, or to taste

$^1/_4$ cup (12.4 grams) cilantro, chopped and loosely packed

This sauce, popular in the northern states of Coahuila and Tamaulipas, is a favorite in Texas restaurants. But the Texas version, usually made with canned ingredients, is inferior to the original.

Heat the oil over medium heat and sauté the *jalapeños*, onion, and garlic until soft but not browned.

Add the tomatoes, vinegar, and salt and simmer, uncovered, for 5 minutes or until the desired consistency is reached. Remove the pan from the heat and add the chopped cilantro.

Cool and serve with *tostadas* or other foods of your choice. Serves 4.

Salsa de jalapeño en escabeche

PICKLED JALAPEÑO SAUCE

This excellent table sauce from Durango is especially good with tostadas. The pickled jalapeños, *even though canned, add a unique flavor that works well with the other ingredients.*

Place the oil and garlic in a small saucepan over very low heat. Cook until the garlic is soft but not browned, 1 to 2 minutes. Add the remaining ingredients, stirring to mix well. Bring the sauce to a boil over medium heat, and, turning the heat to low, simmer for 5 minutes. Allow to cool before serving. Serves 4.

1½ teaspoons (6 milliliters) olive oil

1–2 cloves garlic, minced

3 medium tomatoes, broiled and finely chopped

2–3 pickled *jalapeños*, minced

1½ tablespoons (21 milliliters) juice from *jalapeño* can or jar

¾ teaspoon oregano

¼ teaspoon salt

⅓ cup (48 grams) onion, minced

Salsa de jalapeño o serrano asado

BROILED JALAPEÑO OR SERRANO SAUCE

This simple salsa is one of the best all-purpose table sauces in either of its forms: ground or blended and strained. The charred tomatoes and chiles add a robust flavor, and the texture is yours to determine. Because of the differences between jalapeños *and* serranos *in size and amount of heat, it is difficult to specify the exact number of chiles to be used. A little experimentation will quickly provide the right formula for your taste. A good rule of thumb is 1 chile per tomato for a hot sauce and 1 chile per 2 tomatoes for a sauce of medium heat.*

As mentioned above, there are two ways to make this sauce, each producing quite different results. The easiest method, and perhaps

2 medium to large tomatoes, broiled

1–2 *jalapeños*, or 2–3 *serrano* chiles, broiled

¼ teaspoon salt, or to taste

my favorite, is to put all the ingredients into a blender and blend for about 30 seconds, then strain into a serving bowl. The texture will be smooth and the sauce flecked with tiny bits of the charred tomato and chile skins. The other method requires that the chile seeds be removed, then all ingredients ground to the desired consistency in a *molcajete* or mortar and pestle. (Alternately, a few whirls in a food processor will work, but it is easy to overprocess.) The result makes a chunky, textured sauce with lots of color. Serves 4.

NOTE: To broil tomatoes and chiles, place them 3 to 6 inches (7.6 to 15.2 centimeters) above hot coals on a grill, or below the oven's broiler. Broil until they are soft and the skins are well charred, about 20 minutes.

Salsa para mariscos

SEAFOOD SAUCE

This sauce is delicious with cold boiled shrimp and is an excellent alternative to the usual thick red seafood sauces.

Mix all the ingredients well and allow to stand at room temperature for 1 hour before serving. Serves 4.

2 tablespoons (28 milliliters) lime juice

¼ cup (56 milliliters) olive oil or other good quality cooking oil

2 large *poblano* chiles or Anaheim chiles, minced

3 *serrano* chiles, minced

1 clove garlic, minced

1 teaspoon (.6 gram) oregano

Pinch salt, or to taste

Pinch pepper, or to taste

2 tablespoons (6.2 grams) cilantro, chopped and loosely packed

Salsa de chile piquín

PIQUÍN CHILE SAUCE

Beware! This sauce is made with the fiery little chile piquín, *and these tiny, football-shaped chiles pack quite a wallop. The sauce adds piquancy to mesquite-broiled meats, but be sure to use it sparingly. This recipe comes from San Luis de Río Colorado, a large city 30 miles south of Yuma, Arizona. One fine restaurant there serves nothing but lamb tacos accompanied by this sauce.*

Place all the ingredients in the jar of a blender and blend for 1 minute. Use only a few drops (until you become accustomed to it) on broiled meats, especially lamb. Serves 4.

¹/₄ cup (16.4 grams) *piquín* chiles

2 tablespoons (28 milliliters) mild cider vinegar

¹/₄ cup (36 grams) diced onion

¹/₃ cup (75 milliliters) water

1 medium clove garlic

¹/₄ teaspoon salt, or to taste

1 small or ¹/₂ medium tomato, chopped

Chiles en vinagre

CHILES IN VINEGAR

This delicious condiment is found throughout the states of Nuevo León and Coahuila, where the fiery pequín *and* tepín *chiles are harvested wild. Fortunately, these chiles are one of the easiest and most attractive to cultivate around the home and are particularly adaptable to containers. A few drops of this sauce does wonders for soup and meat dishes.*

Place the chiles, vinegar, and salt in a saucepan, bring to a boil, and simmer for 5 to 7 minutes. Spoon the chiles into a 4-ounce (110-milliliter), sterilized glass container (a restaurant-style oil and vinegar cruet with a cork works well), top with the vinegar, seal, and allow the flavors to develop for several days before using. Serves 4.

¹/₂ cup (33 grams) fresh *pequín* or *tepín* chiles, stems removed

1 cup (225 milliliters) unflavored rice wine vinegar

¹/₂ teaspoon salt

Salsa de chile de árbol

CHILE DE ÁRBOL SAUCE

❖❖❖❖❖

1 ounce (28 grams) *de árbol* chiles or *japonés* chiles
½ cup (110 milliliters) water
2 tablespoons (28 milliliters) cane or cider vinegar
2 cloves garlic
¼ teaspoon cumin
½ teaspoon oregano
½ teaspoon salt

This is one of the hottest sauces I have ever tried. It takes a confirmed "chile head" to enjoy it!

Toast the chiles by heating them in a heavy skillet over low heat until they are fragrant but not burned.

Place the chiles in a blender with ¼ cup (56 milliliters) of the water and the remaining ingredients and blend for 1 minute. Add the remaining water and blend again for 30 seconds. Strain the sauce into a bowl. Serves 4.

Salsa borracha I

DRUNKEN SAUCE I

❖❖❖❖❖

1 small *pasilla* chile or *ancho* chile
2 dried *chipotle* chiles
1 *de árbol* chile
2 medium tomatoes, broiled
½ medium onion, diced
½ tablespoon (6 milliliters) cooking oil
¼ teaspoon salt
½ tablespoon *mescal,* or substitute tequila

This sauce is especially suited to charbroiled meats because it uses the smoked chipotle *chile.*

Toast the chiles by placing them in a heavy skillet over low heat. Turn frequently until they just begin to color and give off a pungent fragrance. Avoid burning them, as this will make them bitter. After toasting, soak the chiles in hot water for ½ hour. Next, seed them and place them in the jar of a blender.

Broil the tomatoes, place 1 of them in the blender with the chiles, and blend for 1 minute. In a small saucepan, sauté the onion in the oil over low heat for 5 minutes. Then add the blended chile mixture, the salt, and *mescal* or tequila and cook another 5 minutes. Crush the remaining tomato in a *molcajete* or mortar and pestle and mix with the other ingredients in a serving bowl. Alternatively, the second tomato may be whirled 2 to 3 times in a food processor. However, be sure not to overprocess. Serves 4.

Salsa borracha II

DRUNKEN SAUCE II

This is the only Salsa borracha *I have found that uses fresh chiles. It is easy to make and excellent.*

Heat the oil in a saucepan over medium heat; add the onion and chiles and cook until the onion is soft but not browned. Add the tomato, beer, and salt; bring to a boil and simmer until the sauce begins to thicken, about 25 to 30 minutes. Remove the sauce from the heat, and when it is cool add the cheese. Serves 4.

¼ **cup (56 milliliters) cooking oil**
1 **cup (142.7 grams) onion, chopped**
4 *serrano* **chiles, seeded and coarsely chopped**
2½ **cups (418 grams) tomato, coarsely chopped**
¾ **cup (170 milliliters) beer**
1 **teaspoon (6.2 grams) salt, or to taste**
½ **cup (54.4 grams) *queso fresco*, grated, or substitute Monterey Jack cheese**

Salsa borracha III

DRUNKEN SAUCE III

This earthy sauce, made of both beer and tequila, which I found in a taqueria *in Saltillo, is one of my all-time favorites. The key is to pulse the blender enough to break the chiles into very small pieces but not so much that it becomes a smooth sauce.*

Preheat your oven to 275 degrees F (135 degrees C).

Rinse off the chiles, toast them in the oven for 5 minutes, then allow them to cool. Remove the stems and seeds and cut the chiles into small pieces. Place the chiles in a blender with the garlic and beer and allow to sit for 15 minutes. Using the pulse mechanism, grind the contents into a chunky sauce made of small bits of softened chile and garlic. Add a little more beer to thin the sauce, if necessary.

6 *pasilla* **chiles**
2 **cloves garlic**
½ **cup (110 milliliters) dark beer**
1 **tablespoon (15 milliliters) cooking oil**
2 **tablespoons (28 milliliters) tequila**
1 **teaspoon (4.5 grams) brown sugar**
½ **teaspoon salt, or to taste**
½ **cup (71 grams) onion, minced**
3 **tablespoons (23 grams) *queso anejo*, crumbled, or substitute feta cheese**

Heat a saucepan over medium heat, add the oil, then add the contents of the blender, the tequila, brown sugar, and the salt. As soon as the sauce comes to a boil remove it from the heat and stir in the onion. When the sauce has cooled, stir in the cheese. Serves 4.

Salsa de chile ancho

ANCHO CHILE SAUCE

3 *ancho* chiles, stemmed, seeded, and deveined
2 cloves garlic
½ teaspoon salt, or to taste
   Water

This is a fairly mild but robust sauce that is particularly good with pork or tostadas.

Soak the chiles in hot water for at least 15 minutes; then place them in a blender with the garlic, salt, and ½ cup (110 milliliters) of the water in which the chiles were soaked. Blend at high speed for 1 minute, adding water and continuing to blend until the desired consistency is achieved. As a variation, add a broiled tomato to the sauce. Serves 4.

Salsa de ajo

GARLIC SAUCE

¼ cup (56 milliliters) cooking oil
1 *ancho* chile, stemmed, seeded, and chopped into small pieces
10 cloves garlic, peeled
¼ cup (56 milliliters) water
   Heaping ¼ teaspoon salt, or to taste

This is one of the most interesting sauces I have come across. It goes well with broiled meats but is particularly suited to broiled seafood.

Heat the oil in a saucepan over low heat and add the chile. Cook, stirring often, until the chile begins to toast and become fragrant, about 2 minutes. Turn the heat to very low, add the garlic, and continue cooking until it is soft and just beginning to brown.

Place the chile, garlic, and oil from the pan in a blender; add the water and salt and blend for 1 minute. Serves 4.

Salsa corriente

COMMON SAUCE

In small grocery stores all over northern Mexico one finds shelves filled with one-liter bottles of commercially prepared hot sauce. This is the sauce that people keep on hand for occasions when they do not have time to prepare a more elaborate one, or where they prefer it. This type of sauce is very easy to make.

Place the chiles in a pot, cover them with water, bring them to a boil, and simmer for 10 minutes or until they are very soft. Strain the chiles, transfer them to a blender, add the remaining ingredients, and blend at high speed for 1 minute. Add some more water, if necessary, to make the sauce a medium to medium-thin consistency. Using a food mill, strain the blended mixture into a bowl, allow it to cool, and refrigerate. Makes about 1½ cups (240 milliliters).

- 4 ounces (112 grams) *guajillo* chiles, stems removed
- 2 cups (450 milliliters) water
- ½ cup (110 milliliters) cane or white vinegar
- 1 teaspoon (6.2 grams) salt, or to taste

Salsa de jalapeño verde

GREEN JALAPEÑO SAUCE

This sauce, made of puréed jalapeños, *is very hot. It is delicious over broiled meats and poultry, if used sparingly.*

Place the chiles in a saucepan and cover them with water. Bring them to a boil and simmer until they are soft, about 15 minutes. Slice open the chiles and remove all the seeds with a small spoon. Next, put the cooked chiles in a blender with the ¼ cup (56 milliliters) of water and the remaining ingredients and blend until puréed, about 30 seconds. Allow to cool before serving. Serves 4.

- 3 ounces (78 grams) fresh *jalapeños*, stems removed
- ¼ cup (56 milliliters) water
- 1 teaspoon (5 milliliters) white vinegar
- 1 teaspoon (6.2 grams) salt
- ¼ teaspoon sugar

Salsa de chile verde

GREEN CHILE SAUCE

3 medium tomatoes
4 green chiles, peeled, seeded, and diced
$^1/_3$ medium onion, diced
1 teaspoon (5 milliliters) vinegar
$^1/_4$ teaspoon salt, or to taste
$^1/_4$ cup (12.4 grams) cilantro, chopped and loosely packed

This sauce is a specialty of the state of Sonora.

Broil and then dice the tomatoes. Mix the tomatoes and chiles with the remaining ingredients. Serves 4.

Salsa de tomatillo

TOMATILLO SAUCE

$^1/_2$ pound (225 grams) *tomatillos*
$^1/_4$ teaspoon sugar
1 *serrano* chile, seeded
$^1/_4$ teaspoon salt
$^1/_3$ cup (75 milliliters) water
1 green tomato (optional)

This sauce is served with tacos, broiled seafood, and chicken and is also used as an enchilada sauce. It is best made with fresh tomatillos, but canned may be substituted. The following recipe is for use as a table sauce. For use as an enchilada sauce, double the quantities to serve 4. Some tomatillos can be a little bitter. To counter this, cook a green tomato with the tomatillos.

If you are using fresh *tomatillos*, cover them with water and bring them slowly to a boil in a small saucepan in order to prevent the skins from breaking. Simmer gently for about 10 minutes or until they are very tender. If you are using the cooked, canned *tomatillos*, omit the simmering but be sure to rinse them thoroughly.

Place the *tomatillos* in a blender or food processor with the remaining ingredients and blend or process until puréed. Return the sauce to the pan and simmer for 5 minutes or until the sauce has thickened slightly. Serves 4.

Salsa cruda de Chihuahua

UNCOOKED SAUCE FROM CHIHUAHUA

This sauce may be misnamed, as the lime juice cooks the chiles, softening the bite, as it does with ceviche.

Place the chiles, onion, green onion, and salt in a glass or other nonreactive bowl with the lime juice. Mix well and refrigerate for 1 to 2 hours. Strain off and discard the lime juice. Next, add the chopped tomatoes and just enough of the broiled, blended tomato to bind the mixture into a sauce. Add more salt, if desired. Stir in the cilantro and avocado, if used. The avocado, although optional, adds a great deal to the sauce. Serves 4.

NOTE: To broil the tomato, place it 3 to 6 inches (7.6 to 15.2 centimeters) above hot coals on a grill or below the oven's broiler. Broil until the tomato is soft and the skin is well charred, about 20 minutes.

¼ cup (30 grams) *serrano* chiles, seeded and chopped

¼ cup (30 grams) *jalapeño* chiles, seeded and chopped

¼ cup (30 grams) *poblano* chiles or *verde*, seeded and chopped

¼ cup (36 grams) onion, chopped

2 tablespoons (10.8 grams) green onion, chopped

¼–½ teaspoon salt, or to taste

½ cup (110 milliliters) freshly squeezed lime juice

2 medium tomatoes, chopped

1 medium tomato, broiled and blended until smooth

¼ cup (12.4 grams) cilantro, minced

1 medium avocado, peeled, seeded, and chopped (optional)

Salsa de cilantro

CILANTRO SAUCE

¼ cup (28 grams)
    serrano chiles,
    seeded and coarsely
    chopped
¼ cup (12.4 grams)
    lightly packed
    chopped cilantro
3 tablespoons (26
    grams) onion,
    coarsely chopped
¼ teaspoon salt
1 teaspoon (5
    milliliters) lime
    juice
5 tablespoons (71
    milliliters) water

This sauce from Coahuila has a fresh, light flavor and goes well with chicken or seafood.

Place all the ingredients in a blender and pulse at low speed until they are well ground but not puréed.

Salsa fresca

FRESH SAUCE

1 cup (227 grams)
    tomatoes, chopped
¼ cup (36 grams) onion,
    chopped
2 tablespoons (16
    grams) *serrano*
    chiles, seeded and
    minced
¼ cup (12.4 grams)
    loosely packed
    cilantro
½ teaspoon salt

This sauce can be ground in a molcajete, *which gives it a fine texture, or it can be blended. Unfortunately, the latter method, which is often used in restaurants, produces an inferior texture. On the other hand, using a blender is a very easy method of making a large quantity of sauce that has a fine fresh taste. One of my favorite restaurants has found a middle ground in that it grinds the ingredients in a meat grinder with a coarse blade. A food processor may also be used for this purpose. If you decide to grind the ingredients by hand, cutting them as finely as possible will make the task much easier.*

Either grind the ingredients together in a *molcajete* or pulse them in a blender or food processor until they reach the desired texture. Makes about 1¼ cups (292 milliliters).

Pico de gallo

TOMATO AND CHILE RELISH

Literally translated, pico de gallo *means "rooster's beak." No one has been able to explain to me the significance of the name. Perhaps it derives from the shape of the* serrano *peppers. In the north of Mexico* Pico de gallo *is the universal table relish. It always accompanies* arracheras *(fajitas, or skirt steak), whether served as an entrée or chopped in tacos. It is delicious with any broiled meat and is an attractive garnish as well.*

Toss all the ingredients until well mixed and serve immediately since this relish does not keep. Serves 4.

1 medium tomato, seeded and finely chopped

3 *serrano* chiles, seeded and minced

2 medium green onions, minced

3 tablespoons (26 grams) onion, finely chopped

$1/8$ teaspoon salt, or to taste

$1/4$ cup (12.4 grams) cilantro, chopped and lightly packed

1 teaspoon (5 milliliters) lime juice (optional)

Salsa de aguacate

AVOCADO SAUCE

◇◇◇◇◇

8 ounces (225 grams) *tomatillos*

3 *serrano* chiles

1 medium to large avocado, about 8 ounces (225 grams)

1 tablespoon (15 milliliters) lime juice

1 green onion, minced

2 tablespoons (17.5 grams) onion, minced

3 tablespoons (9.3 grams) cilantro, minced

½ teaspoon salt, or to taste

Both its texture and taste make this a very special accompaniment to just about anything with which you would serve avocado. Since avocados vary so much in size, you will need to adjust the amount of the tomatillo *mixture you add. To achieve the proper texture the* tomatillo *portion of the sauce should be made in a* molcajete, *but if you are careful it can be made in a blender, using the pulse button at low speed.*

Place the *tomatillos* and *serrano* chiles in a saucepan, cover with water, bring to a boil, and barely simmer until they are tender, about 3 to 5 minutes. Remove the *tomatillos* and place them in a *molcajete* or blender. When the *serranos* are cool enough to handle, remove their stems and seeds, mince, and add them to the *molcajete*, or blender. Either grind the *tomatillos* and *serranos* coarsely in the *molcajete* or pulse a time or two in the blender to achieve the same result. You should have about ¾ cup (170 milliliters) of the *tomatillo* mixture.

Remove the skin and seed the avocado, cut it into ½-inch (1.3-centimeter) pieces, and place it in a bowl. Add the lime juice, green onion, onion, and cilantro and mix well, mashing the avocado slightly in the process. Stir in the *tomatillo* mixture and add the salt. Serves 4 as a table sauce.

Appetizers

◈◇◈

*Aperitivos
y Botanas*

Most cookbooks fail to make clear the real distinction between *aperitivos* and *botanas*, on the one hand, and *antojitos*, on the other. Usually, all three are inaccurately classified as appetizers.

We think of an appetizer as a small first course, served before the entrée, to stimulate the palate. The Spanish word *aperitivo*, "that which has the power of opening the appetite," closely fits this concept. The *botana*, literally the "plug or stopple used to stop up the opening in a leather wine bag," in Mexico refers to snacks taken with cocktails, such as peanuts and *pepitas*. However, both *aperitivos* and *botanas* may be considered appetizers as we know them.

Antojito is a form of the Spanish word *antojo*: a whim, vehement desire, longing, hankering, or fancy. So, *antojitos* could be literally translated as "little whims or fancies," or, as they are often used in Mexico, snacks. However, *antojitos*, as in *antojitos mexicanos*, also refers to typical Mexican dishes. Many Mexican restaurants advertise *antojitos mexicanos* as their specialty. Such foods as tacos, *quesadillas*, enchiladas, burritos, and tamales are included in this category. They are regarded not as appetizers but as snacks, although they are often used as a main entrée, particularly by those in the lower economic strata. The fact that the majority of Mexican immigrants to the United States have come from this class explains the predominance of *antojitos* in Mexican-American restaurants, and why, when most Americans think of Mexican food, they think of *antojitos*.

Because the use of both *aperitivos* and *botanas* in Mexico fits our perception of appetizers, I have included both in this section. However, because of the real differences between them and *antojitos*, the latter will be found in a separate section. This placement also more accurately reflects our conception of *antojitos* in the United States.

Aperitivos and *botanas* are very special elements of all regional Mexican cuisines. Although many Mexican appetizers, such as peanuts, *chicharrones*, and *tostadas*, are fairly simple, they are used in distinctive ways and with unusual seasonings that make them truly special.

Tostadas or Totopos

TORTILLA CHIPS

Tortilla chips, or tostadas, are the appetizer universally provided in Mexican-American restaurants. Often called totopos in the south of Mexico, they are difficult to resist. The problem is that a basket or two takes the edge off one's appetite.

In Mexico tostadas are used more sparingly. Most restaurants do not serve them automatically, although this is changing. One reason may be that they are not usually as good as those made north of the border. Mexican tortillas are usually thicker and contain more moisture than ours, making them more difficult to fry properly. Also, thermostat-controlled fryers that produce consistent results are not yet as common in Mexico as they are in the United States.

Tostadas should be made from the thinnest possible corn tortillas, cut into 8 quarters, then fried in deep oil at 350–375 degrees F (177 to 190 degrees C) until they are crisp. They are ready to serve when they are golden brown and have stopped sputtering. If this does not happen simultaneously, adjust the temperature.

Serve *tostadas* with your favorite salsas, guacamole, and as a garnish for refried beans. Leftover *tostadas* are used to make *chilaquiles*.

Nachos

GARNISHED TORTILLA CHIPS

6 corn tortillas, cut into
   quarters
4 ounces (112 grams)
   cheddar or
   Monterey Jack
   cheese, thinly sliced
24 thin slices of pickled
   jalapeños

A small restaurant in Piedras Negras, Coahuila, known as Nacho's, claims to have originated the nacho. Regardless of who served the first nacho, its popularity as an appetizer or cocktail snack has spread throughout Mexico and the United States. In this country, we have "nacho-flavored tortilla chips," which do not even approximate the great taste of the real thing.

Deep-fry the tortilla pieces as for *tostadas* (p. 53). Drain on paper towels and arrange in an ovenproof serving dish. Top each fried chip with a slice of cheese and a slice of *jalapeño*.

Place the dish of prepared chips about 6 to 8 inches (15.2 to 20.3 centimeters) under a preheated broiler for 1 to 2 minutes, or until the cheese is just melted. Serves 4.

Nachos compuestos

SPECIAL NACHOS

Compuesto means "fixed up," and these nachos certainly are. They sometimes are called nachos supremos *by ambitious restaurateurs.*

Do everything as for regular Nachos (see above) except add 1½ cups (381 grams) Refried Beans (p. 107) and ¾ cup (190 grams) Guacamole (p. 83) to the list of ingredients. Top each *tostada* triangle with: 1 tablespoon (16 grams) Refried Beans, a slice of cheese, and a slice of *jalapeño*. Place the *Nachos compuestos* under the broiler until the cheese has melted, then remove. Garnish with ½ tablespoon (7 grams) Guacamole. Serves 4.

Queso flameado

FLAMING CHEESE

Queso flameado, *or* Queso fundido *(burned cheese) as it is often called in the south of Mexico, are two names for the same delicious dish. There is really no substitute for* queso asadero, *or the Mennonite* queso de Chihuahua, *as the principal ingredient. If these are not available, the best substitute for this dish is mozzarella. At restaurants such as the México Típico in Nuevo Laredo, Queso flameado is served flaming at the table.*

Fry the *chorizo* until it is well browned. Place the cheese in a flame-proof, medium-sized serving dish. Top with the crumbled *chorizo* and set 6 to 8 inches (15.2 to 20.3 centimeters) under a preheated broiler. Cook until the cheese is melted and bubbling but not browned. While this is cooking, warm the brandy, if used, in a small pan.

When the cheese is ready, remove it from the oven, pour the warmed brandy over the cheese, and light it. Set the serving dish and an ample supply of corn and/or flour tortillas and salsa on the dining table. Each person can then spoon individual portions of cheese onto the tortillas. Serves 4.

½ **pound (225 grams)** *chorizo*

1 **pound (450 grams)** *asadero, queso de Chihuahua,* **mozzarella, or farmer cheese, grated**

½ **ounce (15 milliliters) brandy (optional)**

Chile con queso

CHILE WITH CHEESE

2 tablespoons (30 grams) butter

1 large onion, coarsely chopped

4 green chiles, roasted, peeled, seeded, and chopped

1 clove garlic, minced

2 large tomatoes, peeled, seeded, and chopped

1 pinch oregano

1 pound *asadero, queso de Chihuahua,* or mozzarella cheese, grated

The prevalent—and mistaken—idea of Chile con queso *probably derives from the variety served at cocktail parties that is made with concentrated cheddar cheese soup. The authentic dish, such as this recipe from the state of Chihuahua, is far superior.*

Sauté over medium heat, the onion, green chiles, and garlic until they just begin to soften. Add the tomatoes and oregano and continue to cook over medium heat for about 5 minutes.

Preheat the oven to 425 degrees F (220 degrees C). Place the cheese in an ovenproof bowl, top with the sautéed vegetables, and bake until the cheese is melted and running into the vegetables but not browned.

Unless it is to be eaten immediately, serve the *Chile con queso* in a chafing dish or on a plate warmer. Spoon the cheese mixture onto flour or corn tortillas, roll up, and eat. Serves 4.

Chicharrones

FRIED PORK RINDS

Chicharrones *are made from pork rinds that are deep-fried until crisp and puffy, then lightly salted. A favorite Mexican snack in the north, they are often accompanied by lime halves and Tabasco or a similar sauce.*

Chicharrones *also are used to flavor* Frijoles de olla *or* Frijoles a la charra, *or softened in a sauce as a filling for tacos. In the open-air market in Chihuahua City, there is stall after stall of large iron cauldrons set over gas fires, filled with bubbling lard in which* Chicharrones *are cooking. The counters are piled high with cooked rinds of all sizes, from about 1 inch (2.54 centime-*

ters) to more than 1 foot (30.5 centimeters), priced according to quality and sold by weight.

Chicharrones are not difficult to make if you can find uncooked pork rinds. Cook them in oil heated to 350 degrees F (177 degrees C) in a deep fryer until they puff up and become crisp. This takes about 10 minutes. However, Chicharrones are easier to buy than to make, and the commercial products are of acceptable quality.

To serve, place the Chicharrones on a serving dish, squeeze some lime juice over them, and add a few drops of Tabasco sauce. They are also an excellent accompaniment to oysters on the half shell. (See also Tacos de chicharrones [p. 170]) Serves 4.

Cacahuates con chile

HOT PEANUTS

Probably the most popular cocktail appetizer in northern Mexico is peanuts. The hot peanuts and garlic peanuts made in Coahuila are truly extraordinary. On trips to the interior, we always stopped at the modest house of an old man in Piedras Negras, across the border from Eagle Pass, Texas. This was the home and factory of the "Hot Peanut Man." We would emerge with brown sacks of delicious, piquant, freshly roasted peanuts. Roasting peanuts is still a cottage industry in that area, although major corporate food companies are now getting into the act with the predictable result—a drop in quality.

Garlic may be added to this recipe, to make hot garlic peanuts. See the following recipe for the full garlic version.

½ **cup (110 milliliters) cooking oil**

¼ **cup (16.4 grams)** *piquín* **chiles**

8 **cloves garlic, peeled (optional)**

2 **cups (232 grams) raw Spanish peanuts, shelled**

Salt, to taste

Place the oil, chiles, and garlic in a small pan and warm over low heat for 3 minutes. Do not allow the mixture to approach the simmering point.

Blend the mixture for 2 minutes and let it stand for 1 hour. Blend again for 1 minute; then strain the mixture into a small glass jar or plastic container.

Next, toss the peanuts with 2 teaspoons (7 milliliters) of the flavored oil until they are well coated and place them in a large heavy iron skillet.

Place the skillet with the peanuts into an oven preheated to 300 degrees F (148 degrees C) and roast them, stirring every 5 minutes, for a total of 30 minutes. (The process may take a little longer, depending upon the freshness of the peanuts.)

Remove the skillet from the oven and allow to cool for 30 minutes, salt to taste, and serve. Serves 4.

Cacahuates con ajo

GARLIC PEANUTS

This is a slight variation on the preceding recipe for hot peanuts.

Toss the peanuts with the oil and garlic in a medium-sized, heavy skillet and place them in a 300-degree F (148-degree C) preheated oven for 30 minutes, stirring every 5 minutes.

Remove the nuts from the oven, pour them into a small bowl, and allow them to cool for 30 minutes. Salt to taste and serve. Serves 4.

2 **cups (232 grams) raw Spanish peanuts, shelled**

1 **tablespoon (15 milliliters) cooking oil**

8 **medium cloves garlic, minced**

Salt, to taste

Pan de maíz

FRIED CORN BREAD

This fried corn bread from Coahuila makes a delicious appetizer when served with guacamole.

Mix the cornmeal, flour, salt, and baking powder. Add the lard or oil and egg and mix well. Then add the remaining ingredients to form a thick batter.

    Heat oil to 375 degrees F (190 degrees C). Deep-fry the bread by immersing it in the oil 2 tablespoons (30 grams) of batter at a time in a large serving spoon. They are finished when puffed, crispy, and golden brown. Serve immediately with Guacamole (p. 83) and salsa. Serves 4.

½ cup (64 grams) yellow cornmeal

½ cup (75 grams) all-purpose flour

½ teaspoon salt

1 teaspoon (3.3 grams) baking powder

1 tablespoon (14.25 grams) melted lard or oil

1 egg, lightly beaten

2 pickled *jalapeños*, seeded and minced

2 tablespoons (28 milliliters) liquid from *jalapeño* jar

½ cup (110 milliliters) milk

Oil for deep-frying

Bacon and Guacamole

This dish makes an appetizer, light lunch, or supper that I have often enjoyed in the state of Coahuila. It could hardly be easier to prepare, and the smoke from the fire gives the bacon an extra-special flavor, especially if you use mesquite wood.

Broil the bacon slowly over mesquite coals, or over charcoal-flavored wood chips, setting the grill about 10 to 12 inches (25.4 to 30.5 centimeters) above the fire. The distance from the heat and the cooking time are important because of the high fat content of the bacon. Serve with Guacamole, *Bolillos*, and butter for an appetizer. With the addition of rice and/or beans, this makes a lunch or supper dish. Serves 4.

¾ pound (340 grams) bacon, cut extra thick

Guacamole (p. 83)

Bolillos (p. 96)

Olivos encurtidos

CURED OLIVES

◇◇◇◇◇

3 tablespoons (36 grams) lye

5 gallons (18 liters) water

1 gallon (3 kilograms + 600 grams) ripe green olives

3 tablespoons (60 grams) Noniodized salt

Until an old friend of my family, Ray Salcido, brought us some of his homecured olives, I had always found them too salty and strong-tasting. Ray's olives have a wonderful texture, tender but firm. Their flavor is mild but subtly full, without the overpowering taste of salty brine.

In doing research for this book, I found similarly delicious olives throughout Sonora, where they are sold in bulk from tubs in markets and grocery stores. Ray has kindly allowed me to use his recipe, which follows. Please note that this recipe requires lye, which, if used improperly, can cause injury. Read and carefully follow all directions on the package.

Olives are ready for curing when they just begin to turn a dark purple.

In a nonreactive container, dissolve the lye in 1 gallon (3,600 milliliters) of water and add the olives. Soak for 24 hours. Rinse the olives with cold water.

Mix 3 heaping tablespoons (60 grams) salt into 1 gallon (3,600 milliliters) of water, add the olives, and soak for 24 hours. (Be sure to use noniodized salt, as iodized salt will spoil the flavor.) Rinse the olives and repeat the procedure twice.

After the final rinsing, prepare another solution of salt water. Place the olives in sterilized jars, fill with the salt water solution, seal, and refrigerate. Makes 1 gallon.

Jalapeños en escabeche

PICKLED JALAPEÑOS

The title of this recipe does not really do it justice. From Saltillo's fantastic La Canasta restaurant, this version of this popular appetizer is simply the best I have ever had. Although you may use any type of vinegar, I suggest rice wine vinegar to better duplicate the lower acid content of those found in Mexico.

With a pin or needle prick the skins of the *jalapeños* every $\frac{1}{8}$ to $\frac{1}{4}$ inch (.3 to .6 centimeter), then stem, seed, and cut them into $\frac{1}{4}$- to $\frac{1}{2}$- inch (.6- to 1.3- centimeter) slices. In a nonreactive bowl mix together the water, salt, vinegar, and lime juice; add the *jalapeños* and refrigerate overnight.

Add the corn oil, oregano, thyme, marjoram, peppercorns, bay leaves, and softened garlic to the chiles. Parboil the carrots until they are just beginning to soften, put them in cold water to stop the cooking process, then also add them to the bowl with the *jalapeños*.

Using a strainer, dip the onions and zucchini, if using, into boiling water for 15 seconds, rinse with cold water, and add to the bowl. Add the *jícama*, if using, return the bowl to the refrigerator, and marinate for about 3 hours. Serves 4 as an appetizer or snack.

$3\frac{1}{2}$ ounces (100 grams) *jalapeño* chiles (about $\frac{2}{3}$ cup when sliced)

$\frac{1}{3}$ cup plus 3 tablespoons (126 milliliters) water

$1\frac{1}{2}$ teaspoons (9–10 grams) salt

$\frac{1}{4}$ cup (56 milliliters) rice wine vinegar

2 teaspoons (7 milliliters) lime juice

$\frac{1}{4}$ cup (56 milliliters) corn oil

$\frac{1}{4}$ teaspoon oregano

$\frac{1}{4}$ teaspoon thyme

$\frac{1}{4}$ teaspoon marjoram

$\frac{1}{4}$ teaspoon whole black peppercorns

2 bay leaves

2 cloves garlic, fried until soft but not browned

11 ounces (310 grams) carrots, sliced into pieces $1\frac{1}{2}$ inches (3.8 centimeters) by $\frac{1}{4}$–$\frac{1}{2}$ inch (.6–1.3 centimeters), about $\frac{2}{3}$ cup

4 ounces (112 grams) onions, sliced into $\frac{1}{4}$–$\frac{1}{2}$-inch slices (.6–1.3-centimeter) slices (about $1\frac{1}{2}$ cups)

$2\frac{1}{2}$ ounces (70 grams) zucchini, sliced very thin (optional)

$2\frac{1}{2}$ ounces (70 grams) *jícama*, peeled and sliced very thin (optional)

Verduras en escabeche

PICKLED VEGETABLES

This appetizer, similar to the preceding recipe, has a mild and pleasant but rather vinegary taste. Other types of squash or other vegetables may be substituted.

Slice all the vegetables, except the *jalapeños*, to about ⅛ inch (.32 centimeter) thickness. Blanch the potatoes and squash until just barely tender and reserve. Heat the oil in a large pot over low heat and add the *jalapeños* and onion. Cook, stirring often, until they just begin to soften, 5 to 10 minutes. Add the garlic, cook for 30 seconds, then add the remaining ingredients, including the reserved potatoes and squash. Bring the liquid to a boil, then pour into a large ceramic or glass bowl and allow to cool. Refrigerate overnight before serving. Serves 4.

½ **pound (225 grams) white salad or red potatoes**

4 **medium-sized squash, such as zucchini, crookneck, or Mexican** *calabasa*

2 **tablespoons (28 milliliters) olive oil**

5 *jalapeños*, **seeded and halved**

1 **small onion, sliced**

2 **cloves garlic, crushed**

½ **cup (110 milliliters) white vinegar**

1¼ **cups (280 milliliters) water**

2 **teaspoons (1.2 grams) oregano**

½ **teaspoon salt**

2 **bay leaves**

⅓ **cup (43 grams)** *jícama*, **sliced thin and coarsely chopped**

Jícama

Jícama *is a tuberous root-type vegetable that resembles a giant free-form potato, basically round but with angular planes. It has a similar texture to water chestnuts but with a slightly sweet, fruity taste. Having achieved popularity in the United States some years ago,* jícama *is found in many grocery stores in major cities.*

In northern Mexico jícama *is usually peeled, sliced, and served with chile powder or hot sauce and limes and taken as a snack. It is also an ingredient in* Verduras en escabeche *(p. 62).*

Nopales

PRICKLY PEAR CACTUS

Nopales *are the leaves or paddles of the nopal cactus.* Nopalitos *are the* nopales *that have been julienned or chopped.* Nopales *are similar to okra in terms of texture and can be unpleasant if not properly cooked.* Nopales *are often prepared by charbroiling and boiling. Charbroiled* nopales *are served with meats and poultry. The boiled version is also served with entrées or as a salad with vinegar and oil. If the leaves have not had their thorns removed, you must do so. Then slice off ⅛ inch (.32 centimeter) from the perimeter of the leaf. If charbroiling, place the leaves over coals and cook, turning once or twice, for about 15 minutes. To boil, either julienne or chop coarsely and boil with lots of salt until tender. I have discovered that harvesting the cactus paddles very early in the morning reduces the viscousness of the end product to a considerable degree.*

Coctel de camarones

SHRIMP COCKTAIL

❖❖❖❖❖

¾ **pound (340 grams) small to medium-sized shrimp**

2 **tablespoons (28 grams) catsup**

½ **cup (113 grams) mayonnaise (preferably homemade)**

1 **tablespoon (15 milliliters) lime juice**

¼ **cup (32 grams) celery, minced**

6 *serrano* **chiles, seeded and minced, or to taste**

2 **green onions, minced**

¼ **teaspoon salt**

½ **teaspoon pepper, coarsely ground**

¼ **cup (12.4 grams) cilantro, chopped and loosely packed**

As in this country, shrimp are a favorite cocktail appetizer in Mexico, especially in Baja California and on the coast of Sonora. This recipe for sauce, from a restaurant in the coastal resort of Mazatlán, is far superior to the thick catsupy sauce commonly used in this country.

Peel and devein the shrimp. Bring a large pot of water to a boil. Using a large strainer, immerse the shrimp in the boiling water until they begin to turn pink. Avoid overcooking. Remove the shrimp and place under cold running water for a minute or two; then transfer them to a bowl of ice water. These last steps are very important because overcooked shrimp lose their fresh taste and texture. To prevent this, cook the shrimp only until they are just done and chill them immediately to stop the cooking process.

Whisk the catsup into the mayonnaise; then add and combine the remaining ingredients except for the cilantro. When the shrimp are thoroughly chilled, dry them carefully and toss them with the freshly chopped cilantro and the sauce. Serve on small plates or in cocktail glasses. Serves 4.

Soups, Salads & Vegetables

Sopas y Ensaladas y Verduras

Salads are not as generally enjoyed in Mexico as they are in the United States. In the north, mixed green salads are occasionally served, usually with a vinaigrette dressing, but Guacamole and Caesar Salad are more common. Soup, however, is another matter. Mexicans make some of the world's finest and most healthful soups. Mexican soups, and those from the north are no exception, are prepared from natural ingredients cooked so as to best capture their essence and flavor.

Most of these soup recipes provide, in themselves, a satisfying light luncheon or supper.

Sopa de aguacate

AVOCADO SOUP

2 medium avocados

3 cups (675 milliliters) chicken broth

2 teaspoons (4.6 grams) mild chile powder

½ teaspoon cumin

1½ cups (240 milliliters) whipping cream

½ teaspoon salt, or to taste

Dash cayenne pepper

4 3-inch (7.6-centimeter) sprigs of cilantro

I first tasted this soup in a restaurant in the border city of Juárez after a long, hot, dusty drive. It is a refreshing and delicious prelude to a light summer lunch or supper.

Remove the avocado from the skin, chop it coarsely, and place it in the jar of a blender. Add the chicken broth, chile powder, and cumin and blend until smooth.

Pour the mixture from the blender into a medium saucepan and cook over very low heat until very hot. Do not allow to boil. Pour the avocado mixture into a bowl and allow to cool. Stir in the cream, add the salt and cayenne, and chill thoroughly in the refrigerator.

Pour the soup into individual serving bowls, sprinkle with a little cayenne, and garnish with cilantro. Serves 4.

Sopa de ajo

GARLIC SOUP

3 tablespoons (42 milliliters) olive oil

6 cloves garlic, crushed

3 slices French bread, crusts removed

4 cups (900 milliliters) chicken broth

Salt and pepper to taste

Like many other dishes, garlic soup came to Mexico from Spain. It is a tasty accompaniment to the broiled entrées of the north.

Sauté the garlic cloves and bread in the oil over medium heat until they are just browned. Avoid burning. Remove from the heat.

Remove the bread, cut into squares of about 1 inch (2.54 centimeters), and return the cubes to the pan. Immediately add the chicken broth, bring to a boil, cover, and simmer for 20 minutes, or until the bread has disintegrated and mixed well into the broth. Add salt and pepper to taste. Serves 4.

Caldo de pollo

CHICKEN SOUP

To call this just chicken soup is like calling Beef Stroganoff "stew," or Beef Wellington meat pie. This soup is something special and, with a little planning, provides an excellent light lunch when served with hot flour tortillas and butter. Timing is very important, so that each ingredient is properly cooked.

Place the chicken breast in a small pot, cover with water, bring to a boil, and simmer until just cooked through. Remove the chicken to a chopping block and allow it to cool. Remove the skin, shred the meat, and reserve. Bring the chicken broth to a boil, reduce the heat, and bring to a simmer. Add the *ancho* chiles, cover, and simmer for 8 minutes. Then remove and discard the chiles. Add the cumin, the reserved chicken, and the rice. Simmer, uncovered, until the chicken is heated through, about 2 minutes. Now add the zucchini and cook for 3 minutes. Then add the green onions and cook 2 minutes more.

While this is cooking, place ¼ cup (41.5 grams) of the chopped tomato in each of 4 soup bowls. After the onions have cooked for 2 minutes, add the salt and pepper and pour the soup into the serving bowls over the tomatoes. Garnish each bowl with the chopped avocado and a sprig of cilantro. Serve with lime wedges, hot flour tortillas, and butter. Serves 4.

1	whole chicken breast
4¼	cups (1 liter) chicken broth
2	*ancho* chiles
½	teaspoon ground cumin
½	cup (85 grams) cooked Mexican Rice (pp. 101, 102)
¾	cup (106 grams) zucchini, chopped
2	medium green onions, thinly sliced
1	cup (166 grams) tomato, coarsely chopped
½	teaspoon salt, or to taste
	Dash pepper, or to taste
1	medium avocado, diced
4	sprigs cilantro
1	lime, quartered

Caldo de queso de Sonora

SONORAN CHEESE SOUP

◈◈◈◈◈

¼ cup (60 grams) butter

1½ cups (214 grams) onion, diced

2 cups (311.2 grams) potatoes, peeled and diced

2 green onions, diced

2 Anaheim or New Mexico green chiles, peeled, seeded, and chopped

1 cup (167.2 grams) tomatoes, peeled, seeded, and chopped

1¼ cups (280 milliliters) chicken broth or water

3½ cups (750 milliliters) milk, lukewarm

6 ounces (168 grams) Monterey Jack cheese, grated

½ teaspoon salt, or to taste

¼ teaspoon pepper, or to taste

No book on northern Mexican cooking would be complete without a recipe for this rich, creamy soup for which the state of Sonora is famous.

Over medium to medium-low heat, melt the butter and sauté, the onion, potatoes, green onions, and chiles until they are soft but not brown, about 10 minutes. Add the tomatoes and sauté, over medium to medium-high heat for 3 minutes. Next, add the chicken broth or water and bring the soup to a boil; then turn down the heat and simmer, covered, for 15 minutes.

Remove the cover and add the milk and cheese. Stir the soup constantly and heat, without allowing to boil, until the cheese is melted and incorporated with the soup. Overheating the soup will cause it to curdle. Season with salt and pepper to taste. Serve with hot flour tortillas and butter. Serves 4.

Sopa de calabasa

SQUASH SOUP

This delicious and filling soup is a meal in itself.

Boil the chicken and remove the skin. Shred when cool and reserve the meat. Put the broth in a medium-sized pot and add all the ingredients except the reserved chicken meat. Bring to a boil, turn down heat, and simmer, partially covered, for 25 minutes.

Add the reserved chicken to the pot and heat for 5 minutes more. Serve with hot flour tortillas and butter. Serves 4.

2 **chicken breasts**

5 **cups (1,110 milliliters) chicken broth**

²⁄₃ **cup (95 grams) onion, coarsely chopped**

2 **cups (283 grams) zucchini, coarsely chopped**

1 **cup (142 grams) yellow squash, coarsely chopped**

1¹⁄₂ **cups (251grams) tomatoes, peeled, seeded, and chopped**

4 **green chiles, peeled, seeded, and chopped**

1¹⁄₂ **cups (205 grams) fresh or frozen corn kernels**

1 **teaspoon (2 grams) cumin**

1 **teaspoon (.6 gram) oregano**

¹⁄₄ **teaspoon ground black pepper**

¹⁄₂ **teaspoon salt, or to taste**

Sopa de elote

CORN SOUP

◈◈◈◈◈

3 cups (450 grams)
   frozen corn kernels
   (a 1-pound [450-
   gram] bag)
½ cup (110 milliliters)
   chicken broth
3 tablespoons (45
   grams) butter
¼ cup (28 grams) onion,
   chopped
2 small- to medium-
   sized *poblano* chiles,
   peeled, seeded, and
   chopped
1 clove garlic, minced
1 cup (227 grams)
   tomatoes, chopped
2½ cups (560 milliliters)
   whole milk
½ teaspoon salt, or to
   taste
   Cilantro leaves for
   garnish

Although soup made of corn, Mexico's staple, is prevalent in many forms throughout the country, it is found much less often in the north. So it was with great joy that I tested the following recipe from Tamaulipas and found that it is one of the most delicious versions I have tried. Since the recipe calls for frozen corn, I suggest you buy the sweetest, finest quality brand you can; and be sure to measure the corn while still frozen. I should also note that this recipe produces only a scant 1 cup (225 milliliters) per person. This is fine for my taste since it is rather rich, but feel free to double the recipe if you prefer a larger serving or want to ensure the availability of seconds.

Thaw 2 cups (300 grams) of the corn and place it in a blender with the chicken broth. Thaw and reserve the remaining cup.

Melt 1 tablespoon (15 grams) of the butter in a small skillet over medium heat and add the onion, half the chiles, and the garlic and sauté for 3 minutes. Then add the tomatoes and continue cooking until the vegetables have thickened. Next, add the mixture to the blender and blend until the contents are puréed. Then strain the purée through a food mill into a bowl.

Melt the remaining 2 tablespoons (30 grams) butter in a soup pot over medium heat, stir in the strained purée, the reserved whole corn kernels, the milk, the salt, and the reserved chile. Increase the heat until the soup just begins to boil; then keep it at a bare simmer for 20 minutes. Serve the soup garnished with cilantro leaves. Serves 4.

Sopa de elote con arroz

CORN AND RICE SOUP

The addition of cheese to this soup makes it quite rich. As with all soups that use milk, cook it as gently as possible to keep it from curdling.

Melt the butter in a large pot over medium heat, add the rice and sauté, stirring often until the rice just begins to brown. Add the onion and chopped chiles and continue cooking for 2 minutes. Add the corn and cook an additional 3 minutes. Add the broth, milk, and salt and bring the mixture slowly to a simmer. Barely simmer the soup, uncovered, for 20 to 30 minutes or until the corn is tender. If the soup becomes too thick, add a little more broth and/or milk. Just before serving, remove the pot from the burner and add the cheese. Stir until the cheese has melted and serve. Serves 4.

2 tablespoons (30 grams) butter

½ cup (96 grams) rice

½ cup (71 grams) onion, chopped

¼ cup (33 grams) Anaheim, New Mexico, or *poblano* chiles, peeled, seeded, and chopped

4 cups (568 grams) fresh corn, cut from the cob

2½ cups (560 milliliters) chicken broth

1½ cups (240 milliliters) milk

1 teaspoon (6.2 grams) salt, or to taste

2 cups (218 grams) Chihuahua cheese, grated, or substitute Monterey Jack cheese

Sopa de chile

CHILE SOUP

3 *ancho* chiles, stemmed and seeded

3 *de árbol* chiles or *japonés* chiles, stemmed and seeded, or to taste

2 large or 3 small cloves garlic

3 teaspoons (1.8 grams) oregano

1½ teaspoons (3 grams) cumin

1½ quarts (1,350 milliliters) mild beef broth

6 tablespoons (87 grams) butter

6 tablespoons (45 grams) flour

Salt, to taste

6 ounces (168 grams) mild cheddar cheese, grated

Tostadas made from 4 corn tortillas (p. 53)

Place the chiles, garlic, oregano, and cumin in a blender with 1 cup (225 milliliters) of the broth and blend for 1 minute. Melt the butter in a large pot, add the flour, and whisk the roux over medium heat until it begins to brown and gives off a nutty fragrance. Remove the pot from the heat and add 1 cup (225 milliliters) of the broth little by little, whisking well to prevent lumps. Return the pot to the heat and add the remainder of the broth, still taking care to prevent lumping.

Now add the chile mixture and salt and bring to a boil. Reduce the heat and simmer, stirring frequently, until the soup begins to thicken, about 15 minutes.

Place equal portions of the cheese and *Tostadas* (in that order) in each of 4 soup bowls. When the soup has reached the desired thickness, ladle it into the bowls and serve immediately. Serves 4.

Sopa de frijoles

BEAN SOUP

This recipe is one of the few in this book that specifies epazote, *which is an herb found mostly in the cooking of Mexico's more southern regions. If you cannot find it, do not let that deter you from trying this surprisingly sophisticated soup.*

Place the beans and the water in a pot, add 1 sprig of the *epazote*, and simmer, partially covered, until the beans are very tender. There should be about 2½ cups (483 grams) beans and 1 cup (225 milliliters) liquid in the pan when you are done. Add additional water toward the end of the cooking process, if necessary. Place the beans and 1 cup (225 milliliters) liquid in the jar of a blender.

Heat the oil in a skillet over medium heat, add the onion, celery, and garlic and cook until they are becoming soft. Then add the tomatoes and continue cooking until all the vegetables are tender and most of the liquid has evaporated. Place the cooked vegetables in the blender with the beans and their cooking liquid.

Add 2 cups (450 milliliters) of the broth and blend at high speed for 1 minute. Strain the contents of the blender through a food mill and pour it into the pot in which the beans were cooked. Add the remaining 2 cups (450 milliliters) broth, the remaining sprig of *epazote*, and the salt; then bring to a boil and simmer for 15 minutes.

Meanwhile, fry the *chorizo* over medium heat until it is well done and reserve. Also, deep-fry the tortilla strips, then drain and apportion them among 4 soup bowls. When the soup has been cooked 15 minutes, pour it into the bowls over the tortilla strips, sprinkle with the cheese, and garnish with the cooked *chorizo*. Serves 4.

1 cup (182 grams) pinto beans, picked over and rinsed

4 cups (900 milliliters) water

2 sprigs *epazote*

1½ tablespoons (21 milliliters) cooking oil

⅓ cup (48 grams) chopped onion

⅓ cup (38 grams) celery, chopped

1 clove garlic, minced

1 cup (167 grams) tomatoes, chopped

4 cups (900 milliliters) chicken broth

½ teaspoon salt, or to taste

⅓ cup (83 grams) *chorizo* (preferably homemade [p. 154])

2 corn tortillas, cut into strips ⅛ inch (.32 centimeter) wide by 1 inch (2.54 centimeters) long

Oil for deep-frying

1½ cups (164 grams) *queso panela*, grated, or substitute Monterey Jack cheese

Sopa de frijoles negros

BLACK BEAN SOUP

❖❖❖❖❖

½ **pound (225 grams) dried black or turtle beans**

2 **ounces (56 grams) salt pork, chopped**

1 **clove garlic**

1 **teaspoon (.6 gram) oregano**

1 **teaspoon (3 grams) cumin**

1 **tablespoon (15 milliliters) sherry**

1 **tablespoon (15 milliliters) lime juice**

½ **cup (113 grams) sour cream**

1 **large avocado, chopped**

2 **green onions, minced**

¼ **cup (12.4 grams) cilantro, chopped and loosely packed**

2 *serrano* **chiles, minced**

1 **lime, cut into wedges**

Black Bean Soup is not usually thought of as a northern dish. However, this recipe from Chihuahua City is so good that I felt it should be included. The last 6 ingredients, used as a garnish, contrast beautifully in color with the beans for a stunning presentation.

Wash and place the beans in a bean pot or Dutch oven and add water to cover by 2 inches (about 5 centimeters). Add the salt pork and bring to a boil. In a *molcajete* or mortar and pestle, mash together the garlic, oregano, and cumin and add them to the beans.

Turn down the heat and simmer, covered, until the beans just begin to get tender (about 1½ to 2 hours), adding additional water as necessary. Add the sherry and lime juice and continue cooking until the beans are fully tender (about ½ hour). Then remove them from the heat, cool, and put half of the beans in a blender jar with all the cooking liquid and blend. Make sure that none of the salt pork is included. It may be necessary to do this in several stages.

When half the beans and the liquid have been thoroughly puréed, return them to the pot containing the remaining beans. Bring the soup to a boil and simmer about 15 minutes or until it begins to thicken.

Pour the soup into individual serving bowls and garnish with equal amounts of the sour cream, chopped avocado, green onions, cilantro, and *serrano* chiles. Serve immediately with a lime wedge. Serves 4.

Pozole

HOMINY SOUP OR STEW

Pozole is most often associated with Guadalajara, where it is usually made with pork. There it is eaten as a lunch or supper dish, or especially as a late-night, post-cantina fortifier. It ranges from a thin soup to a thick stew. Made with beef, this northern version, which I found in Saltillo, is between a soup and a stew and is the best I have had, except in New Mexico, where pozole-*making is a fine art.*

In Mexico, pozole *is usually made from either fresh (undried) hominy or dried hominy. However, it can also be made successfully with canned hominy, which is specified in this recipe since it is easier for most North Americans to obtain. To substitute fresh hominy, simmer it in water until the kernels puff, about 30 minutes. If using dried hominy, soak it overnight and then simmer it in water until it is tender and puffed, about 45 minutes. In either case, strain off the cooking water before adding the* pozole.

Place the meat in a pot with the water and bring it to a boil. Skim off the scum which rises to the surface. Meanwhile, grind the garlic, cumin, and oregano to a paste in a *molcajete* or mortar and pestle and add the mixture to the pot. Add the carrot, onion, chiles, and bay leaves and simmer, covered, until the meat is tender, about 1½ hours.

Remove the meat, and, when it is cool enough to handle, shred it in a food processor (using a plastic blade) and reserve. Pour the cooking broth into another container, reserving the carrot, onion, and chiles. Place the cooked carrot, onion, and chiles in a blender with ½ cup (110 milliliters) of the cooking broth and blend for 1 minute. Strain the mixture through a food mill and return it to the pot with 4½ more cups (1 liter) of the broth. Add the canned or cooked fresh or dried hominy, the tomato purée, and the salt and simmer, uncovered, for 15 minutes. Just before serving bring the soup to a high boil, add the reserved, shredded meat, and heat for about 30 seconds. (If you add the meat sooner, it will tend to form unpleasant clumps.) Ladle the soup into bowls and top with the shredded lettuce. Serves 4.

1 pound (450 grams) beef brisket, trimmed of all fat, (weighed *after* trimming) and cut into 1-inch (2.54-centimeter) pieces

10½ cups (2 liters + 240 milliliters) water

3 cloves garlic, minced

¼ teaspoon cumin

½ teaspoon oregano

1 carrot, peeled and cut into 3-inch (7.6-centimeter) pieces

¼ onion

2 *ancho* chiles, stemmed and seeded

2 bay leaves

2 15-ounce cans (425 grams) white hominy, 4 cups (720 grams) fresh hominy, or 3½ cups (676 grams) dried hominy

¼ cup (59 grams) tomato purée

½ teaspoon salt

4 cups (380 grams) shredded lettuce

Caldo de carne seca

DRIED BEEF SOUP

3 tablespoons (36 grams) lard or olive oil (42 milliliters)

2½ cups (357 grams) onion, thinly sliced

3 cloves (15 grams) garlic, minced

1⅓ cups (125 grams) shredded *Carne seca*, or Dried Beef (p. 140)

1½ cups (251 grams) tomatoes, finely chopped

¼ cup (12.4 grams) chopped and loosely packed cilantro

8 cups (1,750 milliliters) beef broth

4 cups (622 grams) potatoes, peeled and cut into ¾-inch (1.9-centimeter) pieces

2 cups (225 grams) carrots, peeled and sliced crosswise into ¼-inch (.6-centimeter) rounds

½ teaspoon salt, or to taste

½ teaspoon ground pepper

Simple to prepare and a great way to use leftover dried beef, Caldo de carne seca *is a delicious addition to any meal. Please note that the amount of salt specified assumes that you made the* Carne seca *with the lower amount called for in the recipe for it. If not, or if you are using a commercial product, please adjust the salt accordingly. In fact, in Mexico when preparing this dish cooks often presoak the meat to remove excess salt. In this regard, please remember also that canned broth usually has a very high salt content, so if you use it be careful.*

Heat a large pot over medium heat, add the lard or olive oil, and cook the onion until it is a rich golden brown but not burned. Add the garlic and beef and continue cooking for 3 minutes, stirring often. Add the tomatoes and cilantro and cook an additional 3 minutes. Add the broth, potatoes, and carrots, and bring the soup to a boil; then simmer it for 20 minutes. Add the salt and pepper, cook an additional 5 minutes, and serve. Serves 4.

Caldillo canasta

SOUP CANASTA

Like everything else served at Saltillo's La Canasta restaurant, this soup is first class. The complexity and sophistication of this dish go far beyond what could be expected from its simple ingredients. The recipe calls for fideo, *which usually refers to the little rolled "nests" of spaghettini-sized pasta. It also calls for* Carne seca machacado, *which is dried beef that has been processed until light and fluffy. If you do not have a Mexican grocery that carries this product, either make your own or purchase some naturally flavored beef jerky, chop it into small pieces, and process it in a food processor until it is the proper texture. Depending on the source of your dried beef and chicken broth, you want to be very careful about the dish's salt content. If you follow the recipe in this book for* Carne seca *and make your own broth, you will probably need to add salt; but if you use commercial beef and canned broth, the result can be much too salty. One solution to this dilemma is to use a low-sodium broth diluted with water.*

¼ cup (56 milliliters) cooking oil

4 ounces (112 grams) *fideo*, broken into 1-inch (2.54-centimeter) pieces

4 ounces (112 grams) *Carne seca*, chopped (p. 140)

1 cup (170 grams) *Pico de gallo* (p. 49)

1 quart (900 milliliters) mild chicken broth

Salt, to taste

Heat a pot over medium heat, add 2 tablespoons (28 milliliters) of the oil and sauté the pieces of *fideo* until they are just golden brown. Remove the *fideo* to a strainer to drain. Add the remaining 2 tablespoons (28 milliliters) oil and sauté the *Carne seca*, stirring often, for 3 minutes. Add the *Pico de gallo* and cook an additional 3 minutes. Then add the broth and salt, if used, bring to a boil, and simmer until the pasta is al dente, about 8 to 9 minutes; serve with some *Chiles en vinagre* (p. 41) on the side. Serves 4.

2 cups (312 grams) soft wheat grains
   Water
1½ tablespoons (21 milliliters) cooking oil
1 pound (450 grams) very lean bottom round beef, cut into ½-inch (1.3-centimeter) pieces
½ cup (57 grams) onion, chopped
3 cloves garlic, minced
3–4 Anaheim or New Mexico chiles, peeled, seeded, and chopped
1½ cups (255 grams) potatoes, peeled and chopped
1½ cups (255 grams) sweet potatoes, peeled and chopped
¾ cup (96 grams) carrots, peeled and chopped
1½ cups (212 grams) zucchini, chopped
1 cup (145 grams) green beans, cut into 1½-inch (3.8-centimeter) pieces
1 cup (95 grams) cabbage, chopped
2 cups (454 grams) tomatoes, chopped
1 cup (30 grams) fresh spinach, washed thoroughly and chopped
   Salt to taste

"Pozole" de trigo

WHEAT, VEGETABLE, AND MEAT STEW

I have found this dish only in the state of Sonora, where wheat is king. This is not really pozole, *which is the Mexican word for hominy, but a fine Sonoran version of that ubiquitous corn-based soup or stew. This particular version calls for wheat grains plus a produce department full of vegetables and just enough lean meat to provide flavor. It is, therefore, both nutritious and low in calories. I suggest you use soft wheat if you can find it or substitute barley, because hard winter wheat which resembles brown rice takes longer to cook and is not nearly as tasty.*

Bring the wheat to a boil in 1½ quarts (1,350 milliliters) water and simmer, covered, until it is tender and the grains are starting to burst; reserve.

Heat a large pot over high heat, add the oil, and brown the meat, stirring constantly. Strain off any excess oil and add 2 quarts (1,300 milliliters) water to the pot. Bring the liquid to a boil, skimming off any scum that rises to the surface. Then add the onion, garlic, and chiles; cover and simmer the meat for 45 minutes to 1 hour or until it is becoming tender. Add the remaining ingredients and simmer, covered, for 15 minutes. Add the reserved wheat and continue simmering, uncovered, for 10 minutes more. Serve with flour tortillas, lime wedges, and hot sauce. Serves 4.

Sopa de pescado estilo Baja California

BAJA-STYLE SEAFOOD SOUP

This seafood soup is simple to make and has a fresh, clean taste made particularly interesting by the addition of fried onion. Any mild fish will do. In fact, in the testing I used farm-raised catfish with great success.

Place the fish scraps and bones in a large pot, cover with the water, and simmer for 20 minutes. Discard the fish and bones and strain the broth. Bring the liquid to a boil, poach the ¾ pound (340 grams) fish filets until just done and remove them. When they have cooled, cut the fish into ½-inch (1.3-centimeter) pieces and reserve.

Add the bay leaves, rice, potatoes, cabbage, celery, carrots, and tomato and simmer, uncovered, for 15 minutes.

Meanwhile, heat a skillet over medium heat; add the oil and sauté, the onion until it is becoming golden brown. Add the garlic and cook another 1 or 2 minutes, but do not allow the onion to burn.

After the vegetables have cooked for 15 minutes, stir the fried onion and garlic into them, add salt and pepper, and simmer another 5 minutes. Place equal portions of the reserved fish filets in each of 4 soup bowls and ladle the vegetable mixture over them. Serves 4.

1 pound (450 grams) fish scraps and bones

8½ cups (2,110 milliliters) water

¾ pound (340 grams) mild, firm fish filets

2 bay leaves

¼ cup (48 grams) uncooked long grain rice

2 cups (312 grams) potatoes, peeled and cut into 1-inch (2.54-centimeter) pieces or slightly larger

¾ cup (58 grams) cabbage, chopped

½ cup (56 grams) celery, minced

½ cup (64 grams) carrots, minced

1 medium to large tomato, chopped

1½ tablespoons (21 milliliters) olive oil

2 cups (285 grams) onion, thinly sliced

2 cloves garlic, minced Salt and black pepper to taste

Ensalada Caesar

CAESAR SALAD

3 anchovy filets, or to taste

2 cloves garlic

5 teaspoons (22 milliliters) lime juice

2 tablespoons (12 grams) green olives, pitted and sliced

2 tablespoons (12 grams) artichoke hearts, chopped

1 teaspoon (5 milliliters) Worcestershire sauce

Pinch salt, or to taste

¼ teaspoon coarse black pepper

3 tablespoons (42 milliliters) garlic oil (see p. 16); small additional amount to make croutons

3 slices bread

1 egg

8 ounces (225 grams) romaine lettuce

¼ cup (12 grams) Parmesan cheese, grated

No book on the cooking of northern Mexico would be complete without a recipe for this famous salad. It originated at Caesar's Restaurant in Tijuana during the 1930s. This was an era when, because of Prohibition, many Americans flocked to the border towns for fun—and many creative entrepreneurs developed new ways to supply it. The original recipe has been widely published, but there are countless variations. This appetizing one from Chihuahua maintains the "flavor" of the original.

In a *molcajete* or mortar and pestle, mash together the anchovies and garlic, transfer to a large salad bowl, and add the lime juice. Whisk in the olives and artichoke hearts, then the Worcestershire sauce, salt, and pepper. Lastly, add the garlic oil, a little at a time.

To make the croutons, brush the bread slices on one side with garlic oil, place on a baking sheet, and bake at 350 degrees F (177 degrees C) until they just begin to brown. Turn the bread over, brush with garlic oil, and bake until this side begins to brown. Allow the toast to cool and cut into 1-inch (2.54-centimeter) squares.

Place the egg in a small bowl or saucepan and cover it with boiling water. After 1 minute remove it to a pan of cold water.

Next, break the egg into the salad bowl and whisk in the dressing from the *molcajete*. Add the lettuce, Parmesan cheese, and croutons. Toss well and serve immediately. Serves 4.

Requesón el norte

RICOTTA CHEESE SALAD

Requesón is Mexico's version of ricotta cheese, which makes an excellent substitute. This salad, in one form or another, is served widely in homes and in upscale restaurants.

Place all the ingredients in a large bowl and stir until they are well combined. Serve as a first course or with soup for a light meal. Serves 4.

2 cups (477 grams) ricotta cheese

2–4 *serrano* chiles, seeded and minced

1 cup (167 grams) tomatoes, seeded and finely chopped

4 green onions, minced

½ cup (48 grams) cilantro, minced and loosely packed

¼ cup (56 milliliters) olive oil

¼ teaspoon salt, or to taste

Ground black pepper, to taste

Ensalada de garbanzos

GARBANZO BEAN SALAD

❖❖❖❖❖

3 cups (509 grams)
   cooked garbanzo
   beans
2 *poblano* chiles,
   roasted, seeded,
   peeled, and sliced
1 red bell pepper, sliced
½ cup (71 grams) onion,
   minced
¼ cup (12.4 grams)
   cilantro, minced
1 cup (109 grams) *queso
   Chihuahua*, or
   substitute Monterey
   Jack cheese
2 tablespoons plus 2
   teaspoons (35
   milliliters) lime
   juice
¼ cup (56 milliliters)
   olive oil
   Heaping ¼ teaspoon
   salt, or to taste
   Enough spinach
   leaves to make beds
   for the salad

The combination of the nutty garbanzo beans with the tangy olive oil and lime juice dressing makes this salad from Baja California quite special. Interestingly this is the same combination of flavors that has made hummus from the Middle East an international favorite. The salad can be made with canned garbanzos or garbanzos which you prepare from dried beans.

In a salad bowl combine the beans, chiles, bell pepper, onion, cilantro, and cheese. Make the dressing by combining the lime juice, olive oil, and salt and add it to the bowl, tossing well. The salad can be prepared up to 2 hours before serving if kept refrigerated. To serve, make beds of spinach on 4 salad plates, mound the salad on them, and serve. Serves 4.

Guacamole

Guacamole is the universal salad, appetizer, and condiment in northern Mexico. It is made by mashing ripe avocados with lime juice and various herbs and chiles. There are many varieties of avocado in Mexico, but the California haas is the best (see "Basic Ingredients"). As an appetizer or salad, Guacamole is served with tostadas (fried tortilla chips), or it can be served in a Tortilla Cup (p. 84). Experiment with the various combinations of chiles and herbs to find your favorite. Here are a basic recipe and the spicier version I prefer.

NOTE: Some cooks add about 1 tablespoon of very thick cream (not sour cream) to the recipe, which creates an extra-rich product.

For Basic Guacamole, mash the avocado in a *molcajete* or large bowl with the lime juice until well mixed but not too smooth. Fold in the chopped tomato and cilantro, if used. Serves 4.

For Spicy Guacamole, mix all the ingredients as for Basic Guacamole. Serves 4.

BASIC GUACAMOLE

1 medium-ripe avocado

½ tablespoon (7.5 milliliters) lime juice

½ medium tomato, coarsely chopped (optional)

1 tablespoon (3 grams) cilantro, chopped and loosely packed (optional)

SPICY GUACAMOLE

1 medium-sized ripe avocado

1 teaspoon (2 grams) chopped, canned *jalapeño* pepper

1 teaspoon (5 milliliters) liquid from *jalapeño* can

2 teaspoons (7 milliliters) lime juice

1 tablespoon (3 grams) cilantro, chopped and loosely packed

½ medium-sized tomato, coarsely chopped (optional)

Tortilla Cups

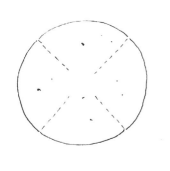

Tortilla Cups are corn tortillas fried in the shape of a cup, to be filled with Guacamole (p. 83). They are easy to make and a very attractive addition to any plate. Making the cups requires a 6- or 8-ounce (170- or 225-milliliter) soup ladle approximately 3 inches (7.6 centimeters) in diameter, which is used to form the cups.

First, cut the tortillas as shown in the diagram. Next, heat oil to 350 to 375 degrees F (177 to 190 degrees C) in a deep fryer or Dutch oven. Place a cut tortilla flat into the oil and immediately press the soup ladle's rounded bottom into the middle of the tortilla, maintaining pressure until the tortilla has wrapped itself around the ladle and is totally immersed in the oil. Hold the ladle in place for about 30 seconds; then remove it, being careful to avoid spilling any hot oil. Repeat this process for as many cups as desired. Allow the now formed cups to continue cooking, turning once or twice with kitchen tongs, until they are crisp (about the time they stop sizzling). Remove the cooked cups to drain on paper towels. When cool, store in plastic bags until ready for use. If properly sealed, the bags will keep the cups crisp for up to 24 hours.

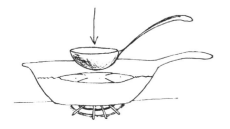

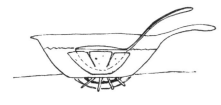

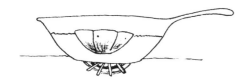

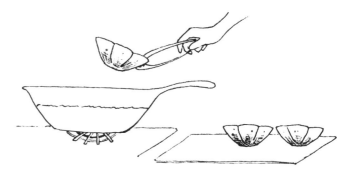

Fiambre

MEAT AND VEGETABLE SALAD

Fiambre is a cold meat and vegetable salad that is usually marinated. This particular recipe, a "pickled" version from Sonora, makes a terrific buffet dish. It can also be kept in the refrigerator for several days and used for snacks.

Boil the chicken until just done and remove. When it is cool enough to handle, coarsely shred the chicken and place it in a layer on the bottom of a 2½- to 3-quart (225- to 2,700-milliliter) dish.

Boil the potatoes until they are just tender, drain, cool them, and place them on top of the chicken.

Cut the apples and place them in a layer on top of the potatoes. Place the olives on top of the apples, and sprinkle the raisins over them. Boil the zucchini for about 30 seconds, strain, cool, and place on top of the raisins. Sprinkle the cheese over the zucchini.

Combine the vinegar and salt and whisk in the oil. Pour the dressing over the ingredients in the dish, cover it, and refrigerate from 4 hours to overnight. An hour before serving remove the dish from the refrigerator and allow the salad to come to room temperature. At serving time, drain off most of the dressing, mix the salad, and either place on the table for diners to help themselves or serve on individual plates. Serves 4.

1 pound (450 grams) boneless, skinless chicken breast

2½ cups (425 grams) boiling potatoes, peeled and sliced ⅛ inch (.3 centimeter) thick and into 1½-inch (3.8-centimeter) pieces

2 cups (227 grams) apples, peeled and sliced ⅛ inch (.3 centimeter) thick and cut into 1½ inch- (3.8-centimeter) pieces

1 cup (180 grams) black olives, pitted and sliced

1 cup (56 grams) raisins

1½ cups (212 grams) zucchini, sliced ⅛ inch (.3 centimeter) thick and cut into 1½-inch (3.8-centimeter) pieces

12 ounces (340 grams) *asadero* cheese, grated, or substitute Monterey Jack cheese

1 cup (225 milliliters) vinegar

1 teaspoon (6.2 grams) salt

1 cup (225 milliliters) cooking oil

Salpicón de mariscos

SEAFOOD SALAD

◇◇◇◇◇

½ pound (225 grams) firm-fleshed, mild fish filet

½ pound (225 grams) shrimp, peeled and deveined

½ pound (225 grams) lobster tail, peeled

¾ cup (85 grams) celery, cut in julienne strips

¾ cup (96 grams) carrot, cut in julienne strips

¼ cup (36 grams) onion, minced

¼ cup (43 grams) green onion, chopped

3 *serrano* chiles, stemmed, seeded, and minced

6 tablespoons (84 milliliters) lime juice

6 tablespoons (84 milliliters) olive oil

½ teaspoon salt, or to taste

¼ teaspoon black pepper, or to taste

1 large avocado, peeled, seeded, and chopped

1½ cups (251 grams) tomatoes, chopped

Lettuce leaves

This seafood salad from Baja California can also be served as an appetizer. While the recipe calls for fish, shrimp, and lobster in equal quantities, it can be made with any combination or any one of these items. For the fish portion of the recipe, use a firm, mild filet. Grouper or sea bass work well as does swordfish, especially when served by itself.

Poach the fish, shrimp, and lobster in separate batches until they are just cooked through; then strain and allow them to cool. Using your fingers or two forks, shred the fish and lobster and combine. Cut the shrimp into ¼-inch (.6-centimeter) pieces and mix it into the fish and lobster. Add the celery, carrot, onion, green onion, and chiles and chill. About 15 minutes before you are ready to serve the salad mix together the lime juice, olive oil, salt, and pepper, and stir it into the seafood mixture. Just before serving, stir in the avocado and tomatoes. Serve on a bed of lettuce. Serves 4 as a salad or 6 as an appetizer.

Papas rellenos

STUFFED POTATOES

This is the Mexican version of the stuffed baked potato that is familiar to most of us in the United States. However, it is a far different product because the first phase of cooking calls for boiling the potato rather than baking it. This creates a much more interesting texture, not to mention the terrific combination of the stuffing ingredients. It is preferable to use white boiling potatoes for this dish because baking potatoes become mealy and tend to fall apart.

Simmer the peeled potatoes in water to cover until they are soft enough to pierce fairly easily with a skewer except toward the center. This will take about 20 minutes. Remove the potatoes from the water, and when they are cool enough to handle slice a ¼-inch (.6-centimeter) piece lengthwise from one side to create a level surface. Using a paring knife and medium-sized spoon, cut and scoop out the interior of the potatoes from the flattened side, leaving a ¼- to ⅓-inch (.6- to .85-centimeter) wall all around. It is important that the interior portion of the potatoes, which is removed and which will be used in the stuffing, be firm and cut into fairly equal-sized pieces of about ½ inch (1.3 centimeters). Place the chopped potato centers in a bowl and add the chopped *poblano* chiles.

Heat a skillet over medium heat and fry the bacon until it is crisp; then remove and reserve it. Fry the *chorizo* until it is golden and remove and reserve it. Toss the oil with the chopped potato centers and chiles and fry until the potatoes are crisp and golden brown; then place them in a bowl. Chop the bacon and add it and the *chorizo* to the potato/chile mixture, and allow it to come to room temperature. Stir in the *queso fresco* or Monterey Jack cheese and the sour cream.

Fill the reserved potato shells with the above mixture and bake until they are hot and cooked through, about 25 to 30 minutes. Place the potatoes on serving plates and sprinkle on the *queso panela* or feta cheese. Serve with broiled meats or poultry. Serves 4.

- **4 8–9-ounce (225–250 grams) white potatoes, peeled**
- **2 *poblano* chiles, stemmed, seeded, peeled, and finely chopped, about ½–⅔ cup (65.7–87.6 grams)**
- **4 pieces bacon**
- **¼ cup (56 grams) *chorizo***
- **1 tablespoon (15 milliliters) olive oil**
- **½ cup (54 grams) *queso fresco* or Monterey Jack cheese, grated**
- **½ cup (113 grams) sour cream**
- **½ cup (54 grams) *queso panela* or feta cheese**

Jalapeños rellenos

STUFFED JALAPEÑOS

◈◈◈◈◈

12 large *jalapeño* chiles,
     peeled but stems
     left on
¹/₃ **pound (150 grams)**
     ***asadero* or**
     mozzarella cheese
 2 **eggs**
 1 **tablespoon (15**
     milliliters) olive oil
 1 **tablespoon (15**
     milliliters) milk
     Flour for dredging
     the chiles
     Dried bread crumbs
     Oil for deep-frying

Unless you can find the mild jalapeños *grown from the seeds developed by Texas A & M University serve this dish only to confirmed chile-heads because it is very hot. Nevertheless, it makes a delicious appetizer or accompaniment to broiled meat.*

Peel the chiles using one of the methods suggested in the section on chiles (see "Basic Ingredients"). Cut a slit in the side of each chile and, using a small spoon, scoop out the seeds and veins. Fill the chiles with pieces of cheese cut so that the chile can be closed completely around them.

Beat together the eggs, the oil, and the milk.

Dredge the filled chiles in flour, dip them in the egg mixture, then roll them in the bread crumbs until they are well coated; refrigerate them for at least 1 hour.

Heat oil in a deep fryer or deep pot to about 250 degrees F (118 degrees C) and deep-fry the chiles in batches until they are golden brown but not burned. Serves 4 as an appetizer.

Maria's Corn

The following recipe is from Maria Jiménez, who comes from the village of La Ciénega de las Flores in Nuevo León, just north of Monterrey. It is a delicious vegetable dish that should be made with tender white corn if possible.

Heat a large skillet over medium to medium-high heat, add the oil, and sauté the corn until it is well browned. Turn the heat to medium and add the onion and bell pepper and continue cooking for 2 minutes. Add the tomatoes, salt, cumin, and water and simmer for 30 minutes. Serves 4.

$1/3$ cup (83 milliliters) cooking oil

5 cups (690 grams) fresh white corn, cut from the cob

$1/3$ cup (48 grams) onion, thinly sliced

$1/3$ cup (44 grams) green bell pepper, thinly sliced

2 medium-sized tomatoes, coarsely chopped

1 teaspoon (6.2 grams) salt

$1/8$ teaspoon cumin, ground

3 cups (675 milliliters) water

Elotes al carbón

CHARBROILED CORN

◈◈◈◈◈

4 **ears of unhusked
    sweet corn,
    preferably white
    corn**
2 **tablespoons (28
    milliliters) melted
    lard or olive oil**
2 **limes**
2 **tablespoons (13
    grams) chile powder**
   Aluminum foil

One of the most typical sensations in northern Mexican towns and villages is the smell of corn roasting over mesquite fires. This is also one of the most delicious ways of preparing corn on the cob. It goes particularly well with charbroiled foods and is made while the wood is burning down to coals. The secret of this dish is leaving the husks on during the roasting process, which keeps the corn moist and makes a beautiful presentation.

Prepare a fire, preferably of mesquite or mesquite charcoal, but do not light it.

Slice off the end of each ear of corn on the side opposite the stalk. Peel back the husks and, under running water, remove the silk. Then soak the corn in cold water for ½ hour. Dry and place each ear of corn on a piece of aluminum foil about 8 inches by 12 inches (20.3 by 30.5 centimeters). Brush the corn with the lard or olive oil, sprinkle on some lime juice, and dust with the chile powder. Replace the husks and wrap the ears in the foil.

Light the fire and allow it to burn about 8 minutes or until it is roaring. Place the corn on a grill about 4 inches (10.2 centimeters) above the burning wood or charcoal and cook for 20 minutes, turning every 5 minutes. Then put the corn on the side of the grill and prepare the rest of the meal. Serves 4.

NOTE: If you double-wrap the corn in foil, you can place it directly on the coals.

Tortillas & Bread

❖❖❖

Tortillas y Pan

Tortillas and chiles undoubtedly are the most distinctive and essential elements of Mexican cuisine. The corn tortilla is one of the most ancient forms of bread, known in what is now Mexico nearly as long as there has been corn. Even today, in many parts of Mexico tortillas are still made as they have been since the advent of Indian culture. Corn is dried, cooked with dolomitic lime, and ground into *masa*, or dough, on stone *metates*. Tortillas are then patted out by hand and cooked on a *comal*, the Mexican griddle.

The flour tortilla, important to northern Mexican cuisine, is a later variant, following the introduction of wheat and lard by the Spanish.

Today, flour and corn tortillas are mostly machine-made, although in some restaurants and in homes with plenty of servants they are still made the superior way, by hand. Whether of flour or corn, handmade or not, tortillas hot from the griddle make the most delicious and versatile of breads.

Because of the popularity of tortillas, *Bolillos*, an excellent, more traditional type of bread, are often overlooked. Very much like small French or Italian dinner rolls, they are served with meals or with such fillings as ham and cheese for delicious *tortas* (sandwiches).

Tortillas de harina

WHEAT FLOUR TORTILLAS

❖❖❖❖❖

2 cups (280 grams)
    flour
¹/₂ teaspoon salt
1 heaping ¼ teaspoon
    double-acting
    baking powder
2 tablespoons (30
    grams) lard, or
    rendered beef suet
    or shortening
2 tablespoons (30
    grams) butter
²/₃ cup (166 milliliters)
    very hot water

In most parts of northern Mexico, flour tortillas are preferred to corn tortillas. The tortillas of Sonora are huge, often 10 to 18 inches (24.5 to 45.7 centimeters) in diameter, and paper-thin. In the state of Coahuila they are often rather small and much thicker, about 4 inches (10.2 centimeters) in diameter and ¹/₈ to ³/₁₆ inch (.3 to .5 centimeter) thick.

While making a good flour tortilla is easy, making a really great flour tortilla is an art, but one that, with a little practice, is easily learned. Watching an expert is a little like watching a magician: a few quick moves and a small piece of dough becomes a delicate tortilla. The secret to forming flour tortillas, whether they are thick or thin, is allowing the dough to rest, which makes it pliable and easy to work. Without this step you will never create ultra-thin Sonora-style tortillas. The secret to cooking flour tortillas is to have the right temperature. Too low a heat will produce hard tortillas resembling shoe leather; too high a heat will burn the tortillas before they have a chance to puff. Start by following the directions exactly; later experiment with the heat and cooking time and you soon will be making world-class tortillas.

NOTE: For the diet conscious, shortening may be substituted for the lard and butter. (See also Appendix B: Nutrition and Northern Mexican Cooking.)

Mix the flour, salt, and baking powder. Heat the lard and butter or shortening over very low heat. Add to the flour mixture, stirring until well combined.

Beat the water into the flour, salt, and baking powder, adding a little at a time until the dough is well combined. Knead the dough for 1 minute, wrap in a dampened towel, and allow to rest for 15 minutes.

NOTE: If you have a food processor, combine the dry ingredients and, with the blade in and the machine going, first pour in the melted fat, then the water until the dough just forms a ball.

Next, heat an ungreased *comal* or heavy skillet over medium to low heat. Lightly flour a smooth countertop or other work surface. For normal 6-inch tortillas, divide the dough into 12 pieces and form into balls. To make a 10-inch, Sonoran-style tortilla, divide the dough into 6 pieces (rewrapping the remaining dough to prevent it from drying out). Next, shape the pieces into balls, and flatten them slightly. Cover the formed dough with a damp towel. Allow the dough balls to rest for at least 30 minutes or up to 1 hour.

Now, place a dough ball on the lightly floured surface. Push down to flatten it with the palm of your hand and dust the top lightly with flour. Using a small rolling pin (which can be made from a broomstick), roll out the tortilla in the following manner: beginning at the center, roll away from you, stopping just short of the edge of the dough. Now, roll back toward yourself, again stopping just short of the edge of the dough. Now, turn the dough a half turn and repeat the process. Turn the dough and repeat the process once or twice more.

Next, lift the tortilla, reflour the work surface, turn the tortilla over, and repeat the whole process. With a little practice the entire procedure takes only a few seconds. If necessary, turn the tortilla and continue rolling until it is $\frac{1}{8}$ inch (.3 centimeter) thick or the thickness and diameter you prefer.

Next, place the tortilla on the ungreased *comal* or skillet and cook until air bubbles begin to form, about 20 to 30 seconds. (At this point the cooked side should show some browned spots. If it shows some burning, the heat is too high; if there is no browning, it is too low.) Now, turn the tortilla and cook for an additional 20 to 30 seconds, during which time the tortilla should continue to puff. Turn again and cook for 10 seconds, or until the tortilla stops puffing. Remove the cooked tortilla to a tortilla warmer or wrap it in a towel. Repeat the process for the remaining tortillas. Makes 12 small tortillas or 6 large tortillas.

Tortillas estilo Sonora

SONORA-STYLE TORTILLAS

To make the paper-thin tortillas found in Sonora, prepare the dough as for flour tortillas (see p. 92). Then make the dough balls about twice as big as for regular flour tortillas (6 instead of 12 pieces), and let them rest a full hour.

Tortilla factories in Mexico first pass the dough through a dough-roller that looks very much like the handwringer on old washtubs. This forms the dough into a very thin, round tortilla. Finally, and most importantly, the tortilla is stretched by hand into its final shape in much the same way as pizza dough is stretched.

Make sure that the dough is not too damp or too dry (practice will be your best guide) and sprinkle your work surface and dough ball with flour to keep them from sticking together. Roll the dough as thin as possible. Next, begin stretching it by pulling one side and then the other until you have the desired size and thickness.

In Sonora tortillas are cooked on huge gas-fired griddles. However, few of us have utensils that will accommodate a tortilla of 15 or more inches (38 centimeters) in diameter. Keep the size of your skillet or *comal* in mind when shaping your dough. As stated in the preceding recipe, dividing the dough into 6 pieces should allow you to make 6 tortillas 9 to 10 inches (22.9 to 25.4 centimeters) in diameter, about the size of a large skillet or griddle. Finally, cook as for regular flour tortillas. Because of their thinness, these tortillas cook very quickly and can easily be overcooked. Makes 6 large tortillas.

Tortillas de maíz

CORN TORTILLAS

Corn tortillas are much easier to buy than to make and are now available throughout most of the United States. That is the good news. The bad news is that most corn tortillas sold in this country are of a decidedly inferior quality. In Mexico corn tortillas are made by soaking dried yellow or white corn in water overnight, with a little lime added to soften the corn. It is then boiled, ground to a paste called nixtamal, *or* masa, *shaped into tortillas, and cooked. Most Mexican corn tortillas are made by machine daily in the* tortillerías *(tortilla shops), where they are sold fresh. In this country (and regrettably in Mexico) many commercial tortillas are made from corn flour instead of fresh* masa, *which gives an inferior texture. In any case, most of our tortillas often are not really fresh, and lack the robust flavor and texture that are necessary to get the most out of Mexican recipes. Our tortillas, however, because they usually are thinner and have a lower moisture content, make far better* tostadas *and other items calling for crisp-fried tortillas. However, many cities in the United States do have* tortillerías *which make their* masa *from corn rather than from corn flour or Masa Harina.*

If good corn tortillas are not available where you live, it is well worth your while to buy some packaged Masa Harina, made by Quaker, and try making your own. With a little practice you will be pleased with the results. The only equipment you will need is a tortilla press, waxed paper or plastic garbage bags, and a heavy skillet. Follow the directions on the package and experiment with various levels of heat and timing to find the method that gives the best results. When making corn tortillas, try adding 2 tablespoons (17.5 grams) white flour to each cup of Masa Harina. This is a "secret" ingredient used by many Mexican cooks and results in a lighter, more flexible, smoother tortilla.

Bolillos

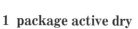

1   **package active dry yeast**

2¼ **cups (506.3 milliliters) water**

2   **tablespoons (30 grams) butter**

2   **pounds (900 grams) bread flour**

3   **tablespoons (36 grams) sugar**

1   **tablespoon (18.6 grams) salt**

   Heaping ¼ teaspoon ground cinnamon (optional)

MEXICAN ROLLS

After tortillas, Bolillos, or other such rolls made in different shapes, are undoubtedly the most popular bread in Mexico. They are served with entrées, in continental breakfasts, or as tortas (sandwiches). Most often in the south of Mexico Bolillos are light and crunchy, much like French rolls. I have also found this version in the north, but just as frequently northern Bolillos are a heavier, more country-style bread, sometimes with a touch of cinnamon. One of the meanings of the word bolillo *in Spanish is bobbin, and it is from that shape that these rolls get their name.*

Bolillos can be made by hand, in a food processor, or with a mixer with a dough hook; the procedure of adding the wet ingredients to the dry is basically the same. Also, I have specified the amount of flour by weight as I have found it to be much more accurate than measurement in cups. However, the 2 pounds specified equals approximately 6½ cups.

Mix the yeast in ⅓ cup (75 milliliters) of the water until dissolved. Allow to sit until bubbly, about 10 minutes. Stir the yeast mixture into the remaining water and add the melted butter.

Place the flour in a large mixing bowl or in a food processor fitted with a plastic blade. Add the sugar, salt, and cinnamon (if using it) and mix well. Add the yeast mixture to the flour, a little at a time, and form into a dough, which should be just slightly on the damp side. Add a little more water or flour as required to achieve this consistency. Knead the dough on a well-floured work surface for 8 to 10 minutes by hand or with a dough hook, or for about 45 seconds in a food processor. Place the kneaded dough into a large bowl that has been lightly greased with butter; turn it to coat with the butter, cover with a damp towel, and allow to rise until doubled in volume, about 1½ hours.

After the dough has risen, punch it down and divide it into balls of about 4 ounces (112 grams) each. Form the balls into oblong rolls about 4 to 5 inches (10.2 to 12.7 centimeters) long, 2½ to 3 inches (6.4 to 7.6 centimeters) wide, and 1½ to 2 inches (3.8 to 7.6 centimeters) high. Pinch each end into a little point to give the roll its distinctive shape. Allow the *Bolillos* to rise until nearly doubled in size, about 1 hour.

Preheat your oven to 375 degrees F (190 degrees C). Then, using a sharp knife or razor, slash the rolls across the top lengthwise about ¼ inch (.6 centimeter) deep, brush with cold water, and place them in the preheated oven. Bake the *Bolillos* until they are golden brown and the bottoms sound hollow when tapped, about 15 to 20 minutes. Makes 12 to 14.

Rice & Beans

❖❖❖

Arroz y Frijoles

The preparation of rice in northern Mexico is nearly identical to that in other parts of the country. It is soaked in hot water, dried, then fried in oil until lightly browned. It is then often fried with a blended tomato mixture before water is added for the final cooking. The end product is light and dry, with each grain of rice expanded to its maximum size. It can be made in advance and then heated in either a conventional or microwave oven.

Northern bean recipes also are similar to those in other regions, except for one of the most popular versions, *Frijoles a la charra* (Beans in the Fashion of the Horsewoman [p. 106]), which is much more common in the north. This variation uses fried chiles, onions, tomatoes, and garlic, which are added toward the end of the cooking time. It is the standard accompaniment to *al carbón* entrées.

Arroz

RICE

Mexicans are serious about rice. This staple, which was introduced by the Spanish, is often a meal in itself, particularly in the case of a dish like Arroz huérfano, *or Orphan's Rice (p. 104).*

In Mexico rice is normally sautéed in oil or lard before broth or water is added and the boiling process begun. To prepare Arroz mexicana *(pp. 101, 102), probably Mexico's most popular rice dish, tomato, puréed with onion and garlic, is added to the rice after it has been browned in oil. It is then cooked until virtually all the moisture has evaporated and the grains of rice no longer stick together, before the broth or water is added. If this is not done, the rice will be soupy. Although rice can be boiled in water, either chicken or pork broth makes a much more delicious dish.*

There are two basic ways of preparing Mexican-style rice dishes: with the pot covered and uncovered. The former method, which is probably the most common, yields a light fluffy product with each grain fully "exploded." The second, or uncovered, method leaves the grains more intact. I have provided instructions for both methods in the recipes for Arroz mexicana *(pp. 101, 102) and* Arroz blanco *(pp. 102, 103).*

Many Mexicans wash and soak their rice before frying it. With the more refined, high-quality rice we have in the United States, this step is unnecessary.

Arroz mexicana I

MEXICAN RICE COOKED UNCOVERED

Heat the oil in a heavy pot or Dutch oven over medium heat and add the rice. Cook the rice, stirring constantly, until it is golden brown. Avoid burning. While the rice is cooking, place the tomato, onion, and 2 cloves garlic in a blender and blend until smooth.

Turn up the heat under the rice to medium high and add the tomato mixture. Cook the rice and tomato mixture, stirring constantly, until nearly all the moisture has evaporated and it just begins to stick to the bottom of the pot.

Now, combine the water or broth and salt and add to the rice. Add and stir in all the optional ingredients used except the peas. Bring the water to a boil; then turn the heat down until it just simmers. This is the last time you should disturb the rice until it is cooked. Continue cooking, uncovered, until all the liquid has evaporated, about 18 to 20 minutes. If you are like me and absolutely must test the rice toward the end of the cooking time, take a narrow pointed knife like a boning knife and gently move aside just enough rice to show if any liquid remains in the pot.

When the rice is done, stir it and add the peas if you are using them. Cover and cook an additional 5 minutes on the lowest possible heat. Remove the pot from the heat and allow to stand, covered, for 10 minutes before serving. (Mexican Rice may be prepared well in advance and reheated in a microwave or conventional oven.) Serves 4.

2 tablespoons (28 milliliters) cooking oil

1 cup (192 grams) long or medium grain white rice

1 medium tomato, coarsely chopped

1/3 medium onion, coarsely chopped

2 cloves garlic, peeled

1³/₄ cups + 2 tablespoons (460 milliliters) water or broth

1 teaspoon (6.2 grams) salt

1 small carrot, shredded or cut in julienne strips (optional)

1/2 *ancho* chile, minced (optional)

2 sprigs cilantro (optional)

Additional 4 cloves garlic, peeled and left whole (optional)

4 *serrano* chiles, with only the stems removed (optional)

1/2 cup (68 grams) frozen peas, thawed (optional)

Arroz mexicana II

MEXICAN RICE COOKED COVERED

Prepare the rice exactly as in *Arroz mexicana* I (p. 101), except use 1½ cups (337.5 milliliters) water instead of the 1¾ cups plus 2 tablespoons (460 milliliters) called for in that recipe. Then, after the liquid begins to boil, cover the pot, turn the heat to very low, and cook for 20 minutes. Stir the rice, add the peas if you are using them, replace the cover, and allow the rice to steam for 10 minutes. Serves 4.

Arroz blanco I

WHITE RICE COOKED UNCOVERED

2 tablespoons (28 milliliters) cooking oil

1 cup (193 grams) long grain white rice

2¼ cups (506.3 milliliters) water or chicken broth

1 teaspoon (6.2 grams) salt

1 clove garlic, minced, or to taste (optional)

¼ cup (32 grams) carrots, cut in julienne strips (optional)

¼ cup (32 grams) frozen peas, thawed (optional)

¼ cup (12.4 grams) cilantro, chopped and loosely packed (optional)

White Rice is often served with foods that have a strong or sweet flavor, such as Chicken Mole, *and with very mild dishes such as broiled or sautéed fish.*

Heat the oil over medium heat in a heavy Dutch oven, add the rice, and fry, stirring constantly, until the rice *just* begins to color, about 3 to 5 minutes. Stir the salt into the water or broth and add it to the rice. If you are using garlic and/or carrots, stir them into the rice also at this time.

Bring the water or broth to a boil; then turn the heat down until it just simmers. As with *Arroz mexicana*, do not disturb the rice after combining all the ingredients. Cook until all the liquid either has been absorbed or evaporated. Add the peas and/or cilantro at this time (if used), cover the pot, and cook for 5 minutes over the lowest possible heat. Remove the pot from the burner, stir the rice well, cover, and allow to steam an additional 5 to 10 minutes. Serves 4.

Arroz blanco II

WHITE RICE COOKED COVERED

Prepare the rice exactly as in *Arroz blanco* I (p. 102), except use 2 cups (450 milliliters) water instead of the 2¼ cups (506.3 milliliters) called for in that recipe. Then, after the liquid begins to boil, cover the pot, turn the heat to very low, and cook for 20 minutes. Stir the rice, replace the cover, and allow it to steam for 10 minutes. Serves 4.

Arroz verde

GREEN RICE

This is a rich elegant rice that is delicious served with stuffed chiles, beef, chicken, or seafood. It is particularly good for banquet-style cooking, where a dramatic presentation is important.

Heat a Dutch oven or heavy pot over medium heat, and add the olive oil and butter. When the butter has melted, add the rice and cook, stirring often, until it just begins to brown, about 5 to 8 minutes. Add the onion and garlic and cook for another minute. Meanwhile, place the spinach, cilantro, and chicken broth in a blender and blend until the vegetables are puréed. Add the milk and salt to the blender and blend just until well combined.

 After the onions and garlic have cooked for 1 minute, stir in the contents of the blender, bring to a boil, cover, turn the heat to very low, and cook for 20 minutes. After 20 minutes remove the top of the pot, carefully stir the rice, and continue cooking for 5 minutes. Remove the pot from the heat and allow the rice to steam for 10 minutes. Serves 4.

1 tablespoon (15 milliliters) olive oil

3 tablespoons (45 grams) butter

1½ cups (290 grams) long grain rice

¼ cup (35 grams) onion, minced

1 clove garlic, minced

1 cup (40 grams) tightly packed spinach, washed and dried

½ cup (25 grams) tightly packed cilantro leaves

1¼ cups (280 milliliters) chicken broth

1¼ cups (280 milliliters) milk

1 teaspoon (6.2 grams) salt

Arroz huérfano

ORPHAN'S RICE

❖❖❖❖❖

21 ounces (588 milliliters) chicken broth

¼ teaspoon ground pepper

Scant ½ teaspoon curry powder

3 tablespoons (43 milliliters) cooking oil

1½ cups (290 grams) long grain rice

½ tablespoon (4 grams) onion, minced

1 clove garlic, minced

1½ ounces (42 grams) bacon (about 1 thick slice)

1½ ounces (42 grams) ham, finely chopped (about ¼ cup)

1 teaspoon (5 milliliters) Worcestershire sauce

3 ounces (84 grams) tenderloin steak, cut into ¼–⅓-inch (.64–.85-centimeter) pieces

1 tablespoon (15 grams) butter

¾ cup (86 grams) pecan halves

½ cup (46 grams) blanched, slivered almonds

⅓ cup (38 grams) pine nuts

The Middle Eastern roots of this spectacular rice dish served at Saltillo's La Canasta restaurant are unmistakable. This delicious and versatile dish works beautifully as an accompaniment to just about anything from appetizers to soup to main entrées. Please note that the amount of salt specified is for a light to moderately salted chicken broth, so adjust accordingly.

Mix together the broth, pepper, and curry powder and reserve the mixture.

Heat a heavy pot or Dutch oven over moderate heat, add the oil, and sauté, the rice, stirring frequently, for 3 minutes. Add the onion and garlic and cook 1 minute more. Add the broth mixture, bring to a boil, cover the pot, turn the heat down to low, and simmer for 20 minutes.

Meanwhile, fry the bacon medium crisp, chop finely, and mix with the ham. Just before the 20-minute cooking time is up, toss the Worcestershire sauce with the chopped tenderloin. When the 20 minutes is up, stir the bacon, ham, and tenderloin into the rice and replace the top. Continue cooking the rice for 5 minutes more; then, leaving the top in place, remove the pot from the heat.

Heat the butter in a medium-sized skillet over moderate heat, add the pecans and almonds and sauté, stirring frequently, until the almonds turn a light golden brown. Do not allow the nuts to overcook or they will be bitter.

When the rice is ready, remove the top and stir in the pecans and almonds and mound the rice on a platter or place in a bowl. Sprinkle the pine nuts over the rice and serve. Serves 4.

Frijoles

BEANS

In northern Mexico the frijoles *of choice are pinto beans and bayo beans, or occasionally their cousin, pink beans. While I like the black or turtle beans usually served in southern Mexico equally well, I find pintos a more appropriate accompaniment to the robust northern* al carbón *specialties.*

Pinto beans are prepared in three basic ways. For *Frijoles de olla* (Beans from the Pot [p. 106]), they are simmered with garlic, oregano, salt, pieces of salt pork or bacon, and sometimes cumin. For *Frijoles a la charra* (Beans in the Fashion of the Horsewoman, also sometimes called *Frijoles rancheros* [p. 106]), tomatoes, onions, and *serrano* chiles fried in lard are added toward the end of the cooking period to *Frijoles de olla*. Lastly, there is *Frijoles refritos* (Refried Beans [p. 107]), which is *Frijoles de olla* mashed and fried in lard. (The substitution of oil for lard is not as successful for these recipes.) *Frijoles de olla* and *Frijoles a la charra* are most often served with *al carbón* entrées, while *Frijoles refritos* usually are served with *antojitos* and *Huevos rancheros* (p. 241).

NOTE: Beans, like stew, are better cooked the day before they are to be served, which allows them to absorb the maximum amount of flavor. Be sure to wash and pick over beans carefully to remove dirt and stones.

Frijoles de olla

BEANS FROM THE POT

1 **pound (450 grams) pinto beans, rinsed and picked over**

6 **cups (1,350 milliliters) water**

2 **teaspoons (4 grams) cumin (optional)**

2 **teaspoons (.6 gram) oregano**

3 **cloves garlic**

4 **ounces (112 grams) salt pork or 4 strips bacon, coarsely chopped**

Salt to taste

Place the beans and water in a bean pot or Dutch oven. Grind the cumin, oregano, and garlic to a paste in a *molcajete* or mortar and pestle and add to the pot with the remaining ingredients. Bring the water to a boil and cover, leaving a small space for steam to escape. Simmer until the beans are tender but not mushy. Serve with the cooking liquid in individual bowls. Serves 4.

NOTE: For the health conscious, *Frijoles de olla* can also be made without salt pork or bacon (see p. 274).

Frijoles a la charra or Frijoles rancheros

BEANS IN THE FASHION OF THE HORSEWOMAN

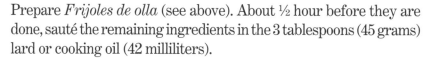

2 **large or 3 medium tomatoes, chopped**

1 **medium onion, chopped**

3–5 *serrano* **chiles, finely chopped, or to taste**

2 **cloves garlic, minced (optional)**

3 **tablespoons (45 grams) lard or cooking oil (42 milliliters)**

Prepare *Frijoles de olla* (see above). About ½ hour before they are done, sauté the remaining ingredients in the 3 tablespoons (45 grams) lard or cooking oil (42 milliliters).

Cook over medium to medium-high heat until the vegetables are soft but not browned, about 15 minutes. Add them to the beans for the last 15 minutes of cooking. Serves 4.

Frijoles borrachos

DRUNKEN BEANS

To make this popular dish, follow the recipe for *Frijoles de olla* (p. 106), substituting 12 ounces (240 milliliters) of dark beer for an equal amount of the water. Serves 4.

Frijoles refritos

REFRIED BEANS

Refried beans are usually not refried at all but fried only once. They are served with entrées or as a filling for tacos and burritos.

Place the garlic, cumin, and onion in a *molcajete* or mortar and pestle and grind to a paste. Heat the lard or oil and fry the garlic-onion purée until it is soft but not browned and gives off a rich aroma. Traditionally, at this stage the beans and enough of their cooking liquid to make a thick soupy mixture are poured into the skillet and mashed into the lard or oil with a tool made expressly for this purpose. If you do not have a bean masher, a large slotted spoon will do. I have found that giving the beans a few whirls in a food processor saves considerable effort in this regard.

Once the beans have been incorporated into the lard or oil, fry them, stirring constantly, over medium-high heat until they have the consistency of mashed potatoes. (See p. 274 regarding how to make Refried Beans without frying.) If they get dry, add more liquid. Serves 4.

NOTE: As with other recipes in this book, an equal quantity of oil may be substituted for lard. However, the reader is advised that this dish will lose something of its character if the substitution is made.

3   cloves garlic
1½   teaspoons (3 grams) cumin
¼   medium onion, coarsely chopped
¼   cup (56 grams) lard or cooking oil (56 milliliters)
½   recipe *Frijoles de olla* (p. 106)

3 **cloves garlic**

¼ **teaspoon cumin**

¼ **medium onion, coarsely chopped**

2 **small *ancho* chiles, soaked in hot water for ½ hour and seeded**

¼ **cup (56 grams) lard or cooking oil (56 milliliters)**

½ **recipe *Frijoles de olla* (p. 106)**

1½ **cups (218 grams) *asadero*, mozzarella, or Monterey Jack cheese, grated**

Frijoles maneados

TIED-UP BEANS

This recipe, like Frijoles refritos, *is a real northern specialty and, when served with tortillas and some* Pico de gallo *(p. 49), is a meal in itself.*

Place the garlic, cumin, onion, and chiles in a *molcajete* or mortar and pestle and grind to a paste.

Heat the lard or oil and fry the puréed ingredients for a few seconds over medium heat. Add the beans and some of their cooking liquid and mash them, turning often, until all the ingredients are well mixed. Fry the beans until they have the consistency of mashed potatoes. Then turn the heat to low, stir in the cheese, and serve. Serves 4.

Entrées

Cooking al Carbón

Cooking *al carbón* is the heart and soul of northern Mexican cooking. This cooking method derives from the area's ranching heritage and sets it apart from the cooking of southern Mexico. Because many of the recipes in this book are cooked *al carbón*, some background and guidelines for this simple but distinctive cooking method are provided here. (More specific directions will be found in the individual recipes.)

Carbón means "coal" and also refers to cooking over natural wood coals or hardwood charcoal. The best fuel by far for broiling northern Mexican foods is mesquite, which imparts a sweet smoky flavor, or related substances such as *huisache* or the Hawaiian *keawe* tree.

Before the introduction of horses and cattle, mesquite was relatively scarce in northern Mexico. Range animals, particularly the horse, regarded the mesquite bean (the tree's seedpod) as a delicacy. When lack of rain produced poor grazing conditions, Mexican ranchers traveled long distances to collect truckloads of mesquite beans for their livestock. As the animals moved across the range, they returned the seeds to the earth in a perfect growing medium, and soon the young mesquite trees were everywhere. However, as a mature mesquite tree requires forty gallons or more of water each day, what at first seemed an ideal food supplement became an unpleasant competitor for this scarce resource. Today, most ranchers on both sides of the border are happy to see a *leñador* (woodcutter) arrive on their doorsteps, chain saw in hand, to thin out the mesquite trees. In the state of Coahuila one cannot drive far without seeing a cart or truck laden with mesquite or *huisache* being transported to homes, to market, or to the *carboneros* (makers of charcoal).

Because of its increasing popularity as cooking fuel, mesquite is now obtainable from markets in most parts of the United States in either wood or charcoal form. If it is not available, oak, hickory, or other hardwood will serve. Each gives excellent results but imparts a different flavor to the food. When cooking with natural woods, I have found that pieces 2 to 3 inches (5 to 7.6 centimeters) in diameter and 1 foot (30.4 centimeters) long will, if properly dried, burn down to coals within 30 minutes. Anything smaller will turn to ash too quickly, and larger pieces take considerably longer. The wood can be placed in a portable barbecue, firepit, or fireplace. On cold days and nights, there is nothing more relaxing than building a fire and enjoying a glass of wine or a cocktail while the wood burns down to perfect coals. A simple fireplace broiler can be made by using three or four bricks on each side to support a barbecue grill.

If wood is not available, use a good charcoal made from hardwood rather than petroleum-based briquettes, which do not provide as much heat and give off an unpleasant odor. For flavoring, add a handful of mesquite chips, sold in many markets, or hickory chips which have been soaked in water for an hour or two. However, never use charcoal for indoor cooking, since it emits poisonous fumes.

Cooking time depends on the heat of the coals, the distance of the grill from the fire, the amount of air circulation, and the shape of the barbecue or firepit. Experience will be your best guide. When cooking outdoors or in the fireplace, set a second grill somewhat farther from the coals to heat beans, rice, and tortillas.

An important difference between the way we and the Mexicans charbroil is that they usually cook their meat over much lower coals for longer periods. I learned this technique years ago on a trip to Múzquiz, Coahuila, where I have a friend, who, although a gringo, is probably the unofficial mayor of the town. One day he took me out to the foothills of the sierra to a large *palapa*, a sort of grass-roofed pavilion situated beside a creek. Each Saturday this is the home of the Pirañas (piranhas), an unofficial men's club so named because of the members' affinity for meat. There they gather to spend the afternoon catching up on the week's events, cooking, and drinking beer (not necessarily in that order).

On a long barbecue constructed of cinder blocks there were large, thin slices of chuck steak cooking over what seemed to be inadequate coals. After about 10 minutes one of the men wandered over and turned the meat. This continued over irregular periods. Finally, after 30 minutes or so, a piece of meat was removed, chopped with a cleaver, and served with hot flour tortillas, *Pico de gallo*, and a wonderful salsa. The meat was tender and had a smoky, almost buttery taste. The advantages of this type of slow cooking soon became evident. Since precise timing is unnecessary, it does not interfere with socializing; cheaper and more flavorful cuts of meat can be used, and less fuel is required. The only tradeoff is that on thicker, more tender cuts the line between degrees of doneness becomes blurred.

When cooking outdoors with wood or charcoal, or with wood in an indoor fireplace, add some "seasoning" to the coals. Mexican cooks often throw a few pieces of onion and/or garlic, chiles, and oregano on the coals. This produces a wonderful aroma and adds flavor to the meat. This is the "secret" ingredient in many of northern Mexico's finest restaurants. A good mix is ⅓ medium onion coarsely chopped, 3 unpeeled cloves garlic, 2 to 3 whole *jalapeño* chiles or 3 to 4 *serrano* chiles, and 1 tablespoon (1.8 grams) oregano. Put the mixture on the coals; then put the meat on to cook as soon as the mixture begins to smoke.

If you cannot cook these dishes over wood or charcoal, use a heavy iron skillet with raised ridges, which will create a similar effect. They can also be broiled in the oven or using a gas or electric grill. The results will still be excellent even though you will miss the tangy smoke flavor.

You will note that some of the following dishes are prepared *al pastor* (shepherd style). In many parts of northern Mexico you will see a whole *cabrito* (kid) attached to iron rods being cooked slowly over hot coals at a 45- to 70-degree angle. Another common sight is food stalls with braziers full of coals, where large, thin pieces of marinated pork are stacked and cooked on vertically placed skewers, with the heat coming from the side. As the outer portion of the meat is done, pieces are sliced off and used to fill steaming hot tortillas. This is cooking *al pastor*, which derives from the campfire cooking of Mexican shepherds of the north, many of whom are of Basque origin. The tacos made in this manner are often called *tacos de trompo* because the cooking meat resembles a spinning top. *Al pastor* cooking is particularly popular in Nuevo León and northern Tamaulipas. The best way of duplicating *al pastor* campfire cooking is to use a barbecue with an electric rotisserie attachment, placed as far from the coals as possible.

Meats

Carnes

Northern Mexico is ranch country, and, as one might expect, beef is by far the most popular meat there. However, kid, lamb, and pork also are important features of the area's cuisine.

While Mexican beef is not normally as tender as American beef, it is often more flavorful. The reason for this is that so many Mexican cattle are grass or range fed instead of being kept in feedlots on a diet of corn and grain. Just as eggs from barnyard chickens that feed on bugs, grass, and other natural foods are superior in taste to mass-produced supermarket eggs, so is the flavor of range-fed beef superior. In fact, so many of our meats produced from scientifically fed animals taste so uniformly bland that eating meat in a country such as Mexico, which raises animals naturally, provides an unexpected treat to a nearly forgotten flavor. In addition to the abundant native grasses, in northern Mexico the cattle graze on wild herbs, such as oregano, which are said to impart a subtle flavor to the meat.

Mexicans like the strong range-fed beef flavor and will often use less expensive cuts like round and chuck, not so much because they are less expensive as because of their more pronounced flavor. This is illustrated by the popularity of *fajitas*, or *arracheras* (skirt steak), and *agujas* bottom chuck, which are often preferred over the more expensive tenderloin or sirloin.

Another popular meat which is not frequently found outside northern Mexico is *cabrito*, or kid. It is particularly enjoyed in the mountainous state of Nuevo León, whose capital, Monterrey, is also the industrial center of Mexico. This *regio montano* (mountain kingdom) has its own cuisine within the regional cuisine, the most prominent feature of which is *cabrito*.

In many parts of northern Mexico, sheep rather than cattle were the first range animals to be introduced. Prominent among the early settlers were sheep ranchers of Basque origin. Basque names such as Elguezabel and Iturría are still common in many places there. While lamb is often cooked *al pastor*, it is more frequently charbroiled and sliced for use in tacos.

While pork is not as popular in northern Mexico as it is in southern Mexico, it is still often used. In every region you will find a cook famous for his *carnitas* (literally, little meats). These cooks will arrive at a party or fiesta with a huge iron cauldron, which is placed on a fire, and into which will be dropped huge chunks of pork and lard. Next to be added are water, spices, fruits, and their juices. As the meat cooks over a period of several hours, it is stirred and turned (often with a shovel) until all the moisture has evaporated and most of the fat has been rendered from the meat. It is then allowed to cook further until it is crisp and golden on the outside, yet moist and tender on the inside.

Carne asada

BROILED MEAT

Carne asada *means "broiled meat" and in northern Mexico also means a cookout or barbecue, a picnic in the country where meat is cooked over an open fire.*

If you order Carne asada *in a restaurant in northern Mexico, you will usually be served a savory plate of thinly sliced, broiled pieces of tenderloin or sirloin steak accompanied by Refried Beans, Guacamole, rice, Pico de gallo, and either flour or corn tortillas, or both. The most distinctive thing about this dish is the manner in which the meat is cut. It is trimmed of all fat and then sliced thinly (¹/₈ to ¹/₄ inch [.3 to .6 centimeter]) with the grain. Elsewhere, when a cut is described as "in the Mexican fashion" or "in the manner of* Carne asada" *this is what is meant. These steaks, because they are so thin, must be broiled very quickly over the hottest possible coals to achieve a rare or medium-rare state. This is especially true for Steak* Tampiqueña *(p. 126) and steak and enchiladas, which are served on a sizzling hot plate. For these dishes, broil the meat on one side only, if you like it rare; then place it uncooked side down on the heated plate, which completes the cooking.*

When making Carne asada, *allow about ½ pound (225 grams) of meat per person and serve with Refried Beans (p. 107) and/or rice, Rajas (strips of fried chile and onion), Guacamole (p. 83), Pico de gallo (p. 49), and hot tortillas or Bolillos (p. 96). Better yet, take the time to prepare Steak* Tampiqueña, *which is the ultimate Mexican combination plate.*

This recipe for Carne asada *is sure to become one of your favorites, especially if you like garlic.*

If the tenderloin is more than about 8 inches (20.3 centimeters) long, cut it in half. Slice it lengthwise, with the grain, into slices about ¼ inch (1.3 centimeters) thick.

Place the garlic, pepper, cumin, and olive oil in a *molcajete* or mortar and pestle and grind the mixture, until the garlic is puréed and the spices are pulverized. Toss the oil mixture with the sliced meat and marinate in the refrigerator for at least 3 hours or overnight.

Broil the meat very close to a very hot fire to the desired degree. Add salt to taste and serve as suggested above. Serves 4.

2 pounds (900 grams) whole tenderloin, completely trimmed of fat

4–5 medium cloves garlic, peeled

1 teaspoon whole black peppercorns, or to taste

½ teaspoon cumin

¼ cup (56 milliliters) olive oil

Salt to taste

Agujas

THIN CHUCK STEAK

2½ pounds (1,100 grams)
 bone-in bottom
 chuck steak, cut no
 more than ½ inch
 (1.3 centimeters)
 thick
Juice of 3 or 4 limes
Salt

Agujas are thin, very flavorful steaks, ½- to ¾-inch (1.3- to 3.4-centimeter) slices cut from the bottom chuck. The protracted cooking time over low heat makes this truly northern dish a favorite at carne asadas, or cookouts, where precise and demanding cooking processes which would interfere with socializing are not favored. Even if you usually prefer steak rare or medium rare, you will soon become addicted to the smoky flavor and almost buttery consistency of this well-done meat. The secret of this dish is that when high-fat meat cooks over a low fire it will be well charred and impregnated with smoke without drying out.

Pour the lime juice onto the meat, salt it well, and marinate in the refrigerator for 1 to 3 hours.

Broil the meat on a grill set at least 6 to 8 inches (15.3 to 20.3 centimeters) away from a slow mesquite fire until it is very well done. Turn the meat every 5 minutes for about 20 minutes. As with similar meat dishes, Agujas are usually served with beans, guacamole, tortillas, and salsa. Serves 4.

T-bone Steak

T-bone and porterhouse steaks are as popular in Mexico as they are in the United States. A T-bone is actually a sort of combination steak, being a New York cut on one side of the bone and a filet mignon on the other.

When broiling T-bones, be sure that the meat is a good distance from the coals. This cut has more fat than any other except rib eye and is therefore susceptible to catching fire. Mexican butchers tend to leave a great deal more fat untrimmed from the steak than we do, often as much as 2 inches (5 centimeters). A steak trimmed in this manner and served on a sizzling iron platter is an impressive sight.

The T-bone is usually served with french fried potatoes, *Frijoles a la charra* (p. 106), or both.

The thinnest possible cut of T-bone will weight about ½ pound (225 grams), but any size up to 1½ to 2 pounds (675 to 900 grams) is manageable. One or two hours before cooking, brush 4 steaks with garlic oil (p. 16) and add a few grinds of pepper. Broil over hot coals, being careful to keep the steaks far enough from the coals to prevent burning. Serves 4.

Fajitas, or Arracheras

SKIRT STEAK

This cut of meat is called Fajitas *in Texas and along the border in Mexico. Further south, it is usually known as* Arracheras. *While still not favored in some parts of the United States, the skirt steak, which a few years ago was used only for hamburger, is becoming more popular here. This is now the preferred steak in many parts of Texas, where there are almost weekly* Fajita *cookoffs. I also have seen* Fajitas *on restaurant menus in California, New York, and numerous other areas. We are learning what the Mexicans have known for years: that, when properly cooked, the skirt steak can be almost as tender as any other cut and always will be more flavorful. Note that, while* Fajitas *are thinner than most of the steaks we usually use, they take somewhat longer to cook. Allow ½ pound (225 grams) of skirt steak per person.*

Fajitas are served whole with rice, Refried Beans *(p. 107), and* Guacamole *(p. 83), or sliced as filling for* Tacos de fajitas *(p. 195). For the latter, the meat is often brought sizzling to the table on a large iron plate or skillet, a dramatic presentation that makes it a winner in restaurants. For* Tacos de fajitas, *broil the meat to one degree less than desired. For example, if you want it medium rare, broil it until just rare. Then slice the meat into bite-sized pieces. While you are doing this, heat a heavy iron skillet over high heat for just a few minutes to avoid damaging it (or yourself, if the heat should cause it to break). Just before serving, transfer the meat to the hot skillet and add the juice of 2 to 3 limes. This is what creates the steam and sizzle. Place the skillet, set on a trivet or other heat-resistant item, on the dining table. Set out bowls of* Guacamole, Pico de gallo *(p. 49), your favorite sauce, and plenty of hot tortillas.*

Another popular variation is Fajitas encebolladas *(Fajitas with Onions). For this variation, thinly slice 1 large onion and fry it in 1 tablespoon (15 milliliters) of olive oil, peanut oil, or lard until very brown, about 20 minutes. During the last 10 minutes add 4 small limes, halved. Add the meat and the cooked onions and lime halves to the heated iron skillet at the same time and mix well just prior to adding the lime juice.*

To be completely tender, Fajitas *should be marinated for a few hours or overnight prior to cooking. The marinade for Chicken Shish Kebabs (p. 166) is a good choice, especially if ½ tablespoon (4.9 grams) of cornstarch, which helps the tenderizing process, is added. An alternate, Mexican-style marinade can be made with ¼ cup (56 milliliters) lime juice mixed with ½ tablespoon (3.5 grams) of garlic powder and ¼ teaspoon of salt, black pepper, and onion powder to taste.*

The following is my favorite marinade, adapted from an Argentine recipe. Although it is not authentically Mexican, it is excellent.

Favorite Fajita Marinade

3 large cloves garlic

½ cup (112 milliliters) water

2 tablespoons (28 milliliters) olive oil

½ tablespoon (7.5 milliliters) red wine vinegar

¼ teaspoon freshly ground black pepper

1 bay leaf

1 sprig rosemary

4 thin slices onion

½ tablespoon (7.5 milliliters) sauce from a can of *chipotle* chiles in *adobo* sauce

3 tablespoons (42 milliliters) lime juice

1 tablespoon (15 milliliters) pineapple juice

½ teaspoon salt

¼ teaspoon Worcestershire sauce

Blend the garlic cloves in the water for 2 minutes at high speed, and pour the mixture into a bowl. Add the olive oil, red wine vinegar, freshly ground black pepper, bay leaf, rosemary, onion slices, and sauce from the can of *chipotle* chiles in *adobo* sauce, and leave, covered and refrigerated for 8 hours or overnight. Then add the lime juice, the pineapple juice, salt, and Worcestershire sauce; stir well and marinate the skirt steak for 2 hours in the refrigerator. Remove from the refrigerator and continue marinating for 1 hour.

Biftec ranchero

STEAK WITH RANCHERO SAUCE

This version of Biftec ranchero *is a real northern specialty. The tomatoes, onions, and chile sauce are also used for Pork Chops* Ranchero *(p. 151) and Eggs* Ranchero *(p. 241). Steak with* Ranchero Sauce *is one of those dishes that require fresh, not canned, ingredients. Any good steak can be used, but a New York cut or rib eye are preferable.*

If broiling the steaks over a fire, start the fire and then prepare the ingredients for the sauce when the coals are about 15 minutes from being ready.

Heat 2 tablespoons (30 grams) of the lard or olive oil (30 milliliters) in a large heavy skillet. Add the onion, garlic, green onions, and chiles. Cook over medium heat, stirring frequently, until they are just soft but not browned, about 5 to 10 minutes.

Add and melt the remaining 1 tablespoon (15 grams) of lard or add 1 tablespoon (15 milliliters) of olive oil, and the tomatoes, stirring well to combine with the other ingredients. Reduce the heat to medium and cook, stirring often, until all the liquid has evaporated. Now broil the steaks to the desired degree and place them on individual serving plates. Remove the sauce from the heat, stir in the cilantro, and spoon the sauce over the steaks. Serve with Refried Beans (p. 107) and rice. Serves 4.

3 tablespoons (45 grams) lard or olive oil (45 milliliters)

1 medium onion, coarsely chopped

2 cloves garlic, minced

4 green onions, coarsely chopped

1 *poblano* chile, peeled, seeded, and chopped; or substitute 1 Anaheim chile or bell pepper

2 *serrano* chiles, finely sliced

4 medium tomatoes, seeded and coarsely chopped

4 6–8-ounce (168–225 grams each) New York or rib eye steaks

½ cup (25 grams) cilantro, chopped and loosely packed

Biftec a la plancha

PAN-BROILED STEAK

**4 8-ounce T-bone or
porterhouse steaks
(225 grams each
[the porterhouse
has the larger filet])
Salt and pepper to
taste**

Although charbroiling is by far the most popular method of cooking steaks in most parts of northern Mexico, many people, there as here, prefer their steaks pan-broiled for reasons of convenience or taste. In pan-broiling, the meat is cooked in a heavy skillet over medium to medium-high heat (depending on thickness), using just enough fat to keep it from sticking. The best source of fat for this purpose is rendered suet from the fat trimmings of the steaks. This is done while the skillet is heating. Biftec a la plancha *is particularly popular in the state of Chihuahua, where adequate-sized mesquite is often not available. There it is served with the same accompaniments as steaks* al carbón. *In Chihuahua City and Juárez, the steaks often are cooked and served in individual iron or steel plates that have wooden bases made especially for this purpose. This creates a spectacular, sizzling presentation. Heat-resistant gloves should be used for serving, and care should be taken to avoid burns from the popping fat.*

This recipe is for T-bone or porterhouse steaks, which, because of their fat content, are particularly easy to pan-broil. The same is true for rib eye steaks. The instructions may also be applied to other cuts of beef and to pork. The recipe here calls for 8-ounce steaks, which is about as thin as it is practical to cut a T-bone. In Mexico this thin cut is often preferred, I suspect, because it is so economical.

Salt and pepper the steaks and trim them of excess fat. Place 2 to 3 ounces (56 to 79 grams) of the fat in a large iron or other heavy skillet over medium-high heat. Using kitchen tongs, turn the fat pieces frequently as they begin to sizzle to prevent them from burning. When the skillet is very hot and the rendered fat is beginning to smoke, remove any remaining pieces of fat and add the steaks. Cook them about 1½ minutes on each side for rare to medium-rare steaks, more for other degrees of doneness, and serve immediately with Guacamole (p. 83), beans, *Rajas* (strips of fried chile and onion), and rice.

If you have individual steel or iron cooking plates with wooden bases, cook the steaks individually in the plates. Then, after adding the accompaniments, use heat-resistant gloves to set them in their insulating wooden bases on the table. For variation, heat the individual plates in the oven at 350 degrees F (177 degrees C), cook the steaks in the large skillet, place them on the hot plates, and serve them as above. If you are using either of these techniques, remember that the steaks will continue to cook long after they are served. To avoid overdone steaks, cook them on one side and then turn and cook them 15 seconds on the other side before placing them, lightly cooked side down, on the serving plates. Serves 4.

Biftec pimental

MEXICAN-STYLE PEPPER STEAK

Biftec pimental *is steak topped with strips of seeded and peeled chiles that have been sautéed in butter. A perfectly ripe, red Anaheim chile is usually used. The flavor of the ripened chile is more rounded and mellow than when it is green, and it is almost sweet. These ripe chiles are rarely available in the United States. If you cannot grow your own, substitute a good red bell pepper. This way of serving steak is common in Chihuahua, where steaks are usually pan-broiled instead of charbroiled. However, either method may be used for this dish.*

Choose your favorite steak; T-bone, rib eye, or New York are good choices. Cook the steaks *al carbón* or pan-broil them and serve them topped with the chiles or peppers.

To prepare the topping, heat the butter in a medium-sized skillet over medium heat. Then add the garlic, if used, and the chiles and peppers and sauté them until they are soft and serve over the steaks. Serves 6.

6 steaks

2 tablespoons (30 grams) butter

1 clove garlic, minced (optional)

1 cup (131 grams) red, ripe Anaheim chiles, peeled, seeded, and chopped; or substitute 3 red bell peppers, seeded but not peeled, and sliced into thin strips

Black pepper, to taste (to be added if using bell peppers)

Steak Tampiqueña

1 pound (450 grams) filet steak, cut with the grain in the Mexican fashion (see *Carne asada*, p. 117)

½ pound (225 grams) shredded, cooked chicken

2 dozen tortillas (only 1 dozen is needed but allow for mistakes)

1 recipe *Mole* Sauce (p. 170)

4 Tortilla Cups (p. 84)

Guacamole, made with 2 avocados (p. 83)

1½ cups (380 grams) Refried Beans (p. 107)

1 recipe Mexican Rice (pp. 101, 102)

Rajas (strips of fried chile and onion)

Shredded lettuce or cabbage

Chopped tomatoes

Steak Tampiqueña *is the aristocrat of Mexican combination plates and is a favorite restaurant meal. Introduced in Mexico City's Tampico Club in the 1940s by José Inéz Loredo, a native of Tampico, Steak* Tampiqueña *has been adapted and changed by chefs throughout the republic. The original recipe called for a thin, pan-broiled filet to be served with enchiladas in green chile sauce and crispy, browned* quesadillas, *garnished with sautéed* Rajas *(fried chile and onion strips). This dish is now presented accompanied by different types of enchiladas, tacos, gorditas, chalupas, rice, beans, and guacamole, but almost always with the original fried onions and chiles.*

The prospect of a good filet tampiqueña *has often tempted me to make the 150-mile drive from San Antonio to one of three nearly equidistant border towns: Nuevo Laredo, Piedras Negras, or Ciudad Acuña. Each one has many fine restaurants with just as many versions of this famous dish. Two of the best may be found at the México Típico restaurant in Nuevo Laredo and Martino's in Ciudad Juárez, across from El Paso.*

Since the recipe for Steak Tampiqueña's *accompaniments are given elsewhere in this book, only the final preparation and assembly is described here. It takes a little planning and practice to get the timing right, but the result is well worth the effort.*

Using the shredded, cooked chicken and *Mole* Sauce, make 4 *Enchiladas de mole* (p. 219), or substitute cheese of your choice, and place on an ovenproof plate in a 375-degree F (190-degree C) oven for 8 to 10 minutes. While this is cooking, make 4 Tortilla Cups and fill them with the Guacamole. Make *Tostadas* from 2 tortillas (p. 53), as a garnish for the beans. Next, make 4 Crisp Chicken Tacos (p. 205) with either crisp or medium-fried tortillas. Make the *Rajas*.

Remove the plates with the enchiladas and arrange the tacos, *Rajas*, Guacamole (in Tortilla Cups), Refried Beans, and Mexican Rice as shown in the color photograph. Place 2 *Tostadas* in each serving of beans.

Using a very hot fire, broil the steaks very quickly, about 1½ to 2 minutes on the first side and 1 minute on the second (as they will be placed against the sizzling hot plates) and set them on the plates. Garnish the plates with the lettuce or cabbage and tomatoes and serve, using hot dish holders. Be sure the table is protected with heat-resistant place mats. Serves 4.

Costillas de res

BEEF SHORT RIBS

This dish makes a hearty addition to any carne asada *(barbecue) and also is delicious and filling by itself. Since the ribs are very thick and fatty, keep the grill well away from the coals to prevent burning on the outside.*

Score the beef short ribs by slicing them, at ¼-inch (.6-centimeter) intervals, one way and then the other, as though you were trying to set up a crossword puzzle across the fatty tops. Then marinate, refrigerated, for 2 hours.

To prepare the marinade, remove the seeds and stems from the chiles, soak them in hot water for 10 minutes, and place them in a blender with the remaining ingredients. Blend for 60 seconds. If the mixture is a little too thick to blend satisfactorily, add a little water and continue to blend.

Broil the marinated ribs for 30 to 45 minutes, setting them far enough from the coals to prevent flareups and burning on the outside.

Good accompaniments are hot corn tortillas, *Pico de gallo* (p. 49), and any of the *jalapeño* sauces. Slice the meat into small pieces and wrap it with the other ingredients in hot tortillas. Serves 4.

4 **pounds (1,800 grams) beef short ribs**

MARINADE
4 *ancho* **chiles**
4 *japonés* **chiles**
1 **tablespoon (1.2 grams) oregano**
4 **cloves garlic**
1 **tablespoon (6 grams) cumin**
¹⁄₃ **cup (83 milliliters) mild red wine vinegar**
¹⁄₃ **cup (83 milliliters) cooking oil**
¹⁄₂ **teaspoon salt**

Carne guisada

BEEF STEW

◇◇◇◇◇

4 **cloves garlic**
1 **tablespoon (1.8 grams) oregano**
½ **teaspoon cumin**
¼ **cup (60 grams) lard or cooking oil (56 milliliters)**
2 **pounds (900 grams) very lean round steak or stew meat, cut in 1-inch (2.54-centimeter) pieces**
1½ **tablespoons (13 grams) flour**
 Water
1 **teaspoon (6.2 grams) salt**
3 *ancho* **chiles, stemmed and seeded, but left whole**
3–6 *japonés* **chiles or** *de árbol* **chiles, stemmed and seeded**
¼ **cup (42 milliliters) tomato sauce**

Carne guisada *is a delicious Mexican-style stew that somewhat resembles Texas-style chile.* Carne guisada *has recently become very popular in south Texas, where it is made with potatoes, carrots, and celery and thickened with flour toward the end of the cooking process, very much as we do our stews.* Carne guisada *is usually eaten with flour tortillas.*

The following is an authentic northern Mexican recipe which I picked up while participating in a cattle drive on a friend's ranch. There it was made with airmailed chiles and neighbor's meat.

My friend flew me to the cow camp, where he also delivered some supplies. The unhappy cook pointed out that the chiles had been forgotten. Later in the day my rancher friend returned and, circling just above us, dropped several well-wrapped bags of chiles. As I watched him prepare the stew, I asked the cook what cut of meat he was using. He replied with a grin "carne de vecino," which literally means "neighbor's meat." He quickly assured me that he was not a rustler but had traded some dry provisions to the neighboring ranch foreman for the steer.

Mash the garlic, oregano, and cumin together in a *molcajete* or mortar and pestle.

Heat the lard or oil over medium heat in a heavy iron pot or Dutch oven. Place the beef and flour in a paper bag and shake until the beef is well coated.

When the lard or oil is hot, add the beef and cook, stirring continuously to prevent scorching, until it is well browned. Pour off any excess lard or oil and add enough water to just cover the meat. Then add the remaining ingredients.

Bring the mixture to a boil, cover, and simmer 1½ hours, or until the meat is very tender and most of the cooking liquid has evaporated. (There should be very little gravy.) If necessary, add more water. If it is too watery, remove the cover and continue cooking until the proper consistency is reached. Serve with flour tortillas and your favorite sauce. Serves 4.

Cortadillo de carne de res

"CUT-UP" BEEF STEW

This is a truly traditional northern dish, dating back to the seventeenth century. It combines regional ingredients in a simple manner but one which produces a surprisingly complex blend of flavor and texture. As its name, deriving from the verb cortar, *"to cut," suggests, it is made by cutting up ingredients which are then fried in a manner similar to Chinese-style stir-frying.* Cortadillo *is served in its juices or somewhat thin gravy, accompanied usually by Refried Beans and corn or flour tortillas to "clean" the plate. It is not often found on restaurant menus, where it is sometimes called* Biftec a la mexicana *or* Guisada a la mexicana, *but is nearly always available on request.* Cortadillo *is particularly favored in Coahuila and Nuevo León as an early morning "fortifier" after a bout in the* cantinas.

This recipe, which I adapted from the one served at Saltillo's La Canasta restaurant, is a delight after a lot of more complicated dishes. It epitomizes the best of simple comfort food, Mexican style. But it is not without its own subtleties and is certainly the Rolls-Royce of cortadillos. *(If, like me, you find it hard to use the expensive tenderloin cut for what is essentially a stew, albeit a special one, substitute top sirloin, but do not use a tougher cut.)*

Heat a large skillet over medium-high to high heat, add 2 tablespoons (28 milliliters) olive oil, then add the meat. If you do not have a large skillet (about 12 to 13 inches [30.5 to 33 centimeters] in diameter]), you should cook the meat in 2 batches so that it will brown properly. Allow the meat to brown for a few seconds before touching it; then turn it and allow it to brown again. Continue cooking the meat, turning constantly, stir-fry fashion, until it is just browned all over; then remove the meat to a bowl.

Turn the heat to medium to medium high, add the remaining 2 tablespoons (28 milliliters) olive oil, the green pepper, onion, tomatoes, and chiles, if used, and sauté until the vegetables are soft. Return the meat to the pan with any accumulated juices, add the salt, pepper, and tomato purée and cook until the liquid in the pan bubbles and the meat is heated through.

Serve with Refried Beans (p. 107) and corn and/or flour tortillas. Serves 4.

¼ cup (56 milliliters) olive oil

1¼ pounds (560 grams) very lean beef tenderloin, or substitute top sirloin, cut into ⅛–¼-inch (.3–.6-centimeter) pieces, about ½ inch (1.3 centimeters) long

2 cups (263 grams) green pepper, finely chopped

⅔ cup (95 grams) onion, finely chopped

2 cups (334 grams) tomatoes, finely chopped

2 *serrano* chiles, seeded and minced (optional)

½ teaspoon salt

¼ teaspoon ground pepper

½ cup (116 grams) tomato purée (not paste)

Milanesa

BREADED VEAL CUTLET

1 pound (450 grams)
  veal, tenderloin, or
  tenderized round
  steak, sliced ⅛ inch
  (.3 centimeter)
  thick
  Flour
2 **eggs beaten with 3
  tablespoons (12
  milliliters) water
  and salt and pepper
  to taste**
  Bread crumbs
  Cooking oil

You will find this dish on the menu of almost any good restaurant in northern Mexico. It is also used as a filling for tacos. Since veal is not often used in Mexico, tenderloin sliced thin as for Carne asada *or round steak, pounded to tenderize it, is commonly substituted. As with many other northern Mexican foods, particularly the steaks, it is not so much the entrée of breaded veal that makes this dish special but the choice of items which accompany it.* Milanesa *is usually served with Refried Beans (p. 107) and/or Mexican Rice (pp. 101, 102), Rajas (fried strips of chile, onion, and sometimes squash), Guacamole (p. 83), and a lime half. This combination is delicious and uniquely Mexican.*

NOTE: While *Milanesa* is often served with additional flour rather than bread crumbs for the second coating, I much prefer the breaded version.

Dip the pieces of meat (veal if you prefer) into flour and shake off the excess. Next, dip the floured meat into the egg mixture and coat it with the bread crumbs. Refrigerate the meat for at least 1 hour.

Heat ¾ inch (1.9 centimeters) of cooking oil in a heavy skillet until it is very hot, or until just before it begins to smoke. Cook the meat for about 20 to 30 seconds on each side, or until done. The trick is to cook it so that the coating is nicely browned and the meat inside is still moist and tender. Serve as suggested above. Serves 4.

Albóndigas en salsa de chile

MEATBALLS IN CHILE SAUCE

Several kinds of chiles may be used for this dish. I prefer either the canned *chipotle chiles or* ancho *chiles. If neither is available, use chile powder.*

To make the meatballs, mix well all the ingredients except the cooking oil. An electric mixer or food processor will do this efficiently. Form the mixture into 1- to 1½-inch (2.5- to 3.8-centimeter) balls. Then, heat the cooking oil in a large heavy pot or Dutch oven over medium-high heat. Add the meatballs and fry, turning often, until they are well browned. Then remove them and drain them on paper towels while you prepare the sauce.

Pour off the remaining oil and return the pot to the burner. Turn the heat to low and melt the butter. Add the onion and fry, stirring often, until it becomes soft and translucent. Add the carrots and flour and cook, stirring often, for about 3 minutes, being careful not to let the flour burn. Remove the pot from the heat and add the broth a little at a time, stirring well after each addition. When about half of the broth has been added, return the pot to the burner and add the remaining broth in a stream while stirring constantly.

Next, grind the garlic, cumin, oregano, and chiles in a *molcajete* or mortar and pestle and add them and the tomatoes to the pot. Add the reserved meatballs and bring the liquid to a boil. Then turn the heat to low or medium low and simmer for 30 minutes, uncovered, or until the sauce is thickened. Add a little salt to taste and serve with Mexican Rice (pp. 101, 102) or white rice. Serves 4.

MEATBALLS

- 2 slices stale or dried bread, crumbled
- 2 small eggs
- ⅓ cup (48 grams) onion, minced
- 2 canned *chipotle* chiles or *ancho* chiles, seeded and finely chopped
- ¼ cup (48 grams) uncooked rice
- 1 teaspoon (6.2 grams) salt
- ¼ teaspoon pepper
- 1½ pounds (675 grams) ground beef
- ⅓ cup (83 milliliters) cooking oil

SAUCE

- 4 tablespoons (60 grams) butter
- 1 medium onion, thinly sliced
- 2 medium carrots, cut in julienne strips
- 3 tablespoons (26 grams) flour
- 3 cups (675 milliliters) beef broth
- 1 clove garlic
- ¼ teaspoon cumin
- ½ teaspoon oregano
- 2 canned *chipotle* chiles or *ancho* chiles, seeded and finely chopped
- 4 tomatoes, peeled, seeded, and finely chopped

  Salt to taste

1½ pounds (675 grams) sirloin steak

MARINADE
½ cup (110 milliliters) red wine vinegar

¼ cup (56 milliliters) dry vermouth

3 tablespoons (43 milliliters) cooking oil

5 cloves garlic, minced

½ teaspoon salt

½ teaspoon black pepper

1 tablespoon (3 grams) unflavored meat tenderizer

SHISH KEBABS
Thin steel or wooden shish kebab skewers

4 medium tomatoes, quartered, or 16 cherry tomatoes

2 medium onions, cut into ½-inch (1.3-centimeter) pieces

3 large *poblano* chiles; Anaheim chiles, or bell peppers may be substituted

4 thick slices of bacon, cut into 1-inch (2.54-centimeter) pieces

Marinated beef

Alambres de carne de res

BEEF SHISH KEBABS

In northern Mexico, Beef Shish Kebabs are usually made from the tenderloin or filet and are normally not marinated. Because of the cost of this cut in the United States, I usually substitute sirloin, which, when marinated, is sufficiently tender.

BEEF

Use either unmarinated tenderloin or marinated sirloin. If you are using sirloin, trim all fat from it and cut it into pieces approximately 1½ inches (3.8 centimeters) square and ½ inch (1.3 centimeters) thick. Then marinate the meat, refrigerated, overnight or for at least 3 hours.

MARINADE

Use this marinade or the one for Chicken Shish Kebabs (p. 166) or any other marinade you like that does not contain soy sauce or a sweetener. Mix all marinade ingredients well.

Thread ingredients on the skewers in the following order: 1 piece pepper; 1 piece tomato (or 1 cherry tomato), 2 pieces onion, 1 piece bacon, 2 pieces beef, 1 piece bacon, 2 pieces onion. Repeat until all ingredients have been threaded.

Broil the shish kebabs over hot coals, on both sides, until they are well charred but the beef is still moist and tender in the middle. This takes about 3 to 5 minutes on each side if the coals are really hot. If cooking over fire is not feasible, or a charbroiler is not available, broil in the oven 2 to 3 inches (5 to 7.6 centimeters) from the heating element for the same amount of time.

Shish kebabs are usually served with Guacamole (p. 83) and rice and/or *Frijoles a la charra* (p. 106). Serves 4.

Alambres con zanahorias

SHISH KEBABS WITH CARROTS

After you have trimmed, pounded, and sliced the sirloin, combine the lime juice, garlic, salt, and olive oil and marinate the meat in it for ½ hour (any longer and the lime juice will start to "cook" the meat as in *ceviche*). Meanwhile, prepare a wood or charcoal fire in your barbecue.

When the meat has marinated, prepare the shish kebabs as follows:

Thread on a piece of *poblano* chile, a piece of carrot, a piece of onion, a piece of bacon, then 3 pieces of meat. Add a piece of bacon, a piece of onion, a piece of *poblano* chile, 2 pieces of carrot, a piece of onion, a piece of bacon, and 3 more pieces of meat. Continue in this manner until you have 4 sections of meat (3 pieces each), then end with a piece of bacon, a piece of onion, a piece of carrot, and a piece of *poblano* chile. Prepare the remaining 3 shish kebabs in the same manner.

Brush some of the marinade over the prepared shish kebabs and cook over a very hot fire until the meat is cooked through, turning 4 times, about 8 to 10 minutes in all. Serve the shish kebabs with your favorite sauce and hot tortillas and/or Mexican Rice. Serves 4.

1½–2 **pounds (675–900 grams) trimmed top sirloin, cut into 48 pieces 1½–1¾ inches (3.8–4.4 centimeters) in diameter, ⅛ inch (.3 centimeter) thick**

¼ **cup (56 milliliters) lime juice**

3 **cloves garlic, minced**

½ **teaspoon salt**

½ **cup (110 milliliters) olive oil**

32 **¹⁄₁₆ inch (.2 centimeter) thick pieces of carrot about 1 to 1½ inches (2.5–3.8 centimeters) in diameter**

32 **1-inch (2.54-centimeter) slices of onion**

16 **1-inch (2.54-centimeter) pieces of sliced bacon**

20 **1–1½-inch (2.54–3.8-centimeter) pieces of *poblano* chile**

4 **shish kebab skewers Hot sauce Fresh corn or flour tortillas and/or Mexican Rice (pp. 101, 102)**

Sábanas del norte

"SHEETS" NORTHERN STYLE

4 4½-ounce (126 grams each) filet mignons, cut about 1 inch (2.54 centimeters) thick

¼ cup (60 grams) butter

2 tablespoons (28 milliliters) medium sherry

2 tablespoons (28 milliliters) liquid from canned *chipotle* chiles

1 cup (109 grams) *asadero* cheese, grated, or substitute mozzarella or provolone cheese

Sábanas *means sheets, and that is exactly what these huge wafer-thin pieces of filet mignon resemble. Usually associated with the cooking of central Mexico, this recipe, which I found in Zacatecas, is excellent and goes well with other northern dishes. The technique and presentation are also very interesting.*

I have tried several methods of forming the meat but have found the one suggested by Diana Kennedy in *The Art of Mexican Cooking* to be the best. Place a filet between sheets of plastic wrap, and, using a meat pounder or the side of a heavy cleaver, pound it until it is oblong shaped and about ⅓ inch (.85 centimeter) thick. Fold the meat in half or into a circular bundle and continue pounding until the meat is wafer-thin. At this point it will be 9 or 10 inches (22.8 or 25.4 centimeters) in diameter. Pound from the center out and be careful not to shred the edges. Other than that the process is pretty easy.

Remove the top sheet of plastic wrap and replace it with a sheet of waxed paper. Then turn the meat over so that the waxed paper is on the bottom. Replace the remaining sheet of plastic wrap with another sheet of waxed paper. Treat the remaining filets in like manner and place them in the refrigerator.

About 15 to 20 minutes before you cook the meat, place it in the freezer so that it will stiffen, making it much easier to handle.

Preheat your broiler. Also, at this time melt the butter and stir in the sherry and liquid from the *chipotle* chiles.

Next, heat a griddle or heavy skillet over very high heat. The pan must be very hot, the way it should be for blackened red fish and similar dishes. When the griddle is hot enough, pour on just a little oil or use a spray coating. Immediately place 1 of the *Sábanas* on the griddle for just a few seconds; then flip it over and cook a few seconds more. Remove the meat to a serving plate and cook the remaining meat in the same manner. When all the steaks are done, brush them with the butter mixture, top with the cheese, and place 2 to 3 inches (5 to 7.6 centimeters) under the broiler to melt the cheese. This should take no more than 1 to 1½ minutes.

Serve the meat with Refried Beans (p. 107). Serves 4.

Combination Meat Plates

PARILLADAS

Parilladas *are typical of Argentinean cooking and also of the cooking of northern Mexico. Most people in the United States are, by now, familiar with the sizzling platter of* fajitas. *Picture that same platter with the addition of broiled chicken, ribs, sausage, pork, lamb, sweetbreads, and perhaps tamales and* quesadillas *and you have an idea of what a northern Mexican* parillada *can be.*

Parilladas, *which are usually served with* Frijoles a la charra *(p. 106) but can also be served with Refried Beans (p. 107) and/or rice, are featured in some restaurants, particularly in Nuevo León and Coahuila, but are most often found at private gatherings.*

Parillada zacatecana

MEAT PLATTER ZACATECAS STYLE

12 ounces (340 grams) sirloin, cut no thicker than ¼ inch (.6 centimeter)

Juice of 2 limes

2 tablespoons (28 milliliters) olive oil (plus additional oil for sautéeing the meat)

2 large onions, sliced very thin

8 *serrano* chiles, stems removed

2 cloves garlic, minced

½ teaspoon salt (plus additional salt for the sirloin)

½ recipe *Adobo estillo Zacatecas* (p. 150)

1 recipe Guacamole (p. 83)

1 recipe Refried Beans (p. 107)

1 recipe *Quesadillas* (p. 229)

Flour and/or corn tortillas

Salsa

This is one of my favorite meals. It is a delight to serve because the pan-broiled adobo *and beef go so well together and with the other ingredients, and the plate looks so appealing.*

One-half hour before serving sprinkle the sirloin with the lime juice and set aside.

Heat a heavy skillet over medium heat, add 2 tablespoons (28 milliliters) of the olive oil, then add the onions and *serranos*. Cook, stirring frequently, until the onions are soft and beginning to brown. Add the garlic and salt, cook 2 minutes more, then set the pan aside while you prepare the meats.

Heat another heavy skillet or griddle over medium-high heat, add enough oil to grease the surface, then pan-broil the sirloin to the desired degree of doneness. Remove the sirloin to a warm dish and sprinkle on salt to taste. Add a little more oil to the cooking surface and pan-broil the *Adobo estillo Zacatecas* until it is browned and cooked through.

Chop the two meats into bite-sized pieces and mix them together; then mound them onto the center of an oval platter. Mound the fried onion on top of the meat. Place a mound of Guacamole at one end of the platter and a mound of Refried Beans at the other. Place *Quesadillas*, cut into nacho-sized pieces, along the sides of the platter and serve with small flour and/or corn tortillas and salsa. Serves 4.

Lengua de res estilo norteño

NORTHERN-STYLE BEEF TONGUE

The sauce for this dish is both subtle and delicious, and is as good with poached chicken as with tongue. For the most tender results, select a tongue of no more than 3 pounds (1,350 grams). Also, remember to peel the skin from the meat while it is still warm since this will be nearly impossible once it is chilled.

In a large pot bring to a boil sufficient water to cover the tongue. Add the tongue, onion, carrot, garlic, and bay leaves and simmer for 2 to 3 hours or until the tongue is very tender.

Remove the tongue from the pot (leaving the cooking liquid in it), and when it is cool enough to handle peel and discard the skin. Replace the tongue in the pot and allow it to cool in the broth. At this point the dish can be refrigerated for several days.

To prepare the sauce, tear the chile (or chiles) into small pieces and place them in a blender. Bring ½ cup (112 milliliters) of the tongue broth to a boil, add it to the blender, and allow the contents to soak for 15 to 20 minutes. Add the cinnamon and blend for 1 minute. Add the tomatoes and blend an additional 15 seconds.

Meanwhile, melt 1½ tablespoons (22.5 grams) of the butter over medium heat and sauté the pecans and almonds until the almonds are beginning to turn golden. Add the browned nuts to the blender with the remaining 1 cup (225 milliliters) of broth, cloves, thyme, raisins, and salt.

Melt the remaining 1½ tablespoons (22.5 grams) butter in a medium-sized saucepan and stir in the contents of the blender. Bring to a boil and simmer the sauce until thickened, about 15 minutes.

Meanwhile, slice the tongue thinly. When the sauce has thickened, add the sliced meat and continue cooking until it is heated through, about 3 minutes. Serve with white rice. Serves 4 to 6.

1 beef tongue of 2½–3 pounds (1,000–1,350 grams)

1 small onion, halved

1 carrot, cut into several large pieces

4 cloves garlic

2 bay leaves

1 large *pasilla* chile, stemmed and seeded, or 2 smaller ones

1½ cups (337.5 milliliters) tongue broth

1 1½-inch (3.8-centimeter) piece stick cinnamon or a heaping ¼ teaspoon ground cinnamon

10 ounces (280 grams) tomatoes (1 large or 2 small)

3 tablespoons (45 grams) butter

¼ cup plus 2 tablespoons (44 grams) pecan halves

¼ cup plus 2 tablespoons (35 grams) blanched, slivered almonds

⅛ teaspoon ground cloves

¾ teaspoon thyme

3 tablespoons (11 grams) raisins

½ teaspoon salt, or to taste

Menudo

TRIPE STEW OR SOUP

2 pounds (900 grams)
   beef tripe
1½ pounds (675 grams)
   calf's foot
5 cups (1,125 milliliters)
   chicken broth or
   water
3 *ancho* chiles
1 onion, chopped
1 teaspoon (.6 gram)
   oregano
2 tablespoons (28
   milliliters) lime
   juice
¼ teaspoon pepper
3 cloves garlic, minced
1 cup (225 milliliters)
   water
1 15-ounce can (425
   grams) hominy
2 teaspoons (12.4
   grams) salt

CONDIMENTS
Minced green onions
Oregano
Lime wedges
Crushed *piquín* chile
Chopped cilantro
Salt

Depending on its thickness, Menudo *can be either a delicious, hearty soup or a stew. It is consumed any time of the day or night. Northern Mexicans can be hard drinkers, and* Menudo *is the favorite hangover remedy after a night at the* cantinas. *This dish is sold by street vendors for breakfast and at all-night restaurants. Endorsing hangover cures is risky, but I will say that it does seem to work.*

Menudo *is made of honeycomb beef tripe, which is the lining of the cow's stomach, and a calf's foot. This may not sound very appetizing, but when it is properly cooked and seasoned even the most squeamish find it delicious. So universal is its appeal that in Texas and other parts of the Southwest* Menudo *cookoffs are held. While tripe is universally available, and most Southwest supermarkets carry frozen calves' feet, the latter may prove difficult to find elsewhere. While it is an important ingredient for the flavor and final texture of the dish, it is better to cook* Menudo *without it than not to cook it at all.*

If frozen, thaw the tripe and soak it for several hours or overnight in water. After soaking, which should be done also for fresh tripe to remove unpleasant flavors, slice the tripe into bite-sized pieces about ½ inch (1.3 centimeters) thick and place them in a heavy pot or Dutch oven.

Add the calf's foot and chicken broth or water and bring to a boil. Place the chiles, onion, oregano, lime juice, pepper, garlic, and cup of water in a blender and blend for 1 minute or until puréed.

Add the chile mixture to the pot, bring to a boil, and then reduce the heat so that the soup barely simmers. Cover and cook for 4½ hours, checking often to prevent boiling, which makes the tripe tough. If too much liquid appears to be evaporating, add more broth or water as needed. Now add the hominy, including the liquid from the can, and the salt. Cover and continue simmering for ½ hour. Serve the soup with the listed condiments, which are passed around the table and added, to taste, to the soup. Serves 4.

Barbacoa

BARBECUED HEAD OF COW, GOAT, OR SHEEP

This is a weekend dish in northern Mexico. Proper preparation requires a special pit. It is often prepared by meat markets on weekends and during fiestas.

First, a large quantity of mesquite is burned down to coals, half of which are placed in a pit lined with volcanic rock or fire brick and several times larger than the head. The head is then wrapped in several layers of wet burlap, and a wire is placed around it to facilitate its later removal. The package is then lowered onto the coals. The remaining coals are then placed on top of the head. A cover, usually made of clay or iron, is fitted over the head but well below the ground surface. Earth is piled over the cover and tamped down to seal the pit and make it airtight.

The process usually is begun in the afternoon or evening, and the head is allowed to cook until morning (12 to 18 hours). After the head has been lifted from the pit, the brains, tongue, cheeks, and other parts considered edible are removed and served with hot tortillas and sauce.

This method of cooking produces a unique smoky taste. In the United States, Hispanic restaurants and tortilla factories often make *Barbacoa* by steaming the heads in large kettles over water. I do not recommend that version. Serves 4.

1 cow, goat, or sheep's head, skinned but with nothing else removed

Carne seca

DRIED BEEF

◇◇◇◇◇◇

2 **pounds (900 grams)
    lean round steak,
    cut very thin**
⅓ **cup (83 milliliters)
    lime juice**
¾ **teaspoon–½ tablespoon
    (4.7–9.3 grams) salt**

This Mexican-style beef jerky is often called Machaca, *or* Machacado *when it is pounded and shredded and mixed with other ingredients. It is a very versatile item and is used as a filling in a famous egg dish called* Machacado *(p. 241), as an appetizer, and in soup.* Carne seca *is made by cutting and/or pounding lean cuts of beef into very thin slices. It is then sprinkled with lime juice and salt and left to bake under the dry desert sun. For those of us who live in cooler and more humid climates, this method of preparation is often not an option. Fortunately, excellent* Carne seca *can be made in a food dehydrator in about three hours.*

Please note that the following recipe gives a broad choice for the amount of salt. The upper amount is close to that used in most parts of northern Mexico while the lesser amount still produces an authentic taste and is more acceptable in these health-conscious times.

Regarding the cut of meat to use, I suggest the thin-sliced and extremely lean round or sirloin steaks commonly called "breakfast steaks" in supermarkets. These should then be pounded as thin as possible between sheets of plastic wrap using a meat pounder or the side of a heavy cleaver.

Pound the meat as thin as possible between sheets of plastic wrap. Mix the lime juice and salt and pour it over the meat, making sure both sides are coated; then allow the meat to sit for ½ hour.

Place the meat in a food dehydrator and dry at 145 degrees F (63 degrees C) for approximately 3 hours or until the meat is quite dry.

You can leave the meat whole to be used as a snack, or process it for use in fillings. For the latter, cut the meat into small pieces and shred using the steel blade of a food processor until it is light and fluffy.

Makes approximately 10 ounces (280 grams) *Carne seca* or a little over 3 cups (280 grams) of *Machaca.*

Mochomos

SHREDDED, FRIED BEEF OR PORK

Mochomos is a popular way of preparing beef and pork in northern Mexico. It can be used as a filling for burritos or chimichangas, *or served by itself with guacamole and limes as an appetizer or main dish. The meat, which is boiled until tender, shredded, then fried crisp, makes a good substitute for* Machaca *or* Carne seca *(p. 140). If you use pork, which is popular in Chihuahua and Sonora, use a lean cut such as the loin. If you use beef, which is popular in Sinaloa, you can use any lean cut, but I suggest you try either brisket or boneless short ribs. The brisket will have a superior texture, but the ribs will cook more quickly.*

Place the pork or beef in a pot and cover with water by 2 inches (5.08 centimeters); then add the whole onion, garlic, bay leaf, oregano, and salt. Bring to a boil and simmer until the meat is tender. This will take 45 minutes to 1 hour for pork and 1½ to 2 hours for beef. If necessary, add more water.

When the meat is done, allow it to cool in the water, discard the onion, and mince the garlic; then shred the meat. Pulling it apart by hand or with two forks or grinding it in a *molcajete* creates the best texture. But a food processor fitted with a plastic blade is much easier and yields an acceptable result.

Heat a skillet over medium heat, add the lard, rendered beef fat, or olive oil, then add the minced onion. Cook the onion, stirring frequently, until it is soft but not browned. Stir in the meat and minced garlic and allow it to cook undisturbed until it browns on one side. Stir; then allow the meat to brown once again, and then stir it almost constantly until it is very brown and crisp. Add the salt and serve, either as a filling for burritos or *chimichangas* or on a plate accompanied by Guacamole (p. 83), lime quarters, shredded lettuce, salsa, and small, thin flour tortillas. Serves 4.

1¼ pounds (560 grams) pork or beef, cut into 1-inch (2.54-centimeter) pieces

1 whole small onion, peeled

3 whole cloves garlic, peeled

1 bay leaf

1 teaspoon (.6 gram) dried oregano or 2 4-inch (10.1-centimeter) stems fresh oregano

½ teaspoon salt, or to taste

2 tablespoons lard (30 grams) if using pork, or rendered beef fat, if using beef, or substitute olive oil (28 milliliters)

⅔ cup (95 grams) onion, minced

Cuajitos

◇◈◇◈◇

BEEF AND LAMB STEW

1½ **pounds (675 grams) stew beef, cut into** ¾-**inch (1.9-centimeter) pieces**

½ **pound (225 grams) lamb, cut into** ¾-**inch (1.9-centimeter) pieces**

⅓ **cup (44 grams)** *poblano* **chiles, seeded and minced**

2 *serrano* **chiles, seeded and minced**

2 **cloves garlic, minced**

½ **medium onion, minced**

½ **pound (225 grams) tomatoes, chopped**

½ **teaspoon salt**

½ **cup (110 milliliters) water**

The origin of the name of this dish from Nuevo León is a bit of a mystery. Alicia Gironella De'Angeli and Jorge De'Angeli point out in El gran libro de la cocina mexicana *that in some parts of Mexico the word* cuajo *refers to a school recess and surmise that it is associated with a time of rest and relaxation. This dish used to be commonly cooked in a pit like* Barbacoa, *and fortunately we can easily simulate this effect by using a clay cooker.*

Cuajitos *is a very simple stew, and, like* cortadillo, *which it somewhat resembles, it is made with fresh rather than the dried chiles used in similar dishes in Texas. (My theory is that in Nuevo León this and similar dishes are usually prepared in villages where fresh chiles are available in contrast with the ranch and trail drive cooking common to Texas that relied on dried, preserved foods.)*

Cuajitos *can be made entirely with beef, but it is much more interesting with the addition of some lamb.*

Completely submerge a clay cooker and soak it for at least 15 minutes.

Mix all the ingredients together and place them in the cooker. Put the cooker in your oven and turn the heat to 425 degrees F (220 degrees C). (Do not preheat the oven as the clay may crack.) Cook for a total of 2 hours and serve the *Cuajitos* with Refried Beans (p. 107) and corn and/or flour tortillas. Serves 4.

Cordero al pastor

ROASTED LAMB SHEPHERD STYLE

The best ways to duplicate al pastor *cooking are to use a barbecue with a rotisserie attachment or a grill placed about 2 feet (61 centimeters) from the coals. If you choose the former method, ask the butcher to bone and tie the lamb so it can be threaded onto the skewer.*

To make the marinade, grind all the ingredients into a paste in a *molcajete* or mortar and pestle. Rub the paste onto the lamb and marinate, covered, in the refrigerator overnight.

If you are using a barbecue with a rotisserie, cook as far from the coals as possible until done, 45 minutes to 1¼ hour per pound. If you are using the method with a grill 2 feet (61 centimeters) from the coals, cook for the same time or use an electric or charcoal smoke cooker, following the directions for leg of lamb; or bake in a 350-degree F (177-degree C) oven for 30 to 40 minutes per pound. No matter what method you choose it is prudent to check the lamb occasionally with a meat thermometer.

If you are using the meat for tacos, slice it diagonally into bite-sized pieces and serve with *Frijoles de olla* (p. 106) or *Frijoles a la charra* (p. 106), *Pico de gallo* (p. 49), your favorite table sauces, and plenty of hot tortillas. Alternatively, serve as a main meat course with rice and/or beans. Serves 4.

1 leg of lamb

MARINADE
1 teaspoon (1.4 grams) *piquín* chile
5 cloves garlic
½ teaspoon oregano
6 fresh mint leaves or ½ teaspoon dried
½ teaspoon mild chile powder
½ teaspoon salt
½ teaspoon pepper
¼ cup (12 grams) cilantro, chopped and loosely packed
3 tablespoons (26 grams) minced onion
¼ cup (56 milliliters) olive oil
2 tablespoons (28 milliliters) lime juice

Cordero a la griega

GREEK-STYLE LAMB

❖❖❖❖❖

1½ pounds (675 grams) boneless steaks, cut from the leg of lamb, ½ inch (1.3 centimeters) thick

2½ pounds (1,100 grams) lamb ribs

Juice from 3 large limes

2 tablespoons (28 milliliters) olive oil

3 onions, sliced to between ⅛ and ¼ inch (.3 and .6 centimeter)

2 cloves garlic, minced

Heaping ¼ teaspoon salt (plus salt for the lamb)

Corn tortillas

Salsa de ajo (p. 44), or your favorite hot sauce

Guacamole (p. 83)

This is not a dish that will bring a smile to the face of your cardiologist. But its name notwithstanding, it is one of the most satisfying and popular entrées in and around Monterrey, especially in upscale restaurants. While one variation consists of lamb pan-broiled until crisp, my hands-down favorite is this rendition, which is charbroiled over mesquite and served sizzling on an iron platter with fried onions, guacamole, and thin, soft corn tortillas (made that way by adding some wheat flour to the masa—*see instructions for corn tortillas, p. 95). In restaurants in Mexico often the lamb comes heaped on the platter to such a height that you wonder how you will possibly be able to make a dent in it. In fact, you quickly discover that because the restaurant has used the cheaper cuts of lamb such as the shoulder and ribs, you have to work to extract a meal from between the fat and bones. But you do, and it is rich and delicious, providing ample meat to roll in the tortillas with some guacamole and hot sauce. However, to make eating this dish more effortless, for this recipe I have specified a combination of boneless steaks cut from the leg of lamb and ribs, a less fatty and certainly less troublesome version, but one that retains the authentic taste.*

Start a fire of mesquite wood or charcoal. Brush a little of the lime juice over the lamb and allow it to rest at room temperature while the wood or charcoal burns to coals.

To make the fried onions, heat a skillet over medium heat, add the olive oil and the onions. Cook, stirring often, until the onions are soft and begin to brown. Then, add the garlic and salt, turn the heat to low, and cook 5 minutes. Keep the onions warm.

Sprinkle some salt on the lamb and broil it over medium to low heat until it is cooked through and crusty on the outside. Meanwhile, heat individual iron steak platters in the oven at 550 degrees F (288 degrees C) or heat a large iron griddle or skillet over high heat. When the lamb is done, put it on the individual platters or griddle and pour the remaining lime juice over it to create the "sizzle." Serve the lamb with corn tortillas, sauce, Guacamole, and reserved onions. Serves 4.

Carnitas

PORK TIDBITS

Carnitas *are usually associated with the south of Mexico, especially the state of Michoacán. However, they are also enjoyed in the north, particularly at barbecues and fairs.*

There are two basic methods of making Carnitas: *The first is the traditional way in which large cuts of pork are placed in huge copper pots with enough melted lard to cover them plus a little water, milk or juice, garlic, and herbs. The meat is cooked for a long time until the exterior is crisp and the meat is nearly falling apart. While there is nothing to compare with the crisp texture and succulent taste of* Carnitas *cooked in this fashion, they are undeniably contrary to virtually all dietary guidelines. Fortunately, there is another alternative, which, depending on the cut of pork chosen, can be quite low in fat. In this method the pork is cut into small pieces, then simmered in water with spices until the liquid has evaporated and the meat is very tender. The* Carnitas *are then browned in the rendered fat or, if a very lean cut is used, in a little added lard or oil. I have provided recipes for both alternatives.*

Carnitas I

TRADITIONAL CARNITAS

◆◇◆◇◆◇◆

2 pounds (900 grams) lard

¼ cup plus 1 tablespoon (71 milliliters) milk

¼ cup plus 1 tablespoon (71 milliliters) water

1 sprig thyme, or ½ teaspoon

1 head garlic, whole and unpeeled

1 bay leaf

2 teaspoons (12.4 grams) salt

2½ pounds (1,100 grams) pork butt or shoulder, cut into pieces ¾ inch (1.9 centimeters) thick by 2 inches (5 centimeters). You can also use country-style spareribs, cut into 2-inch (5-centimeter) pieces.

The secret of cooking this type of Carnitas *is to boil rather than fry the meat until it is just tender, then to increase the heat and continue cooking until it is golden and crisp.*

Melt the lard in a large pot over low heat. Stir in the remaining ingredients and increase the heat until the meat just simmers. Continue cooking at a bare simmer, stirring every 5 minutes or so (Mexicans using their huge copper cauldrons often use a shovel to perform this task) until the meat is tender, about 1 hour. Remove the bay leaf and garlic and increase the heat to the low side of medium to medium-high and continue cooking, stirring frequently, until the meat is brown and crispy, about 7 to 10 minutes. Remove the meat, drain, then partially shred it (this means that there should be some small whole pieces of meat along with the shredded portion). The plastic blade of a food processor is ideal for this operation.

Serve the *Carnitas* with Guacamole (p. 83) for an appetizer or with Mexican Rice (pp. 101, 102) for a main course. Serves 4.

Carnitas II

PORK TIDBITS

This recipe from northern Mexico takes only a short time to prepare and requires no added fat. Country-style spareribs also work very well, especially if you get them cut into sections about 2 inches (5 centimeters) long. For a really low-fat version, use pork tenderloin.

Place the cut-up meat in a large heavy skillet and add just enough water to cover. Grind together the cumin, oregano, garlic, and chiles in a *molcajete* or mortar and pestle and add to the skillet with the salt.

Bring the liquid to a boil and reduce the heat to low. Simmer until all the liquid has evaporated. At this point the meat should be very tender, and enough fat should have been rendered to allow it to fry without sticking. If the meat is not yet tender, keep adding more water and cook until it is. If there is not enough fat in the pan, add some lard or cooking oil. Increase the heat to medium and continue cooking, stirring constantly, until the meat is brown and crisp on the outside but still tender and moist on the inside, 5 to 10 minutes. Serve the *Carnitas* with rice or use for tacos. Serves 4.

2 pounds (900 grams) pork loin or boneless pork shoulder, cut into ½–1-inch (1.27–2.54-centimeter) pieces
Water
2 teaspoons (4 grams) cumin
2 teaspoons (1.2 grams) oregano
4 cloves garlic
4 *piquín* chiles
½ teaspoon salt, or to taste

Carnitas de jugo

CARNITAS WITH JUICE

Follow the basic recipe for *Carnitas* II (p. 146) but add 1 cup (225 milliliters) of orange juice or pineapple juice, or a combination of both, before covering the meat with water. Also, keep the heat low for the final frying since the sugar from the juices burns easily, imparting a bitter taste.

Serve *Carnitas de jugo* with flour tortillas, charbroiled green onions, rice, and your favorite sauce. Serves 4.

Cochinita píbil del norte

PIT-COOKED PORK NORTHERN STYLE

3½ **pounds (4,725 grams) boneless pork loin roast**

MARINADE
2–3 *ancho* **chiles, seeded and deveined**
 2 *de árbol* **chiles, seeded and deveined**
 ¾ **cup (170 milliliters) orange juice**
 3 **cloves garlic**
 ½ **tablespoon (.9 gram) oregano**
 ¾ **teaspoon salt**
 ½ **teaspoon black pepper**
 Juice of 1 small lime

Cochinita píbil is a famous dish from the Yucatán, a long way from northern Mexico. This recipe is included not only because it is excellent but also as an example of how recipes from other regions can change and become a part of the northern cuisine.

A few years ago I stopped at a small roadside stand in the village of Magdalena, Sonora. Since I was not familiar with the area, I picked the one open-air stall that seemed to be the busiest. The owner was carving delicious-looking slices from a large piece of smoked pork which had obviously been marinated. The pork was cooked in a huge pit barbecue which sat beneath a thatched roof. The sliced pork was placed on flour tortillas that had been heated over the barbecue. Sliced green onions, which had also been charbroiled, and a spoonful of guacamole topped the pork.

This taco, with the smoky texture and flavor of the pork, was ambrosia. When the lunch crowd had thinned, I asked the stall owner about the meat. He said it was the Yucatán specialty. There it is made with a paste that contains achiote, *ground from the seed of the annato tree. However, I was pretty certain that there was no* achiote, *which gives the Yucatán dish its character, in the marinade. He said I was right, that since* achiote *was difficult to find he used other ingredients. These he kindly identified for me. After some experimentation, I was able to duplicate the flavor of his tacos, which is different from the classic Yucatán version but to me just as good, if not better.*

This dish is best cooked in a water-smoker, or other barbecue that cooks with indirect heat (not directly over the coals) but also may be prepared on a rotisserie or in an oven.

Put all the marinade ingredients in a blender and blend at high speed for 1 minute. Place the pork and marinade in a nonreactive bowl and marinate in the refrigerator for at least 3 hours or overnight.

Smoke the meat in the barbecue for 45 minutes to 1 hour per pound, or bake at 350 degrees F (177 degrees C) until a meat thermometer registers 150 degrees F (66 degrees C).

Use for tacos, as described above, or as a main course with rice or beans. Serves 4.

Adobo estilo Zacatecas

ZACATECAS-STYLE SEASONED PORK

❖❖❖❖❖

6 tablespoons (42 grams)
  chile powder made
  from *ancho* chiles
½ teaspoon cumin
  Heaping ¼ teaspoon
  ground cinnamon
1 teaspoon (.6 gram)
  oregano
1 bay leaf, crumbled
1 teaspoon (6.2 grams)
  salt
½ teaspoon ground
  pepper
¼ cup (56 milliliters)
  cider vinegar
1½ pounds (675 grams)
  lean pork, thinly
  sliced
  Cooking oil

This recipe for pork adobo *comes from Zacatecas. While it is debatable whether Zacatecas can be considered part of northern Mexico, this dish is so good as is the* Parillada zacatecana *of which it is a part, that it does not really matter.*

Place all the ingredients except the meat and cooking oil in a blender and blend to a paste.

Using either the side of a heavy cleaver or a meat pounder, pound the meat between pieces of plastic wrap until it is no more than ⅛ inch (.3 centimeter) thick, or less.

Coat both sides of the meat with the paste, place it in a covered dish, and refrigerate it overnight.

Heat a heavy skillet, *comal,* or griddle over medium-high heat; add just enough oil to grease the surface and pan-broil the meat until it is done, but not overcooked. Serve the *adobo* with rice and sliced tomatoes and onion, chopped for tacos, or as part of the *Parillada zacatecana* (p. 136). Serves 4.

Costillas de puerco

PORK RIBS

These are prepared in much the same way as beef ribs except that they are not scored. I would also suggest substituting cider vinegar for the wine vinegar in the beef marinade, as it enhances the flavor of the pork.

Marinate the ribs at room temperature for 1 hour or in the refrigerator for 3 hours.

Broil the ribs, keeping them far enough from the coals to prevent burning, turning often. Broiling time is about 30 minutes for spareribs and 45 minutes for country-style ribs.

Serve with hot tortillas, *Pico de gallo* (p. 49), and your favorite hot sauce. Serves 4.

4 **pounds (1,800 grams) pork spareribs or country-style ribs**
Marinade for beef ribs, substituting cider vinegar for wine vinegar (p. 127)

Chuletas de puerco ranchero

PORK CHOPS RANCHERO

This dish is made in exactly the same way as Steak with *Ranchero* Sauce (p.123), except that 8-ounce (225-gram) pork chops are substituted for the steaks. Serves 4.

Chilorio

◈◇◈◇◈

¼ **cup (56 milliliters) rice wine vinegar**

6 **tablespoons (42 grams) chile powder made from *ancho* chiles**

3 **cloves garlic, minced**

½ **teaspoon cumin**

1 **teaspoon (6.2 grams) salt**

2 **pounds (900 grams) lean pork loin, cut into 1-inch (2.54-centimeter) pieces**

Water

½ **cup (113 grams) lard, cooking oil (112 milliliters), or a mixture of both**

Flour tortillas

Guacamole (p. 83)

Hot sauce

CHILE-INFUSED SHREDDED PORK

Chilorio *is much more common in the south of Mexico than in the north. This version, which I discovered in the state of Coahuila, is simpler than the southern Mexican versions (as are most northern dishes) but every bit as satisfying. It makes a fine filling for flour tortillas and can be reheated for later use.*

This is one of those dishes like tamales where lard is mandatory for an authentic taste. However, cooking oil still produces a nice result. A good compromise is 4 tablespoons (56 grams) lard and 4 tablespoons (56 milliliters) oil.

Place the vinegar, chile powder, garlic, cumin, and salt in a blender and pulse until it forms a thick paste; reserve it. Place the pork in a large skillet or pot and add water until the pork is covered by about ¼ inch (.64 centimeter). Bring the liquid to a boil, skim off any scum, and cook at a bare simmer until the water has evaporated, about 45 minutes, adding additional water as necessary. Remove the pork from the heat, and when it is cool enough, shred it, in a food processor using a plastic blade. Rub the chile powder mixture thoroughly into the meat.

Heat the pot or skillet over medium heat, add the lard and/or oil, and when it is quite hot but not smoking, add the shredded pork. Cook the pork, turning constantly, until it is heated through and just beginning to crisp, about 5 minutes. Remove the pork to a serving platter or individual plates and serve with hot flour tortillas, Guacamole, and your favorite hot sauce. Serves 4.

Asado de boda

WEDDING STEW

Asado de boda, *as its name implies, is traditionally served as part of a wedding feast. The dish is more common in San Luis Potosí and Zacatecas than the more northern states, with the possible exceptions of Coahuila and Nuevo León, where it is often called either* Asado de puerco *or* Asado de cerdo. *This is a delicious recipe, somewhere between a very simple* mole *and New Mexico-style pork chile. Some cooks add a little chocolate during the final moments of cooking, which heightens the dish's resemblance to a* mole. *Select meat from the pork loin with just a little fat, which adds to the flavor.*

Put the pork in a pot, add the water, and bring to a boil, skimming any scum from the surface. Add the bay leaves and simmer for ½ hour or until the pork is tender. Strain the meat, discarding the bay leaves but reserving 3 cups (675 milliliters) of the broth.

Meanwhile, rinse the chiles and place them in a 275-degree F (135-degree C) oven for 5 minutes to toast them. When the chiles are cool enough to handle, remove their stems, seeds, and veins, tear them into small pieces, and place them in a blender. Add the 3 cups (675 milliliters) of reserved broth, the garlic, cumin, oregano, marjoram, cloves, and cinnamon and blend for 1 minute at high speed, or until the mixture is smooth.

Heat a heavy pot or Dutch oven over medium-high heat, add the lard or oil and fry the reserved pork, turning frequently, until it begins to turn golden. Add the onion and cook 1½ to 2 minutes more, or until it is soft. Add the contents of the blender, the vinegar, sugar, salt, and pepper. Bring the liquid to a boil and simmer, uncovered, until the sauce has thickened, about 10 to 15 minutes. Stir in the chocolate, if you decide to use it, and serve with white rice and hot corn tortillas. Serves 4.

2 pounds (900 grams) moderately lean pork loin, cut into ¾-inch (1.9-centimeter) pieces

5 cups (1,125 milliliters) water

2 bay leaves

4 *ancho* chiles

4 cloves garlic

¼ teaspoon cumin

½ teaspoon oregano

½ teaspoon marjoram

¼ teaspoon powdered cloves

½ teaspoon powdered cinnamon

¼ cup (57 grams) lard or cooking oil (56 milliliters)

½ cup (71.4 grams) onion, minced

2 teaspoons (7 milliliters) cider vinegar

2 teaspoons (8 grams) sugar

1 teaspoon (6.2 grams) salt, or to taste

½ teaspoon ground pepper

1 tablespoon (7 grams) bittersweet chocolate, cut into small pieces (optional)

Chorizo

1 pound (450 grams)
   fairly lean boneless
   pork loin or
   tenderloin
1/3 pound (140 grams)
   pork fat
1³/4 ounces (49 grams)
   ancho chiles
   (weighed with the
   stems)
1 *pasilla* chile
1/3 cup plus 1 tablespoon
   (98 milliliters) cane
   or rice vinegar
2 cloves garlic
1 teaspoon (2 grams)
   cumin
1/2 teaspoon ground
   pepper
1 tablespoon (1.8
   grams) oregano
1/4 teaspoon ground
   cloves
   Heaping 1/4 teaspoon
   ground cinnamon
1 teaspoon (6.2 grams)
   salt, or to taste

MEXICAN-STYLE SAUSAGE

While Mexican Chorizo is named after the famous Spanish sausage that is often found in paella, it is a completely different product. Spanish Chorizo is almost always stuffed and dried or smoked while the Mexican variety, especially in the north, is often sold in bulk form. But the biggest difference is that Mexican Chorizo is flavored with chile. Each village in Mexico usually has at least one sausage maker with a following which considers his Chorizo to be the world's best. If you have tried supermarket Chorizo in the United States and been disappointed, please set your impressions aside. For the real thing tastes nothing like the vinegary, salty, cereal-infused type that most commercial Chorizo-makers produce in this country. This recipe from Nuevo León is a favorite and thanks to the food processor is easy to make.

Cut the pork into small pieces (no more than 1 inch [2.54 centimeters]) and cut the fat into pieces as small as possible. Mix the meat and fat together and place in the freezer until just partially frozen, ½ hour to 45 minutes.

Meanwhile, simmer the chiles in water to cover for 10 to 15 minutes or until they are very soft. When they are cool enough to handle, remove the stems and most of the seeds from the chiles and place them in a blender with the vinegar, garlic, and cumin. Blend the mixture for 1 minute; then strain it, using a food mill.

Place the partially frozen meat and fat in a food processor fitted with a steel blade and sprinkle on the pepper, oregano, cloves, cinnamon, and salt; then pour in the chile mixture. Process the meat, 1 or 2 seconds at a time, until it is coarsely ground. Allow the mixture to season overnight in the refrigerator; then use wherever *Chorizo* is needed. Makes about 1½ pounds (660 grams).

Chorizo verde

GREEN CHORIZO

This is a unique dish which I first sampled at La Parilla, a restaurant in Chihuahua City. I find that I now prefer it to the traditional red *Chorizo.*

The pork should have a high fat content, so use pork shoulder or another fatty cut. However, you will still need to add extra fat, so have your butcher do this if the meat is being ground to order, or grind it yourself. (I use a food processor.)

Place all the ingredients, except the pork and fat, in a blender and blend for 1 minute to a smooth paste. Add the chile paste to the pork and fat and mix well. Using a fine blade, put the mixture once through a meat grinder, or whirl it 5 or 6 times in a food processor, using a steel blade.

Refrigerate the *Chorizo verde* for at least 3 hours, or preferably overnight, to allow it to absorb the flavors.

Fry it as you would any bulk-type sausage, and use it as a taco filling, alone, or scrambled with eggs. Makes about 1½ pounds (660 grams).

¼ cup (56 milliliters) mild vinegar

4 green Anaheim chiles, peeled, seeded, and chopped

1 teaspoon (6.2 grams) salt

1 tablespoon (5.3 grams) ground coriander seed

2 teaspoons (1.2 grams) oregano

1 teaspoon (2 grams) cumin

¼ teaspoon black pepper

4 garlic cloves

¼ cup (28 grams) onion, chopped

¼ cup (12.4 grams) cilantro, chopped and loosely packed

12 drops green food coloring (optional)

1 pound (450 grams) pork shoulder, ground

5 ounces (140 grams) pork fat, ground

Longaniza

❖❖❖❖❖❖

MEXICAN-STYLE LINK SAUSAGE

26 ounces (728 grams) of
lean pork loin, cut
into small pieces

8 ounces (225 grams)
pork fat, cut into
very small pieces

8 ounces (225 grams)
bacon, cut into very
small pieces

½ teaspoon aniseed

¼ teaspoon whole cumin

1½ tablespoons (9.8
grams) *ancho* chile
powder

2 tablespoons (13 grams)
sweet paprika

1¾ teaspoons (10.9
grams) salt

½ teaspoon ground
black pepper

¼ teaspoon ground cloves

1 teaspoon (.6 gram)
whole oregano

Natural sausage
casing

Nearly everyone on this side of the border has heard of Chorizo, Mexico's famous sausage, but few are familiar with Longaniza, Mexico's other sausage. Throughout the republic you will find Longaniza in its many regional variations hanging in butcher shops and markets, and being cooked in street-corner food stalls.

After several discussions with sausage-makers and trial and error, I adapted this northern version of Longaniza from a recipe in Horizonte de Ilusiones, a marvelous new book about the history and culture of the state of Coahuila by the noted author and gastronome Sebastián Verti. The result is now my favorite sausage.

A word of advice. If you haven't made sausage, do not be daunted, for the process is quite simple, especially when making small quantities. All you need is a hand sausage stuffer, which is nothing more than a large funnel and some natural casing, available at butcher shops and sausage equipment suppliers. Also, note that pork is being trimmed so lean these days that you will probably have to ask your butcher for some fat. Since the relationship between the lean meat and fat is so important, I suggest you weigh each of these components separately.

To grind the sausage, you can either put it through the medium blade of a meat grinder or process it with a metal blade in the food processor. I prefer the latter method since it best imitates the hand-chopped texture of real country *Longaniza*. If you select the food processor method, it helps to partially freeze the pork, fat, and bacon before processing. In any case, mix together the pork, fat, and bacon in a large bowl. Using a spice or coffee grinder, grind together the aniseed and cumin; then mix them with the remaining ingredients except the sausage casing. Add the blended spices to the meat in the bowl and mix well. Now, either grind or process the meat to the desired texture, which should be slightly coarser than the usual ground meat.

To make the sausage, first soak the casing in water to remove the salt; then run water from the tap completely through the casing you intend to fill. Place the end of a casing over the small end of a sausage-stuffer or a large funnel and, using the pusher provided, stuff the sausage. You can make individual links, tying each one as they are made, or you can stuff the entire casing and twist it into links. *Longaniza* is usually made into links about 3 or 4 inches (7.6 or 10.2 centimeters) long and about 1 inch (2.54 centimeters) thick. Makes about 2½ pounds (1,100 grams) sausage.

Cabrito

SUCKLING KID

Cabrito *is one of the most distinctive dishes of northern Mexico. It is so popular in some areas that many restaurants, including some large ones, virtually serve nothing else. Monterrey, in the northern state of Nuevo León, is the heart of* cabrito *country, a rugged, mountainous region well suited to the raising of goats.*

The meat of the unweaned kid, properly cooked, is considered a delicacy. In typical cabrito *restaurants the cooking is done in the windows facing the street to tempt passersby. There you can watch as ten or more* cabritos *cook over beds of mesquite charcoal or coals. Usually they are prepared* al pastor *(shepherd style). With this method, the whole cleaned animal is spread-eagled on a spit in the shape of a cross, placed at an angle of 45 to 70 degrees over the bed of coals, and turned about every 20 to 30 minutes until done. Once done, the outside is wonderfully crisp, and the meat is juicy and extremely tender. I would describe the taste as somewhere between lamb and chicken.*

There are restaurants specializing in Cabrito al pastor *in the towns of Nuevo Laredo, Ciudad Acuña, and Reynosa along the border with Texas, so if you find yourself in that vicinity, give yourself a treat. Because the whole kid is used, and prepared* al pastor, *this dish is rarely served in homes in Mexico. For these same reasons, it would be even more difficult to duplicate it in the United States. However,* cabrito *is now being sold, in various cuts, in the southwestern United States, particularly in Texas, is older and tougher than desired. In* cabrito *restaurants it is sold by cut. Perhaps the most esteemed cut in Mexico is the* riñonada, *which is basted, as it cooks, with the flavorful fat around the kidneys. After a great deal of experience in introducing* norteamericanos *to* cabrito, *I have found that the* pierna, *or leg, is by far the most enjoyed. So, if you can find* cabrito *where you live, try to get the leg cut.*

The cut of cooked meat is presented on a plate by itself, with hot corn tortillas, sliced onion, and tomatoes, Guacamole (p. 83), Frijoles de olla *(p. 106) or* Frijoles a la charra *(p. 106), and a hot sauce on the side. Alternatively, it is cut up and made into tacos along with the other items.*

If you cannot find cabrito, *you can make a similar dish using either a leg or shoulder of lamb served with the same accompaniments. When you visit northern Mexico, be sure to check the yellow pages of the telephone directory for restaurants that specialize in* cabrito, *and get ready for a special treat.*

While Cabrito al pastor *(Kid Shepherd Style) is a restaurant staple,* Cabrito al horno *(Kid Pot Roast) is often the choice in private homes. There it can be roasted as you would any meat or placed in a covered Dutch oven. The latter method produces the most tender result for kid that is a little old, which is frequently the case in the United States.*

Cabrito al pastor

KID SHEPHERD STYLE

MARINADE

2 **cups (450 milliliters)
    water**
2 **tablespoons (3.6
    grams) oregano**
3 **tablespoons (43
    milliliters) lime
    juice**
1 **teaspoon (6.2 grams)
    salt**
1 **teaspoon (3.3 grams)
    pepper**
²/₃ **cup (116 milliliters)
    cooking oil**
2 **kid legs or hindquarters**

The best way I have found to simulate the spit-cooked cabrito that is almost the national dish of the state of Nuevo León is to barbecue it West Texas style. Throughout most of Texas barbecuing means smoking meat with indirect heat. However, as you move west of Highway 35 it is common to find barbecue that is prepared by placing the meat about 2 feet (61 centimeters) directly above the coals and cooking it for about 1 hour per pound. It is this method that so beautifully reproduces the succulent Cabrito al pastor. Another way of cooking this dish is to use a water smoker.

While many cooks do not marinate cabrito, some of the best do. In the United States, where cabrito is often older than the requisite unweaned 30 days, marinating is desirable. This simple marinade does an excellent job.

Mix all the ingredients except the *cabrito* and marinate the meat for 3 hours or overnight. Prepare a bed of coals about 2 feet (61 centimeters) from a grill and barbecue the meat, turning every 10 minutes for between 1 and 2 hours, or until the meat is very tender. Baste the meat with the marinade each time you turn it. If you need the longer cooking time, you will also need to add coals. It is best to prepare additional coals in another barbecue before adding them in order to prevent flames from scorching the meat.

Serve the meat with *Pico de gallo* (p. 49), Guacamole (p. 83), *Frijoles a la charra* (p. 106), and hot tortillas. Serves 4.

Cabrito al horno

KID POT ROAST

This simple dish is northern Mexico's version of our heartland pot roast.

Place the chiles in a bowl, cover them with boiling water, and allow them to soak for at least 20 minutes. Place the chiles in the jar of a blender, add the remaining ingredients except for the oil, water, and *cabrito*, and blend for 1 minute. You may have to add some of the water in which the chiles were soaked, but use as little as possible since the objective is to create a thick paste. Spread the chile paste on all sides of the *cabrito* and place it in the refrigerator for at least 2 hours or overnight.

Preheat the oven to 300 degrees F (148 degrees C).

Heat a Dutch oven over moderately high heat, add about 2 tablespoons (28 milliliters) of the oil, and brown the *cabrito* in batches. When the meat has been browned, remove the pot from the heat, pour off any remaining oil, and return the *cabrito* to the pot. Add the water to the pot, cover it tightly, and place in the oven for 2½ hours. Serve the *cabrito* with rice and/or hot tortillas. Serves 4.

3 *ancho* chiles, stemmed, seeded, and torn into small pieces

2 cloves garlic, chopped

¼ teaspoon oregano

¼ teaspoon salt

¼ teaspoon ground black pepper

¼ cup (56 milliliters) cooking oil

⅔ cup (166 milliliters) water

2 pounds (900 grams) *cabrito,* cut into 3–4-inch (7.6–10.2-centimeter) chunks

Cabrito con cerveza

KID COOKED WITH BEER

◈◈◈◈◈

¼ pound (112 grams) *tomatillos*

½ pound (225 grams) tomatoes, chopped

1 *ancho* chile, stemmed and seeded

½ cup (71 grams) onion, chopped

2 cloves garlic

¼ teaspoon oregano

¼ teaspoon thyme

¼ teaspoon salt

½ teaspoon ground black pepper

1 12-ounce (240-milliliter) bottle of beer

¼ cup (56 milliliters) cooking oil

2 pounds (900 grams) *cabrito,* cut into 3–4-inch (7.6–10.2-centimeter) chunks

In addition to the Cabrito al pastor *or charbroiled* cabrito *that is found throughout Nuevo León and other parts of northern Mexico in specialty restaurants, there are several other very popular* cabrito *recipes. Found more often in home cooking than in restaurants are the various oven-cooked* cabrito *dishes, and this is one of the best. (Please read the general information on* cabrito *[p. 158] before preparing this or any other* cabrito *recipe).*

Preheat the oven to 300 degrees F (148 degrees C).

Simmer the *tomatillos* in water to cover until they are very soft, about 5 minutes; then place them in the jar of a blender. Add the remaining ingredients except the beer, cooking oil, and *cabrito* and blend for 1 minute.

Heat a Dutch oven over medium-high heat, add about 2 tablespoons (28 milliliters) of the cooking oil, and, in batches, brown the *cabrito* pieces on all sides, adding more oil as necessary. When the last pieces of *cabrito* have been browned, remove them from the pot, turn the heat to medium, and add the blended mixture. Stir in the beer and return the *cabrito* to the pot. Cover the pot tightly and place in the preheated oven for 2½ hours. Serve the *cabrito* with rice and/or hot tortillas. Serves 4.

Fritada de cabrito

KID IN ITS BLOOD

This and the recipe for Barbacoa *(p. 139), are not for the squeamish. Also, their major ingredients are not normally available to most of us. However, both dishes are important in the northern Mexican cooking tradition. I have tried both, and if you can banish disquieting mental images and they are properly prepared, they are delicious.*

This recipe was given to me by my friend Rogelio Chavarría Montemayor of Muzquiz, Coahuila.

Remove the meat from the bones of the kid and cut it into bite-sized pieces. Sauté the meat in the oil in a heavy pot or Dutch oven over medium heat until just browned.

In a separate pan, mix the blood with 1 cup (225 milliliters) water and heat over very low heat for 10 minutes, stirring occasionally.

Seed and devein the chiles and blend for 1 minute, using just enough water to make a purée.

When the meat is browned, add the chile mixture, the blood mixture to cover the meat (add more water, if necessary), then the remaining ingredients. Simmer, covered, until the meat is tender. If the "gravy" is not thickened, remove the cover and simmer to the desired consistency. *Fritada de cabrito* is served with hot tortillas. Serves 4.

1 small kid (under 9 pounds [4 kilograms, 50 grams])
3 tablespoons (43 milliliters) olive oil
  Blood from the kid
  Water
4 *ancho* chiles
½ teaspoon pepper
½ teaspoon cumin
½ onion, chopped
  Salt, to taste

Poultry

◈◈◈

Aves de Corral

Poultry is not nearly as popular in northern Mexico as beef and seafood. There, unless the poultry dish is prepared from young chickens of superior quality, you are likely to be disappointed. Included here are the recipes for the few excellent chicken dishes that I have had in the area. Chicken Shish Kebabs is, in fact, one of the best northern dishes I have ever had.

Alambres de pollo

CHICKEN SHISH KEBABS

◇◇◇◇◇

1¼ **pounds (560 grams) boneless, skinned chicken breasts**

MARINADE
3 **tablespoons (43 milliliters) garlic oil (p. 16)**
1 **tablespoon (15 milliliters) lime juice**
¼ **teaspoon salt, or to taste**
   Pinch cayenne
2 **teaspoons (4.6 grams) mild chile powder**
¼ **teaspoon black pepper**

SHISH KEBABS
   Thin steel or wooden shish kebab skewers
3 **large *poblano* chiles or Anaheim chiles; or substitute bell peppers**
4 **medium tomatoes, quartered, or 16 cherry tomatoes**
2 **medium onions, cut into ½-inch (1.27-centimeter) pieces**
   Marinated chicken
4 **thick slices of bacon, cut into 1-inch (2.54-centimeter) pieces**

Shish kebabs made of chicken and beef are favorites in northern Mexico, where they are called alambres. *There are many northern Mexicans of Middle East descent, and it is probable that Mexican shish kebabs were developed from Arab recipes. My personal favorite is the following shish kebab, in which all the ingredients seem to blend most subtly.*

Cut the chicken breasts into 1-inch (2.54-centimeter) pieces. Toss with the marinade and marinate, refrigerated, for 2 hours.

Thread the ingredients on the skewers in the following order: 1 piece chile, 1 piece tomato (or 1 cherry tomato), 2 pieces onion, 1 piece bacon, 2 pieces chicken, 1 piece bacon, 2 pieces onion. Repeat until all the ingredients have been threaded.

Broil the shish kebabs over hot coals, on two sides, until they are well charred but the chicken is still moist and tender in the middle. This takes about 5 to 8 minutes on each side if the coals are really hot. If cooking over fire is not feasible, or a charbroiler is not available, broil in the oven 2 to 3 inches (5 to 7.6 centimeters) from the heating element for the same amount of time.

Shish kebabs are usually served with Guacamole (p. 83) and rice and/or *Frijoles a la charra* (p. 106). Serves 4.

Pollo al carbón

BROILED CHICKEN

This recipe can be baked in the oven or charbroiled with equal success.

If you are charbroiling, cut the chickens in half lengthwise (or buy them already cut in this manner). If you are baking the chickens, leave them whole. Rinse the chickens well in cold water.

Simmer the *tomatillos* (see "Basic Ingredients") until tender, broil the green chile, and put them both in a blender with the remaining marinade ingredients. Blend the marinade until smooth, about 30 seconds. Place the chickens in a large ceramic bowl, cover with marinade, and marinate, refrigerated, for at least 3 hours or overnight.

If you are charbroiling, set the chicken halves about 8 inches (20 centimeters) from the prepared coals. Turn and baste often with the marinade until the skin is brown and crispy and, when the chicken is pricked with a fork, the juices run clear. If you are baking the chickens, place them in an oven preheated to 400 degrees F (204 degrees C) for 10 minutes. Reduce the heat to 350 degrees F (177 degrees C) and continue to roast them, basting often with the marinade, until they are well browned and, when pricked with a fork, the juices run clear.

Serve with white rice and the remaining marinade as a sauce. Serves 2 to 4.

2 chickens, 3–3½ pounds each (1,350–1,575 grams each)

MARINADE
½ pound (225 grams) *tomatillos*
1 green chile, roasted
½ teaspoon whole *piquín* chile, or ½ teaspoon cayenne pepper
¼ teaspoon cumin
¼ teaspoon black peppercorns
¼ teaspoon oregano
½ teaspoon salt
2 cloves garlic
Pinch cinnamon
⅓ cup (83 milliliters) orange juice
2 tablespoons (28 milliliters) lime juice
¼ onion, chopped

3 tablespoons (45 grams) lard or cooking oil (42 milliliters)

1 3–3½-pound (1,350–1,575-gram) chicken, cut into serving pieces

3 *ancho* chiles

2 *de árbol* or *japonés* chiles

1½ tablespoons (13 grams) sesame seeds

1 heaping tablespoon (9 grams) peanuts

2 heaping tablespoons (12 grams) almonds, blanched and slivered

½ cup (58 grams) pumpkin seeds (see p. 17)

¼ teaspoon cumin

⅓ medium onion, coarsely chopped

1 slice toast, coarsely chopped

1 clove garlic

¼ teaspoon oregano

2½ cups (560 milliliters) chicken broth

1 teaspoon (6.2 grams) salt

¼ teaspoon black pepper

2 teaspoons (4.6 grams) mild chile powder

3 tablespoons (40 grams) tomato purée

Pollo en pipián rojo

CHICKEN IN RED PIPIÁN SAUCE

Pipián, *according to an aged, leather-covered Velásquez Dictionary, means "Indian fricassee." That bare definition hardly does justice to the following two recipes.* Pipián *dishes are braised stews thickened with ground pumpkin seeds, nuts, and other natural ingredients instead of flour. In this respect they are similar to the* moles. *This means of thickening, now so fashionable in the various "nouveau" cooking methods, has been used in Mexico for centuries.* Pipián *dishes, whether prepared as stews or enchiladas, are particularly popular in the state of Sonora.*

Melt the lard or heat the oil in a heavy, deep pot or Dutch oven and fry the chicken pieces, turning often, until well browned. Remove to a plate or dish.

To make the sauce, in a heavy iron skillet toast separately (until fragrant but not burned) the chiles, sesame seeds, nuts, pumpkin seeds, and cumin. When they are cool enough to handle, remove the seeds and stems from the chiles, reserving the seeds. Toast the chile seeds and put them, along with the other toasted ingredients, into the jar of a blender. Add to the blender the onion, toast, garlic, oregano, and 1 cup (225 milliliters) of the chicken broth. Blend at low speed 1 minute.

Cook the sauce in the pot or Dutch oven for 1 minute over medium heat; then add the remaining chicken broth, stirring constantly.

Next, return the browned chicken pieces to the pot and add the salt, pepper, chile powder, and tomato purée. Partially cover the pot and simmer for 20 minutes. Then simmer, uncovered, for 5 minutes. Remove the chicken to individual serving plates, turn the heat to medium high, and reduce the sauce until it begins to thicken, about 5 minutes.

Pour the sauce over the chicken and serve with Mexican Rice (pp. 101, 102). (See also *Enchiladas en pipián rojo* p. 219.) Serves 4.

Pollo en pipián verde

CHICKEN IN GREEN PIPIÁN SAUCE

As with Pollo en pipián rojo, *this recipe is thickened by ingredients other than flour. It probably originated in the south, because the use of Seville, or sour, oranges is rare in the north. However, the chef at the restaurant in the Sonoran border town of Agua Prieta, where I collected this recipe, put his own distinctly northern stamp on it.*

To make the sauce, place all the ingredients except the chicken, lard or cooking oil, and chicken broth in a blender. Blend until well chopped but not puréed.

Heat the lard or cooking oil over medium-high heat in a heavy pot or Dutch oven; then brown the chicken pieces. When browned, remove the chicken to a bowl and pour off all but 1 tablespoon (15 grams or 14 milliliters) of the lard or oil.

Add the sauce to the pot and cook, stirring constantly, for 1 minute. Stir in the chicken broth and return the browned chicken pieces to the pot. Cover and simmer over low heat for 20 minutes. Remove the cover and simmer over medium heat for 5 minutes. Place the chicken on serving plates. Turn the heat to medium high and reduce the sauce until it begins to thicken, about 5 minutes.

Pour the sauce over the chicken and serve with white or Mexican Rice (pp. 101, 102). Serves 4.

8 ounces (225 grams) *tomatillos,* simmered until tender (see "Basic Ingredients")

3 *jalapeño* chiles, broiled and seeded

½ teaspoon cumin

¼ teaspoon black pepper

1 teaspoon (.6 gram) oregano

½ teaspoon salt

2 medium cloves garlic, minced

Pinch cinnamon

¼ onion, coarsely chopped

¼ cup (23 grams) almonds, blanched, slivered, and toasted

¼ cup (29 grams) pumpkin seeds, toasted

2 tablespoons (18 grams) sesame seeds, toasted

1 piece white bread, toasted and coarsely chopped

½ cup (110 milliliters) sour orange juice (see p. 17)

1 3–3½-pound (1,350– 1,575-gram) chicken, cut into serving pieces

3 tablespoons (45 grams) lard or cooking oil (42 milliliters)

1 cup (225 milliliters) chicken broth

Guajolote o pollo en mole

TURKEY OR CHICKEN MOLE

◈◈◈◈◈

- 4 *ancho* chiles
- 1 *de árbol* or *japonés* chile
- ¾ cup (170 milliliters) hot water
- 3 whole cloves
- 3 peppercorns
- ½ stick cinnamon
- 1 teaspoon (2 grams) *ancho* chile seeds
- 1½ tablespoons (13 grams) sesame seeds
- 1 clove garlic
- 5 whole blanched almonds
- ½ corn tortilla
- ½ slice dry white bread
- 2 tablespoons (30 grams) lard or cooking oil (28 milliliters)
- 1 cup (225 milliliters) chicken broth
- ½ teaspoon sugar
- ½ teaspoon salt, or to taste
- 4 semisweet chocolate chips
- 1 3–3½-pound (1,350–1,575-gram) fryer chicken, cut up or 1 8-pound (3 kilogram + 600-gram) turkey
- 3 tablespoons lard (45 grams) or cooking oil (42 milliliters)

There are all manner of legends surrounding the invention of Mole Poblano. *This recipe is a simplified northern version. The most popular is that it originated with a nun who, upon hearing that a clerical dignitary intended to grace the convent with his presence, threw every available ingredient into the pot along with the turkey. Whether her hands were guided by divine intervention we will never know. What we do know is that this dish comes from the southern city of Puebla and is now a Mexican classic. Sadly enough, most restaurants on this side of the border use a ready-made commercial sauce as the base for the* mole, *instead of toasting and grinding the chiles and other ingredients by hand. This is like presenting a packaged French onion soup as the genuine Les Halles original!*

In northern Mexico, a mole *sauce is usually simpler than the Puebla version; it is used on enchiladas as often as it is served as the traditional main dish, and more often with chicken than turkey.* Enchiladas en mole *are one of the accompaniments to our Steak Tampiqueña recipe, the premier Mexican combination plate.*

Toast the chiles over medium heat until pliable and fragrant, taking care to avoid burning. Remove the seeds and stems from the toasted chiles and cover with ¾ cup (170 milliliters) of hot water.

Toast separately: the cloves, peppercorns, cinnamon, chile seeds, sesame seeds, garlic, and almonds, and grind them in a spice or coffee grinder.

Place the chiles and ground spices in a blender and add the water in which the chiles were soaked. Fry the half tortilla in a little hot oil, break it into pieces, and add it to the blender. Toast the bread; then tear it into small pieces and add it to the blender.

Blend all the ingredients in the blender for about 1 minute or until they have the consistency of a smooth paste. Melt the lard or heat the oil in a saucepan, add the sauce from the blender, and cook over moderate heat for 5 minutes. Add the broth slowly, stirring constantly, until it is incorporated into the sauce. Simmer over low heat for 10 minutes, adding more broth if the sauce becomes too thick.

Add the sugar, salt, and chocolate and stir until the chocolate has just melted into the sauce.

This is the basic sauce for enchiladas or base for the traditional Turkey or Chicken *Mole*. For Chicken *Mole*, brown in a Dutch oven 1 3 to 3½-pound (1,350 to 1,575-gram) cut-up fryer in 3 tablespoons (45 grams) lard or cooking oil (42 milliliters). Add the sauce base and enough broth to barely cover the chicken. Simmer, covered, for 45 minutes. Remove the cover and simmer for an additional 15 minutes or until the sauce has thickened.

For Turkey *Mole*, triple the sauce base and use the procedure for Chicken *Mole*, substituting an 8-pound (3 kilogram plus 600-gram) turkey. (See also Enchiladas in *Mole* Sauce, p. 219.) Serves 4.

Palomas asadas

BROILED DOVE

Combine the oil, lime juice, chile powder, and salt and marinate the doves for ½ hour, refrigerated. Wrap each dove in a slice of bacon (if used) and secure with a toothpick. Broil the doves over low coals to the desired degree of doneness. My choice is medium rare, because additional cooking makes them dry. Serves 4.

½ **cup (110 milliliters) garlic oil (p. 16)**

¼ **cup (56 milliliters) lime juice**

2 **teaspoons (6 grams) chile powder**

½ **teaspoon salt**

8 **doves, cleaned and plucked**

8 **slices bacon (optional)**

4–8 **quail, cleaned and**
      plucked
¼ **teaspoon mild chile**
      powder
¼ **teaspoon salt**
1 **cup (140 grams) flour**
1 **egg, beaten**
  Water
  Additional flour
  Oil for deep-frying

Codorniz empanizada

BATTER-FRIED QUAIL

Quail is considered a delicacy in northern Mexico and is particularly popular along the border.

Rinse and dry the quail.

To make the batter, stir the chile powder and salt into the flour; then stir in the egg. Add water, stirring in slowly to prevent lumps, until the mixture has the consistency of a light pancake batter.

Heat the oil to 375 degrees F (190 degrees C). Dip the quail in flour and shake off the excess, dip in the batter, and once again coat with flour. Deep-fry the quail until golden brown. Serves 4 to 8.

Pollo al fresadillas

CHICKEN AND TOMATILLOS

Fresadillas is the regional name for tomatillos in Nuevo León. This dish, which combines tomatillos with tomatoes and chiles, has both an interesting flavor and texture.

Soak the chiles in hot water for 15 minutes, tear into small pieces, and place in a blender.

Heat a saucepan over medium heat and sauté the onion in 1 tablespoon (15 milliliters) olive oil until it is golden brown. Add the garlic and tomatoes and cook an additional 5 minutes. Add the *tomatillos* and the broth, bring to a boil, and simmer until the *tomatillos* are tender, about 5 minutes. Transfer the contents of the pan to the blender and blend with the chiles for 1 minute. Using a food mill, strain the sauce into a bowl.

Preheat your broiler. In the same or another saucepan, heat 1 tablespoon (15 milliliters) olive oil and the butter over medium heat and add the strained sauce, the almonds, raisins, thyme, sugar, salt, pepper, and cilantro. Simmer the sauce until it is quite thick, about 10 to 15 minutes.

Heat a skillet over medium-high heat, add the remaining 1½ tablespoons (21 milliliters) olive oil, and quickly brown the chicken breasts on both sides. Turn the heat to medium, add the sauce and the cream, and simmer until the chicken is just cooked through.

Place the cheese on the chicken breasts and put the skillet under the preheated broiler until the cheese is just melted. Serve the chicken with white rice. Serves 4.

- 2 *ancho* chiles, stemmed and seeded
- ½ cup (71 grams) onion, chopped
- 1 tablespoon (15 milliliters) olive oil
- 1 clove garlic, minced
- ½ pound (225 grams) tomatoes, coarsely chopped
- ½ pound (225 grams) *tomatillos*
- 1½ cups (240 milliliters) chicken broth
- 2½ tablespoons (36 milliliters) olive oil
- 1 tablespoon (15 grams) butter
- ¼ cup (23 grams) blanched, slivered almonds
- ¼ cup (33 grams) raisins
- ¾ teaspoon thyme
- 1 teaspoon (4 grams) sugar
- ½ teaspoon salt
- ¼ teaspoon pepper
- ¼ cup (12.4 grams) cilantro, minced and tightly packed
- 2 boneless, skinless chicken breasts, halved (4 pieces)
- ¼ cup (56 milliliters) heavy cream
- ¾ cup (81.6 grams) *asadero* or mozzarella cheese

Pollo al pasilla

CHICKEN WITH PASILLA CHILES

This dish from Sonora makes a delicious entrée that is interesting because of the sauce's rough texture and the combination of flavors, particularly that of the cheese. If you cannot find panela *cheese, substitute a mixture of $1/3$ cup (34 grams) feta and $1/3$ cup (34 grams) mozzarella or farmer cheese.*

$1/3$ medium white onion, cut into $1/4$-inch (.6-centimeter) slices

2 green onions

$3/4$ pound (340 grams) small, meaty Italian-style tomatoes (regular tomatoes are too watery)

2 cloves garlic, peeled

1–2 *pasilla* chiles

$2^1/2$ tablespoons (35 milliliters) olive oil

$1/3$ cup (36 grams) black olives, pitted and sliced

$1/2$ teaspoon thyme

2 tablespoons (6.2 grams) cilantro, minced

1 tablespoon (4 grams) parsley, minced

1 cup (225 milliliters) chicken broth

Salt, to taste

4 boneless, skinless half chicken breast pieces

$2/3$ cup (68 grams) *panela* cheese, grated

Broil the onion slices, white part of green onions (mince and reserve the green part), and tomatoes by placing them in a small skillet or baking pan 2 to 3 inches (5 to 7.6 centimeters) under the broiler for 15 to 20 minutes or until the tomatoes are slightly scorched and soft. Add the garlic to the pan during the last 10 minutes of cooking.

Meanwhile, toast the chiles by placing them in a 275-degree F (135-degree C) oven for 5 minutes. Make sure the chiles do not scorch or they will give the dish a bitter taste. Remove the seeds and stems from the chiles, tear or cut them into very small pieces, and place them in a blender. Add the broiled tomatoes, onions, and garlic to the blender and pulse until the ingredients are roughly ground together but not puréed. The sauce should be chunky.

Heat $1/2$ tablespoon (7 milliliters) oil in a saucepan over medium heat, add the contents of the blender, the olives, the thyme, the reserved green part of the onion, the cilantro, the parsley, and the chicken broth. Simmer the sauce, stirring frequently, until it thickens, about 20 minutes.

Heat the remaining 2 tablespoons (29 milliliters) of olive oil in a skillet over medium-high to high heat and brown the chicken on both sides. Turn the heat to medium low, add the sauce, and simmer until the chicken is just cooked through. Add salt to taste. Place the chicken on serving plates, top with the sauce, and then the cheese and serve. Serves 4.

Pollo a la naranja

ORANGE CHICKEN

This is a home-style, rather than typical restaurant, recipe in Nuevo León and Tamaulipas. In Nuevo León it, and others like it, are most commonly used with chicken. In Tamaulipas, fish such as red snapper is often the choice. I have specified chicken because that is how this particular recipe is used, but feel free to substitute fish, of course adjusting the cooking times so that it will not be overdone.

When preparing the lime and orange peels, be sure and use only the colored outer parts of the skin as the white inner pith is bitter.

Heat a skillet over medium-high heat, add 2½ tablespoons (35.5 milliliters) of the olive oil and sear the chicken breasts to a golden brown on each side. The heat should be hot enough so the chicken is not cooked through. Remove and reserve the chicken.

Turn the heat to medium, add the remaining 2½ tablespoons (35.5 milliliters) olive oil and sauté the onion, green pepper, and chiles until the onions become golden brown and begin to caramelize. Add the garlic and cook 1 minute more.

Stir in the remaining ingredients, add the reserved chicken, cover the pan, and simmer until the chicken is cooked through, 7 to 10 minutes. Remove the chicken and place ½ breast on each of 4 serving plates. Turn the heat to high and reduce the sauce, stirring constantly until it thickens. Pour the sauce over the chicken and serve with white rice. Serves 4.

5 tablespoons (71 milliliters) olive oil
4 boneless, skinless half chicken breasts
2 cups (285 grams) onion, chopped
1 cup (131 grams) green pepper, chopped
4 *serrano* chiles, stemmed, seeded, and minced
2 cloves garlic, minced
1 teaspoon (2 grams) lime peel, minced
1 tablespoon (7 grams) orange peel, minced
⅔ cup (112 grams) orange, peeled, seeded, and chopped
½ cup (84 grams) tomato, peeled, seeded, and chopped
1 bay leaf
½ teaspoon thyme
½ teaspoon oregano
¼ teaspoon cinnamon
¼ cup (23 grams) blanched, slivered almonds
¼ cup (33 grams) raisins
2 tablespoons (28 milliliters) cider vinegar
1 cup (225 milliliters) freshly squeezed orange juice
2 tablespoons (28 milliliters) dry white wine
2 teaspoons (4.6 grams) brown sugar
½ teaspoon salt
½ teaspoon ground pepper
2 tablespoons (8 grams) parsley, minced
2 tablespoons (6.2 grams) cilantro, minced

Seafood

◈◈◈

Mariscos

Northern Mexico's fresh seafood comes from Baja California and Sonora, particularly Guaymas and Mazatlán. Red snapper, shrimp, lobster, abalone, sea bass, and halibut are some of the preferred offerings. Fresh seafood is not available at all times, but it is very popular all over the north. Almost every fair-sized town has at least one *ostionería* (oyster shop). Since oysters are rarely available, fried shrimp, fish, and seafood cocktails are more often served in these small seafood cafés.

Surprisingly, some of the best and freshest-tasting fish in the area is not found along the coast but in the state of Chihuahua. Here Boquillas and neighboring lakes and reservoirs supply daily loads of freshwater black bass to both Ciudad Juárez and Chihuahua City. Black bass is very good fried whole with only a dusting of flour or, more delicious still, broiled and served *al mojo de ajo* (with garlic sauce). If you are ever near El Paso, I recommend a detour into Juárez, just across the border, to one of the many fine restaurants featuring this wonderful fish.

Huachinango al mojo de ajo

RED SNAPPER IN GARLIC SAUCE

◈◈◈◈◈

Cooking oil for deep-frying

4   1½-pound (675 grams each) whole red snapper or freshwater bass, cleaned

1   cup (140 grams) flour mixed with 1 teaspoon (6.2 grams) salt, ½ teaspoon pepper, and 1 teaspoon (2.3 grams) paprika

¼   pound (113 grams [1 stick]) butter

8   medium garlic cloves, chopped

⅓   cup (18.6 grams) cilantro, chopped and loosely packed (optional)

Limes, halved

Seafood with garlic sauce is a dish served in many parts of Mexico. In the north it is usually made with red snapper or freshwater bass. Like many other northern dishes, it is simple to prepare and tasty eating. The fish can be either deep-fried or charbroiled.

FRYING

In a heavy Dutch oven or deep fryer, heat oil about 1 inch deep until it is very hot, but not smoking.

Using a fish scraper or the blade of a serrated knife, scrape as many scales as possible from the fish. Dredge one of the fish in the flour mixture, shake off the excess, and, using kitchen tongs, place it in the oil. Cook for 1 to 2 minutes on each side, until the fish is well browned but still moist and flakey inside. A little experimenting will yield the best timing for your particular equipment.

Place the cooked fish on a platter in a warm oven. Repeat for the remaining fish. To prepare the sauce, melt the butter in a saucepan, add the garlic, and cook over medium-high heat until the garlic is very soft and just beginning to brown. Place the fish on individual serving plates, add the cilantro to the sauce, if used, and spoon over the fish. Serve with lime halves. Serves 4.

CHARBROILING

Brush the fish with melted butter and broil over hot coals, 5 to 8 minutes on each side, or until the fish begins to flake when tested with a fork. Prepare the sauce as described above. Serve with white rice, Guacamole (p. 83), a garnish made from sliced lettuce and tomatoes, lime halves, and *Bolillos* (p. 96) with butter.

Huachinango a la veracruzana

RED SNAPPER VERACRUZ STYLE

You may wonder what a recipe from the southern seaport city of Veracruz is doing in a book on northern Mexican cooking. This is easily explained by the fact that this recipe, by far the best I have ever experienced, was developed and given to me by Marcy Widdoes, who lives in Saltillo, a capital of northern-style cooking.

Heat the saucepan over medium heat, add ¼ cup (56 milliliters) olive oil and the onions and sauté until they are golden, lowering the heat as necessary. This is very important to the recipe. The onions shouldn't be fully browned, and any burned pieces should be removed. Add the garlic and continue cooking for 1 to 2 minutes.

Add the tomatoes, parsley, *jalapeños*, thyme, marjoram, salt, pepper, beer, and red wine vinegar; bring to a boil, then cook at a brisk simmer until the sauce has thickened, about 15 to 20 minutes.

When the sauce is nearly done, heat a skillet over medium-high to high heat, add ¼ cup (56 milliliters) olive oil and sauté the filets until they are browned on both sides and just cooked through. Place the cooked filets on serving plates.

To make the garnish, place a small saucepan over medium heat, mix ¼ cup (56 milliliters) of the prepared sauce with the sliced olives and capers, bring to a simmer, and reserve.

To serve, spoon the sauce over the fish then top with the garnish. Serve with white rice and steamed squash. Serves 4.

¼ cup (56 milliliters) olive oil

3 cups (383 grams) onions, coarsely chopped

2 cloves garlic, minced

2 cups (454 grams) tomatoes, coarsely chopped

1 tablespoon (4 grams) parsley, minced

1–2 tablespoons (11–23 grams) canned, pickled *jalapeños*, minced

½ teaspoon thyme

½ teaspoon marjoram

½ teaspoon salt

¼ teaspoon ground pepper

½ cup (110 milliliters) beer

2 tablespoons (28 milliliters) red wine vinegar

¼ cup (56 milliliters) olive oil

4 red snapper filets, 6–8 ounces (168–225 grams) each

½ cup (90 grams) green olives, pitted and sliced

¼ cup (35 grams) capers

Camarones asados

BROILED SHRIMP

Broiled shrimp are prepared in several ways in Mexico. They can be marinated in elaborate marinades or simply brushed with melted butter and lime juice during cooking. Whichever method you choose, be sure to use jumbo shrimp (10 to 14 to the pound), since smaller shrimp will be cooked through and dry before they are browned on the outside. For the same reason, shrimp should be cooked very close to a very hot fire. It also helps to use thin shish kebab skewers, as this facilitates handling the shrimp near the heat. My preferred method of broiling shrimp is simply to baste them with a mixture of melted butter, lime juice, and chopped cilantro while they are broiling. However, I would also suggest you try the marinades (pp. 127, 166, 167) for broiled chicken, beef or pork ribs, and chicken shish kebabs. Although many Mexican cooks butterfly the shrimp before cooking, I prefer to leave them whole, which keeps them from drying out.

If using a marinade, marinate from 1 to 3 hours, approximately 6 to 8 ounces (168 to 225 grams) of peeled and deveined jumbo shrimp per person.

Thread the shrimp on shish kebab skewers and broil about 3 inches (7.6 centimeters) from very hot coals, until they are just cooked through and not a moment longer. (Perfecting the timing may take some practice, but it is worth it; there is nothing worse than overcooked shrimp, and nothing tastier than well-cooked shrimp.)

To make the kebabs *al mojo de ajo* (with garlic sauce), sauté 2 chopped cloves garlic per person in 1 tablespoon (15 grams) butter or 1 tablespoon (15 milliliters) olive oil per person. Pour over the shrimp after they have been placed on serving plates.

Serve immediately with white rice, *Bolillos* (p. 96), and lime wedges. Serves 4.

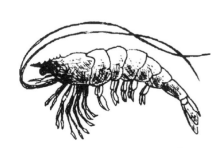

Camarones al mojo de ajo I

SHRIMP WITH GARLIC SAUCE I

This is a favorite in the north, particularly in Baja California and Sonora. Several different excellent variations follow.

Shell and devein the shrimp, leaving the tails intact. Dredge the shrimp with the flour and shake off the excess.

Mix thoroughly the eggs, 2 tablespoons (28 milliliters) of olive oil, milk, salt, and hot chile powder or pepper. Dip the shrimp in this mixture, then coat with bread crumbs. Place the coated shrimp in the refrigerator for about 1 hour before cooking.

Heat oil to approximately 375 degrees F (190 degrees C) in a deep fryer or in a deep heavy skillet or Dutch oven. Fry the shrimp, until golden, in 3 batches. Drain them on paper towels and place them on serving plates.

To make the sauce, cook the garlic in ¼ cup (28 milliliters) olive oil over medium-high heat until it just begins to turn golden. (If the garlic browns, it will have a bitter taste.)

Serve with rice or french fries and lime wedges. Serves 4.

SHRIMP

2 pounds (900 grams) shrimp medium to medium large (26–34 per pound)
Flour for dredging
2 eggs
2 tablespoons (28 milliliters) olive oil
⅓ cup (83 milliliters) milk
¼ teaspoon salt
¼ teaspoon hot chile powder or cayenne pepper
Bread crumbs for coating

SAUCE

¼ cup (56 milliliters) good quality olive oil
2 tablespoons (26 grams) garlic, coarsely chopped

Camarones al mojo de ajo II

SHRIMP WITH GARLIC SAUCE II

2 pounds (900 grams) medium shrimp (35–40 per pound)
Flour for dredging
½ cup (110 milliliters) good quality olive oil
¼ cup (26 grams) garlic, coarsely chopped
½ teaspoon *piquín* chile, pulverized in a mortar and pestle, or substitute ½ teaspoon cayenne pepper
Salt to taste
Lime wedges

This outstanding recipe is very different from the breaded version. It may have originated in the Basque country in Spain, where I have had dishes very similar to this one.

Completely shell and devein the shrimp. Dredge them in the flour, being careful to shake off all the excess. (Too much flour will make the dish soggy; too little will make it lose its crispness.) To achieve the proper texture, the shrimp should be cooked in 2 equal batches.

Heat a heavy deep skillet or Dutch oven over the highest heat until very hot. The pan must be hot enough but not too hot since olive oil burns and catches fire at a lower heat than, for example, peanut oil. With a little experience you will find the right heat, but it is better to err on the side of safety (less heat) at first.

When the skillet is heated, quickly add 2 tablespoons (28 milliliters) oil, 1 tablespoon (7 grams) garlic, ¼ teaspoon of the hot chile or pepper, and half of the shrimp. Stir as rapidly as possible, as for stir-frying, adding up to 2 tablespoons (28 milliliters) more oil (or enough to just keep the shrimp from sticking). Avoid overcooking. When ready, the shrimp will be lightly charred on the outside and perfectly moist and tender on the inside. Place the cooked shrimp on 2 serving plates and repeat the process with the remaining portion of uncooked shrimp.

Serve with rice garnished with lime wedges. Serves 4.

Camarones al mojo de ajo III

SHRIMP WITH GARLIC SAUCE III

This recipe is a particular favorite in the Sonoran seaport of Guaymas, where shrimp often are served within hours of being caught. A good cooking oil or olive oil frequently is used to make the sauce, so feel free to substitute this for the butter.

Make an egg-wash by lightly beating together the egg, 1 tablespoon (15 milliliters) oil, and the milk. Mix together the flour, salt, and pepper.

Heat the oil in a Dutch oven or deep fryer to 350 to 375 degrees F (177 to 190 degrees C). Dip the shrimp into the egg-wash; then dredge them in the flour. Put them in the oil, holding them by the tail for 1 second before releasing. Always use kitchen tongs, being careful to avoid splattering oil, as a severe burn could result.

When all the shrimp are cooked and arranged on serving plates, make the sauce by melting the butter in a saucepan, adding the garlic, and sautéeing until the garlic is soft and just beginning to brown.

Serve with rice and flour tortillas or *Bolillos* (p. 96) and the lime halves. Serves 4.

1 **egg**
1 **tablespoon (15 milliliters) cooking oil**
2 **tablespoons (28 milliliters) milk**
1 **cup (140 grams) flour**
½ **teaspoon salt**
¼ **teaspoon pepper**
  Oil for deep-frying
1 **pound (450 grams) medium (30–35 per pound) shrimp, shelled and deveined, with the tails left on**
4 **tablespoons (60 grams [½ stick]) butter**
4 **medium cloves garlic, minced**
  Limes, halved

Camarones adobados

SHRIMP IN ADOBO

¼ cup (56 milliliters)
  cider vinegar

3 cloves garlic, peeled
  and chopped

1 teaspoon (6.7 grams)
  salt

1 teaspoon (.6 gram)
  oregano

1 heaping teaspoon (2
  grams) cinnamon

3 tablespoons (21
  grams) *pasilla* chile
  powder

3 tablespoons (21
  grams) *ancho* chile
  powder

2 pounds (900 grams)
  medium or large
  shrimp, peeled with
  the tails left on

¼ cup (56 milliliters)
  olive oil

¼ cup (12.4 grams)
  cilantro, minced
  Lime wedges

This recipe from Baja California is one of the most delicious ways of preparing shrimp I have found. It is easily prepared ahead of time and sautéed at the last minute. It goes especially well with white rice and steamed squash tossed with a little heavy cream. To make this dish, you will probably have to make the pasilla *chile powder yourself since it is difficult to find, but this is no problem. All you need to do is remove the stems and seeds from* pasilla *chiles, break them up, and grind them in a spice or coffee grinder.*

Place the vinegar, garlic, salt, oregano, and cinnamon in a blender and blend for 1 minute. Add the chile powders and blend to a thick paste. Using your fingers, massage the paste into the shrimp and allow to marinate for 1 hour.

Heat the oil over medium to medium-high heat and sauté the shrimp until they are just cooked. Just before removing the shrimp from the pan, toss them with the cilantro, then serve with the lime wedges. Serves 4.

Langosta al carbón

CHARBROILED LOBSTER

This recipe calls for langosta, *which is not true lobster but a giant crawfish found in Pacific waters. In any case, it makes delicious eating. If you live on the East Coast, substitute Maine lobster. The fresher the better should be your rule.*

Lobsters
Butter, melted
Paprika or mild chile powder
Lime juice

Split the lobster in half lengthwise, using a cleaver or heavy chef's knife.

Brush the exposed flesh with melted butter, sprinkle with paprika or a mild chile powder, and broil over hot coals, basting often with more melted butter. When ready, the flesh should be well browned on the outside and just cooked on the inside, as for medium steak. Overcooking will cause it to become quite dry and disappointing in flavor and texture, particularly so with frozen lobster. Because lobster is very expensive, whether fresh or frozen, I prefer to do without unless I can get it fresh.

Serve with *Frijoles a la charra* (p. 106) or *Frijoles de olla* (p. 106), corn tortillas, and melted butter flavored with lime juice.

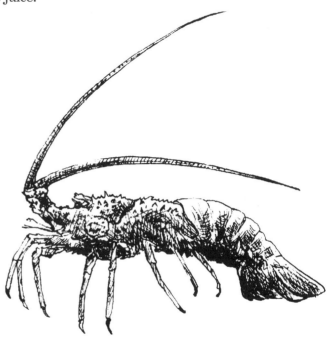

Langosta Puerto Nuevo

LOBSTER

**1 Lobster
Oil for deep-frying**

This dish is named for the tiny village of Puerto Nuevo, which lies between Tijuana and Ensenada in Baja California. Lobster fishermen there used to sell freshly caught lobster from their homes on the sandstone cliffs overlooking the Pacific Ocean. Then four or five fishermen's homes were converted to restaurants. Puerto Nuevo is now a village of restaurants serving lobster with frijoles, *huge paper-thin tortillas (similar to those usually found in Sonora), rice, and beer.*

In Puerto Nuevo lobster is usually fried in shallow pans filled with oil over gas burners. This unusual cooking method produces a marvelous taste and texture.

Split the lobster as for *Langosta al carbón* (p. 185). Preheat a deep fryer to 350 degrees F (177 degrees C). Fry half of the lobster and then the other half. Do not overcook or they will be dry and tough.

Serve with *Frijoles a la charra* (p. 106) or *Frijoles de olla* (p. 106), rice, melted butter flavored with lime juice, flour tortillas, and *Salsa de chile árbol* (p. 42) or *Salsa de chile piquín* (p. 41). Serves 2.

Sopa de pescado

FISH SOUP

Fish soups and stews are greatly enjoyed throughout Mexico, where they are looked upon as a "restorative." One version is called "Vuelva a la vida," or "return to life." This variation, from Guaymas in Sonora, is delicious and very easy to prepare. Since it has the characteristics of a hearty stew, it merits inclusion as a main dish. The recipe calls for white sea bass, but any similar fish may be substituted. In inland areas farm-raised catfish would be an excellent choice.

The soup is served with Mexican Rice (pp. 101, 102) on the side. Diners can then add it to the soup al gusto *(to taste) or eat it separately.*

Broil the tomatoes and *tomatillos* until they are soft and their skins are charred. Remove to a blender.

Make a mild broth by simmering the reserved shrimp shells in 2½ cups (550 milliliters) water for 10 minutes. Remove the shells.

Add the *ancho* chiles to the tomato mixture in the blender, blend for 1 minute, and strain. This should make about 6 cups (1,350 milliliters). (If not, just add more broth to the soup to make a total of 8 cups [1,800 milliliters].)

Heat the olive oil in a soup kettle over medium heat. Sauté the onion, garlic, and *poblano* chile until soft but not browned. Add the zucchini and cook for 1 minute.

Add 6 cups (1,350 milliliters) of the blended, strained tomato mixture to the pot with 2 cups (550 milliliters) of the broth, for 8 cups (1,800 milliliters) in all. Add the bay leaves, cilantro, lime juice, salt, and pepper. Simmer, covered, for 20 minutes.

Uncover the kettle, add the fish, and cook for 5 minutes, with the liquid barely simmering. Add the shrimp, turn off the heat, and allow to sit for 2 minutes.

Remove the bay leaves. Then, using a slotted spoon, remove the seafood and squash to individual soup bowls and top with the broth. Garnish with chopped coriander.

Serve with lime wedges and Mexican Rice in side dishes, to be added to the soup as desired. Serves 4.

3¾ pounds (1,690 grams) tomatoes

4 large or 6 small *tomatillos*

½ pound (225 grams) medium shrimp, shelled and deveined with the shells reserved

1 large or 2 small *ancho* chiles

3 tablespoons (42 milliliters) olive oil

1 medium onion, chopped

3 cloves garlic, minced

1 *poblano* chile, peeled, seeded, and chopped

2 small or 1 large zucchini, sliced in thin rounds and quartered

3 bay leaves

½ cup (25 grams) cilantro, chopped and loosely packed

Juice of 1 lime

½ teaspoon salt, or to taste

Pepper, to taste

1 pound (450 grams) white sea bass or similar fish, cut into ¾-inch (1.9-centimeter) pieces

Chopped coriander for garnish

1 red snapper 4–5
    pounds or 4 1–1½-
    pound fish
    (1,800–2,250 grams
    total), cleaned and
    whole
Juice from 6 limes
½ cup (110 milliliters)
    olive oil
10 garlic cloves, minced
¼ cup (26 grams) mild
    chile powder
1 teaspoon (6.2 grams)
    salt
**Heavy-duty
    aluminum foil**

Fish Steamed in Foil

This recipe is from Guymas, where you can buy fish fresh from the fishing boats when they dock. Often the fish has been caught within the last half hour. The recipe uses any size fish from 1 pound up and is excellent for entertaining. Although red snapper is called for, any similar fish, including catfish, may be successfully substituted.

Place the whole fish on a large double layer of aluminum foil and pour the lime juice over it. Allow to marinate for 1 hour.

Build a wood or charcoal fire (preferably on the beach). This should take 30 to 45 minutes.

Pour the olive oil over the fish, turning it to make sure it is well coated. Sprinkle the garlic, chile powder, and salt over the fish, turning to season both sides.

Wrap the fish tightly in 2 layers of heavy-duty aluminum foil and put it directly on the coals. Cook about 10 minutes on each side for the smaller fish, 20 minutes on each side for the larger one. Place the cooked fish on a serving platter and unwrap it at the table.

Serve with Mexican Rice (pp. 101, 102), limes, *Bolillos* (p. 96), and your favorite sauce. Serves 4.

FISH BALLS
¾ pound (340 grams) sea
    bass or another
    mild, firm fish
3 cloves garlic, minced
¾ teaspoon oregano
1 tablespoon (3 grams)
    fresh mint leaves or
    1 teaspoon dried

Albóndigas de pescado

FISH BALLS

Don't let the translation of this dish put you off, for this is peasant cooking at its best. The flavor of this dish from Baja California is almost more Mediterranean than Mexican. One caveat: the formed balls of fish, spices, and herbs are quite delicate so after placing them in the pot move them as little as possible. But don't worry if one or two break up, they will just become part of the sauce.

Also, to make the fish balls you can spend a great deal of time chopping and grinding the ingredients or you can process them using the metal blade of a food processor. Just remember to process only long enough to mix the ingredients, but not long enough to turn them into a mushy paste.

To make the fish balls, combine the ingredients and process as described above until just mixed. Pat the mixture into balls approximately 1½ inches (3.8 centimeters) in diameter and place them in the refrigerator for at least 1 hour.

To make the sauce, heat the olive oil over medium heat in a large pot or deep skillet and sauté the onion and chiles until they are soft but not browned. Add the garlic and squash and continue cooking until the squash is very soft but not brown. Add the broiled and blended tomatoes. (To broil the tomatoes, place them within a few inches of your broiler and broil until the skins are blackened and they are very soft, about 20 minutes.) Bring the liquid to a boil, then turn it down to a simmer. Add the cilantro and salt.

Carefully add the fish balls, allow the liquid to return to a simmer, and cook for 20 minutes or until the balls are fully cooked and the sauce is thick. Do not disturb the fish balls during the cooking process unless absolutely necessary. Serve with rice. Serves 4.

3 tablespoons (9 grams) cilantro, minced

¼ cup (56 grams) rice, cooked

¼ cup (43 grams) cornmeal

¼ cup (30 grams) dried bread crumbs

2 tablespoons (18 grams) onion, minced

3 small *tomatillos,* boiled until very soft

2 teaspoons–1 tablespoon (10–14 grams) canned *chipotle* chiles, minced

½ teaspoon salt

1½ tablespoons (22 milliliters) lime juice

1 egg, beaten

SAUCE

3 tablespoons (42 milliliters) olive oil

¾ cup (107 grams) onion, chopped

3 ripe, red *serrano* chiles, minced; or substitute green *serranos,* minced

2 cloves garlic, minced

2 cups (283 grams) zucchini or summer squash, chopped

2½ cups (418 grams) tomatoes, broiled and blended (about 1½ pounds [675 grams] fresh tomatoes)

2 tablespoons (6.2 grams) cilantro, minced

½ teaspoon salt, or to taste

1 **pound (450 grams) swordfish, cut into ½-inch- (1.27-centimeter-) thick pieces**

2 **cups (250 grams) green beans, cut into 1½-inch (3.8-centimeter) lengths**

1½ **cups (170 grams) carrots, cut into pieces ¼ inch (.64 centimeter) thick by 1½ inches (3.8 centimeters) long**

8 **whole *jalapeño* chiles, stems removed**

2 **cups (283 grams) zucchini, cut the same as the carrots**

½ **cup (110 milliliters) olive oil**

1 **cup (142 grams) onion, thinly sliced**

2 **cloves garlic, minced**

¼ **cup (56 milliliters) lime juice**

¼ **cup (56 milliliters) white wine vinegar**

1 **teaspoon (6.2 grams) salt**

½ **teaspoon ground pepper**

1 **teaspoon (.6 gram) oregano**

2 **bay leaves**

1 **cup (225 milliliters) water**

Lettuce leaves

1 **large tomato, coarsely chopped**

Pez espada en escabeche

"PICKLED" SWORDFISH

This dish from Baja California is so light and elegant that it is appropriate for almost any occasion. It is especially good as a first or second course or as a light luncheon or supper. The charbroiled swordfish adds a very special taste. Do not allow the relatively large amount of olive oil deter you as most of it is removed at serving time.

Over very hot coals, charbroil the swordfish until it is barely done, and cut it into bite-sized pieces.

Separately, boil the green beans, carrots, and *jalapeños* until they just begin to soften, then plunge them into cold water to stop the cooking process. Immerse the zucchini in boiling water for just a few seconds, then plunge them into cold water.

Heat the oil over moderate heat and sauté the onion and garlic until the onion just begins to soften, about 2 or 3 minutes. Remove the pan from the heat and add the lime juice, vinegar, salt, pepper, oregano, bay leaves, and water. Pour the contents of the pan over the reserved vegetables and swordfish and chill for at least 3 hours. Place some lettuce on each of 4 serving plates and, using a slotted spoon, spoon the swordfish on them. Garnish with tomato and serve. Serves 4.

Light Meals & Snacks

◆◆◆

Antojitos mexicanos

To most Americans "Mexican food" means one special family of foods: *antojitos mexicanos*. This category includes the corn- and tortilla-based specialties such as tacos, *quesadillas*, enchiladas, burritos, and tamales and some other foods, such as *chile rellenos*. Although usually taken as snacks, they also often make up an entire meal. (For a discussion of the relationship of *antojitos* to *aperitivos* and *botanas*, see the introduction to "Appetizers.")

Antojitos mexicanos are a unique feature of Mexican cuisine. They show most clearly the merging of the ancient Indian ingredients and cooking techniques with those of the Spanish. As is often the case with northern dishes, many of these *antojitos* were adapted from southern recipes, becoming something new in the process. The *taco al carbón*, a flour tortilla filled with charbroiled meat, is a good example of this.

In middle- and upper-class Mexican homes, a plate of taco meat is often kept on the kitchen table with warm tortillas and a sauce so that family and servants can help themselves during the day. However, poorer families more often make these items their main meal. In Mexico even expensive restaurants usually serve some *antojitos*, and there are many restaurants that specialize in them. In the Mexican yellow pages listings, you will find restaurants advertising their speciality of *"antojitos mexicanos."*

Tacos

Outside of Mexico, tacos are probably the best known of that country's foods, and it is one of the world's most versatile. Almost anything that is edible probably has been wrapped in a tortilla, and tacos could merit a book to themselves. In the United States, the word taco *calls up images of the fast-food version: boiled hamburger meat in a crisp tortilla shell, topped with lettuce, grated cheese, and some sort of commercial picante sauce. While this popular American item is not too bad, it is very different from the Mexican original.*

In Mexico tacos are made with soft flour tortillas, soft corn tortillas, or corn tortillas that have been fried medium or crisp. If flour tortillas are used, as they often are in northern Mexico, they should be freshly made. Most restaurants have employees who do nothing but make tortillas, which are taken fresh from the comal, *folded around the desired filling, and served immediately. If you are not planning to serve more than 8 people, prepare tortillas in the last few minutes. With a little practice, flour tortillas can be made at the rate of about 2 per minute. If tortillas are made in advance, they should be placed on a medium to medium-hot* comal *or griddle for about 30 seconds on each side, or until they begin to puff, before serving.*

Freshly made soft corn tortillas also are best for tacos. If packaged or other than fresh homemade corn tortillas are used, they should be heated before serving in the same manner as flour tortillas.

When serving soft flour or corn tortillas, wrap them in a hot towel after cooking or heating and place them in a basket. This will keep them hot for some time. In Mexico a basket of tortillas often is taken to the dining table with a platter of the filling and bowls containing various sauces and condiments. Each guest then takes a warm tortilla and fills it with the items of his choice. This method is enjoyable and easy for large informal gatherings.

In the north fried corn tortillas for tacos are most often cooked only to a medium crispness. This makes the tacos much easier to fill, as the shells are not so liable to break, and also provides a marvelous, slightly chewy texture. For either medium or crisp corn tortilla tacos, heat 1 inch (2.54 centimeters) of good cooking oil in a frying pan until it just begins to smoke. For medium-crisp tacos, use kitchen tongs to place a tortilla in the hot oil, immediately fold it as shown in the diagram, and fry it for 15 to 30 seconds until the proper crispness is achieved. Experience will help you perfect the cooking time. Aim for tortillas that are still pliable, but a little crisp on the outside. After one or two tries, you will be making perfect taco shells. Remove the cooked shells to drain on paper towels.

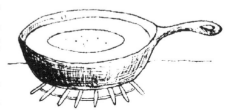

To make crisp tacos, soften the tortilla in the hot oil for a few seconds and remove to drain on paper towels. When the tortilla has cooled sufficiently to permit handling, place the filling in the center and fold. Next, using kitchen tongs, hold the taco in its folded position in the hot oil and cook it until crisp but not browned, turning frequently.

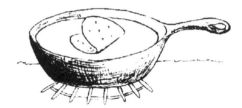

Shredded Meat Filling for Tacos

1½ pounds (675 grams)
  boneless lean beef,
  chicken, pork,
  turkey, or lamb, cut
  into 1-inch (2.54-
  centimeter) pieces
  Water
3 *ancho* chiles,
  stemmed, seeded,
  and left whole
3 *japonés* chiles or *de
  árbol* chiles,
  stemmed and seeded
1½ teaspoons (9.3 grams)
  salt
¼ teaspoon pepper
3 cloves garlic
1 teaspoon (2 grams)
  cumin
1 teaspoon (.6 gram)
  oregano

*In northern Mexico, while many tacos are made from meat cooked
al carbón and then chopped, others are made from shredded meat,
whether from leftovers or meat cooked especially for the purpose.*

*Beef, chicken, pork, turkey, and lamb are shredded to fill medium-
crisp or crisp tacos. While the cooking process for all is the same,
the seasoning combinations are endless. Here is a good, basic recipe
upon which you can improvise.*

Place the meat in a heavy skillet and add just enough water to cover.
Add the chiles, salt, and pepper. Crush the garlic, cumin, and oregano
to a paste in a *molcajete* or mortar and pestle and add to the skillet.

Bring the water slowly to a boil and simmer over moderately low
temperature, uncovered, until all the liquid has evaporated. Remove
a piece of meat and check to see if it shreds easily. If the meat is not
yet tender enough, add more water and continue simmering until it
is properly done.

Allow the meat to cool. At this point most Mexicans shred the
meat by hand, whether it was cooked especially for this purpose or
whether it was meat left over from another dish. Alternatives to
shredding by hand are mashing the meat in a *molcajete* or giving it
a few spins in a food processor, using a plastic blade.

See the section on tacos for instructions for making medium-crisp
or crisp tacos. Serves 4.

Favorite Tacos

The following are some of the best tacos I have found in northern Mexico.

Tacos de fajitas

FAJITA TACOS

Make *Fajitas* according to the recipe (p. 120). Use either the basic recipe or the one for *Fajitas encebolladas* (p. 120). Place slices of the charbroiled meat in hot flour tortillas and top with Guacamole (p. 83), *Pico de gallo* (p. 49), and your favorite salsa. Serves 4.

Tacos de pollo al carbón

CHARBROILED CHICKEN TACOS

Marinate the chicken, refrigerated, for at least 1 hour. Broil over charcoal and slice into bite-sized pieces.

    Place the chicken pieces in hot tortillas and add the remaining ingredients to taste. Top with a dollop of sour cream. Serves 4.

1½ **pounds (675 grams) boneless chicken breasts**
    Marinade for Chicken Shish Kebabs (p. 166
    Flour tortillas
    Guacamole (p. 83)
½ **cup (43 grams) green onion, minced**
2 **tomatoes, chopped**
½ **7-ounce can (100 grams) pickled *jalapeños*, sliced**
    Sour cream

1½ pounds (675 grams)
   rib eye, top round,
   or chuck steak,
   sliced about ¼ inch
   thick
   Juice from 1 lime
   Salt, to taste
   Guacamole (p. 83)
1   medium onion,
   minced
   Cilantro, chopped
   Tomatillo Sauce (p. 46)
   Broiled *Jalapeño* or
   Serrano Sauce (p. 39)
   Corn tortillas

Tijuana Tacos

These tacos are named for the border town where they are sold by street vendors. This is my favorite version. Rib eye or New York strip sliced very thin is the best meat to use in this dish.

About 10 minutes before cooking, sprinkle the lime juice and salt on the meat. Then broil it over charcoal until just done.

Slice the meat into bite-sized pieces and place on heated tortillas. Top with Guacamole, onion, cilantro, and both sauces, to taste. Serves 4.

Tacos de carnitas

Make *Carnitas* according to the recipe (p. 145). Place on hot flour or corn tortillas and top with Guacamole (p. 83), chopped green onion, and *Salsa de chile ancho* (p. 44). Serves 4.

Taquitos de harina

LITTLE FLOUR TACOS

This is one of the few northern Mexican recipes that uses ground meat. I first tasted it at the home of a friend who lives in a small town in the state of Coahuila. The girls in the kitchen would make 20 to 30 of these little tacos and set them on a platter in the middle of the entrance hall, where anyone, including the gardeners and other servants, could stop to enjoy them. I have since had variations on the same delicious snack in many other places.

Crush the garlic, cumin, and oregano together in a *molcajete* or mortar and pestle.

Heat a large heavy skillet over medium heat and add the ground beef, breaking it up with the side of a large spoon or other suitable implement. Add the onions and the mashed garlic, oregano, cumin, chile powder, and cayenne. Fry over medium heat, stirring often, until the meat is well browned and the onions are soft.

Cover the pan, turn the heat very low, and simmer for 20 minutes. While that is cooking, make the tortillas and wrap them in a thick towel to keep them warm. When the filling is done, place a heaping spoonful on each tortilla, fold it over, and set the completed tacos on a warm serving plate. Serves 4.

2 **cloves garlic, mashed**
1 **teaspoon (.6 gram) oregano**
½ **teaspoon cumin**
1 **pound (450 grams) ground beef, lean**
⅔ **cup (95 grams) onions, diced**
2 **tablespoons (14 grams) mild chile powder**
¼ **teaspoon cayenne pepper, or to taste**
12 **flour tortillas, about 4 inches (10.1 centimeters) in diameter**

Tacos de chicharrones

FRIED PORK SKIN TACOS

In addition to serving as an appetizer, chicharrones are often steamed with various sauces and used as a filling for tacos. Served this way, they have a very interesting consistency and flavor. While these tacos are rarely included in cookbooks, they should be, so here are two versions.

Tacos de chicharrones en salsa de tomatillo

FRIED PORK SKIN TACOS WITH TOMATILLO SAUCE

1 pound (450 grams) *tomatillos,* husked and rinsed

2 *serrano* chiles or *jalapeño* chiles, or to taste

½ medium onion, coarsely chopped

2 cloves garlic

2 tablespoons (28 milliliters) cider vinegar

2 teaspoons (4 grams) sugar

½ teaspoon salt

6 cups (91 grams) *chicharrones,* broken into small pieces

Flour tortillas

Sour cream

Put the *tomatillos* in a saucepan, cover them with water, and bring slowly to a boil. Then simmer gently until they are very soft, about 5 to 10 minutes. Place the cooked *tomatillos* in a blender jar; add the remaining ingredients, except the *chicharrones,* tortillas, and sour cream, and blend until puréed, about 30 seconds.

Next, put the blender contents into a medium-sized cooking pot and bring to a simmer. Add the *chicharrones,* stirring well, and cook, covered, over low to medium heat until the *chicharrones* are soft but not too soggy. Serve with hot flour tortillas and sour cream. Serves 4.

Tacos de chicharrones en salsa de tomate

FRIED PORK SKIN TACOS WITH TOMATO SAUCE

Heat the lard or oil in a medium-sized cooking pot and cook the garlic and onion over medium to medium-high heat until the onion is softened but not browned.

Add the tomatoes and cook over medium-high heat for 5 minutes, stirring often. Next, add the hot sauce and *chicharrones,* turn the heat down, and simmer, covered, until the *chicharrones* are soft but not soggy.

Serve with hot flour tortillas and sour cream. Serves 4.

2 tablespoons (30 grams) lard or oil (28 milliliters)

2 cloves garlic, minced

1 medium onion, sliced

4 tomatoes, peeled and chopped

⅓ cup (78 grams) *Salsa de chile ancho* (p. 44), or other hot sauce of your choice

4 cups (65 grams) *chicharrones,* broken into small pieces

Flour tortillas

Sour cream

Tacos de tuétano

MARROW TACOS

◇◇◇◇◇

8 **pounds (3,600 grams)
   marrow bones, cut
   into ¾-inch (1.9-
   centimeter) pieces**
   Cooking oil
8 **thin, 4-inch (10.2-
   centimeter) corn
   tortillas**
   Hot sauce
   Guacamole (p. 83)

Anthropologists tell us that bone marrow was one of prehistoric man's nutritional delights. I can report that this tradition is alive and well in northern Mexico. These delicious tacos, made with very small corn tortillas, are often served as an appetizer in exclusive restaurants. But so rich are they that one or two per guest is sufficient. Marrow comes from the marrow bones of the beef shank. Because of the different sizes of the bones that may be available, it is difficult to estimate quantities precisely, but about 1 pound (450 grams) of bones per taco is a good estimate.

If you have to reheat the marrow after removing it from the bones, simply place it in the oven at 300 degrees F (148 degrees C) for no longer than necessary to warm it, about a minute or less. Do not try to heat marrow in a skillet or overheat it in the oven because it will melt away before you know it.

Place the bones on a baking sheet in an oven preheated to 300 degrees F (148 degrees C) for about 15 minutes. Remove the bones, and using a boning knife, carefully cut out the pieces of marrow from their centers. Cover the marrow to keep it warm.

Heat the oil in a small skillet over medium heat until a drop of water sputters instantly. Immerse the tortillas, one at a time, for just a few seconds and drain on paper towels. Place a small line of marrow down the center of each tortilla, fold it in half, and serve with the sauce and Guacamole. Serves 4.

Tacos a la plancha

PAN-GRILLED TACOS

Lest you think that northern Mexicans cannot cook delicious little treats over anything but charcoal, I offer the following favorite recipe, which is common in taquerías *such as Los Monjitas in Monterrey. There the waitresses are dressed in the habits of Catholic sisters, and the cooks make terrific tacos. You can use chicken, beef, or pork, or a combination of all three meats.*

Please note that these tacos are usually prepared on large commercial griddles that enable the cooks to sauté the ingredients separately for different periods of time. The following instructions duplicate the end result on the typical home stove. Also, it is difficult to specify the exact amount of oil, so just remember that for this dish you want to use as little as possible so that each ingredient is charred and not greasy.

Heat a large skillet over medium-high heat, add just enough oil to film the pan, and fry the bacon until it is nearly crisp. Remove and reserve the bacon.

Mix 1 tablespoon of oil (15 milliliters) with the sliced chicken, beef, or pork, turn the heat to high, and when the pan just begins to smoke add a little oil and sear the meat until it is charred on both sides but not cooked through. Remove the meat and reserve.

Turn the heat to medium high, add a little more oil, and cook the onions, green (and red, if using) pepper, and chiles, stirring often, until they are just soft and charred on all sides. Add the garlic and cook 1 minute more. Add the reserved bacon and meat and the salt and cook, stirring constantly, until it is the desired degree of doneness (cooked through for the chicken and pork and rare to well done for the beef). Sprinkle on the cheese and continue to cook without stirring until it has just melted.

Place equal portions of the filling on each of 4 serving plates and serve with flour and/or corn tortillas, Guacamole, and your favorite salsa. Serves 4.

Olive oil

4 pieces bacon, cut into ½-inch (1.3-centimeter) pieces

1¼ pounds (560 grams) boneless, skinless chicken, sirloin, or pork loin, cut into strips of ⅛ inch by ¾ inch (.3 by 1.9 centimeters)

1¾ cups (250 grams) onions, chopped

2¼ cups (296 grams) green pepper (or half and half green and red pepper), chopped

½–⅔ cup (65.7–98.5 grams) *poblano* chiles or Anaheim chiles, stemmed, seeded, and chopped

2 cloves garlic, minced

1¼ teaspoons (9.3 grams) salt

½ cup (54.4 grams) *asadero* or provolone cheese, grated

12 corn or flour tortillas, or a mixture of both

Guacamole (p. 83)

Salsa

Tacos potosinos

TACOS SAN LUIS POTOSÍ STYLE

◆◇◆◇◆

4 cups (680 grams) potatoes, peeled and cut into ³/₄-inch (1.9-centimeter) pieces

3¹/₃ cups (373 grams) carrots, peeled and cut into ¹/₂–³/₄-inch (1.3–1.9-centimeter) pieces

3 *ancho* chiles, stemmed, seeded, and peeled

1 tomato, broiled

3 cloves garlic

1 teaspoon (.6 gram) oregano

2 tablespoons (30 grams) lard or olive oil (28 milliliters)

¹/₂ teaspoon salt

12 corn tortillas
Cooking oil

12 ounces (340 grams) *queso panela,* grated; or substitute feta cheese

4 cups (350 grams) lettuce, shredded

¹/₄ cup (56 grams) *chorizo*

San Luis Potosí is a place of contrasts. Although this state lies quite far south, its western portion shares the arid landscape and ranching heritage of its northern counterparts. In contrast, to the east where it reaches all the way to the Gulf of Mexico, the state changes dramatically to the tropical region know for the Huasteca Indians which inhabit it. While San Luis Potosí is not usually considered part of northern Mexico by culinary authorities, I have decided to include this dish simply because it is one of my all-time favorites and because versions of it are often served in Nuevo León and Tamaulipas. In San Luis Potosí the tacos are more like enchiladas than in other parts of Mexico.

Making the tacos takes a little practice so be prepared for some trial and error the first time. Please note that feta cheese can be substituted for the queso panela, *but it has a stronger flavor.*

Separately, boil the potatoes and carrots until they are just tender, then drain and reserve them.

To make the sauce, first soak the chiles in hot water for at least 15 minutes; then transfer them to the jar of a blender. Add the broiled tomato, garlic, oregano, 1½ cups (240 milliliters) of the water in which the chiles were soaked, and blend the mixture for 1 minute at high speed. Heat a saucepan over medium heat, add 1 tablespoon (15 grams) of the lard or olive oil (15 milliliters); then pour in the sauce, add the salt, and stir to combine well. Simmer the sauce until it begins to thicken, about 10 minutes; then allow it to cool slightly.

Meanwhile, heat a *comal* or griddle over medium heat. To make the tacos, pour a little oil on the *comal* or griddle; then spread it around with a spatula. Next, using kitchen tongs, dip a tortilla in the chile sauce, allowing it to drain slightly; then place it on the greased griddle. Allow the tortilla to cook until it just begins to harden; then turn it over and continue to cook until it is stiff enough to handle without falling apart. (It should still be quite flexible and not at all crisp.) Place a very small amount of cheese on the middle of the tortilla and roll it as you would for enchiladas. When all the tortillas have been rolled, place them on serving plates on which you have scattered a thin bed of lettuce.

Heat a large pot over medium heat, add the remaining 1 tablespoon (15 grams) of lard or olive oil (15 milliliters), and cook the *chorizo* until it is well browned. Add the reserved potatoes and carrots to the pot and toss them with the *chorizo* until they are heated through. Spoon the vegetables and *chorizo* over the tacos, garnish with a little more lettuce and the remaining cheese, and serve. Serves 4.

Tacos alambres

SHISH KEBAB-STYLE TACOS

Tacos alambres *are a popular dish in Mexico's more elaborate* taquerías. *They make a fine, inexpensive meal, and are prepared in two steps. First, pork, chicken, beef, or lamb (or a combination of meats) is charbroiled with onion,* poblano *chiles, and bacon, either separately or together on a shish kebab. The charbroiled meat and vegetables are then finely chopped and briefly sautéed together on a griddle or in a skillet. To serve, the meat and vegetables are usually mounded on a platter, sometimes topped with grated cheese, and accompanied by hot tortillas which are sometimes placed flat under the ingredients, sometimes on top, and sometimes on the side. A plate of Guacamole (p. 83) and several sauces complete the meal.*

Tacos alambres de pollo

SHISH KEBAB-STYLE CHICKEN TACOS

◇◇◇◇◇

1½ pounds (675 grams) chicken breast, marinated as for Chicken Shish Kebab (p. 166)

2 *poblano* chiles or Anaheim chiles

3 ounces (86 grams) onion, cut in large pieces

2 thick slices bacon

2 cloves garlic, minced

2 tablespoons (28 milliliters) lime juice

1 tablespoon (15 milliliters) olive oil

Salt, to taste

⅓ cup (34 grams) *asadero,* mozzarella, or provolone cheese, grated

3 tablespoons (42 milliliters) extra-thick whipping cream or crème fraîche

Guacamole made with at least 2 avocados (p. 83)

Several hot sauces

Hot flour tortillas

Either cut and skewer the chicken, chiles, onion, and bacon according to the recipe directions for Chicken Shish Kebab or leave them whole. The latter method is easier, especially if you have one of those perforated metal grill pans shaped like a small, square wok to keep the vegetables and bacon from falling through the grill.

Over very hot coals, grill either the prepared shish kebabs or the chicken, chiles, onion, and bacon until they are well charred. Place the cooked ingredients on a chopping board and chop finely. Place the chopped ingredients in a bowl and add the garlic, lime juice, and olive oil.

Heat a skillet over medium-high heat, add the ingredients from the bowl, and cook, turning constantly until they are well heated, but no more than 1 or 2 minutes. Add the salt and place the meat on a platter. Top with the cheese and the cream and serve with the Guacamole, sauces, and tortillas. Serves 4.

Tacos de pollo o guajolote

CRISP CHICKEN OR TURKEY TACOS

These tacos are particular favorites in Sonora, around Guaymas, and in Baja California. It takes some experience to make them properly so I suggest preparing extra ingredients the first time to allow for a few failures.

Heat 1 inch (2.54 centimeters) of peanut oil or another good cooking oil in a heavy skillet. Soften a tortilla in the oil and drain. When the tortilla is cool enough to handle, put 2 to 3 tablespoons (18 to 28 grams) of the shredded meat in the center.

Next, holding the tortilla closed with kitchen tongs, slowly lower the taco back into the hot oil. Cook on one side and then the other until the taco is just becoming crisp. Then, using the tongs, hold the taco slightly open at the top to allow for the later addition of the garnish. Continue to cook until completely crisp and golden.

Remove from the oil and drain on paper towels. As you remove the taco, make sure as much of the oil as possible drains back into the pan. (It is difficult to give precise cooking times because of the variables, but you will soon get the hang of it.)

When all the tacos have been made, add some of the shredded lettuce or cabbage and chopped tomatoes to each one. This will be impossible to do if the tacos were not left slightly open at the top. (If they were not, just place them on a plate and cover them with the garnish and cheese. They do this as often as not in Mexico!)

Sprinkle some of the crumbled cheese on top and serve with hot sauce on the side. Serves 4.

Cooking oil
12 corn tortillas
2½ cups (368 grams) chicken or turkey meat, shredded
2 cups (190 grams) lettuce or cabbage, shredded
2 medium tomatoes, seeded and chopped into small pieces
2 ounces (56 grams) *queso cotija* or feta cheese, crumbled
Hot sauce

Tacos de pescado

FISH TACOS

◇◆◇◆◇◆◇

¾ **cup (170 grams) mayonnaise**

3 **teaspoons (14 grams) American-style mustard**

¾ **cup plus 2 table-spoons (123 grams) flour**

1 **teaspoon (2.3 grams) chile powder**

1½ **teaspoons (10 grams) salt**

1 **cup (225 milliliters) cold beer**

Oil for deep-frying

1½ **pounds sea bass (450–675 grams), or substitute catfish, cut into pieces about 4½ inches (11.4 centimeters) long by 1¾ inches (4.45 centimeters) wide by about ½ inch (1.27 centimeters) thick**

12 **6½–12-inch (16.5–30.4-centimeter) corn tortillas or 24 smaller tortillas**

1½ **cups (142 grams) cabbage, shredded**

Tomato-based salsa

2–4 **limes, cut into wedges**

Guacamole (p. 83)

No book on the cooking of northern Mexico would be complete without a recipe for the famous fish tacos of Baja California. A generation of Californians have enjoyed this product of countless stands before, during, and after assorted revelries.

If your tortillas are smaller than 5½ to 6 inches (14 to 15.2 centimeters) in diameter, use 2 per taco, overlapping them to produce the desired size.

To make the "tartar sauce," mix together the mayonnaise and mustard and reserve.

To make the batter, combine the flour, chile powder, salt, and beer and refrigerate until ready to use.

Heat the oil to 350 degrees F (177 degrees C) in a deep fryer. Using kitchen tongs, dip each piece of fish in the batter and lower into the hot oil, holding it above the bottom of the fryer for a few seconds before letting go. (If you do not do this, the fish will stick to the bottom of the fryer.) Fry the fish until the batter is golden and the fish is cooked through. Remove the fish to paper towels to drain.

Heat the tortillas over a *comal* and place 3 on each of 4 serving plates. Spread some of the "tartar sauce" on one side of each tortilla, top with a little cabbage, and place a piece of fried fish on it. Spoon some hot sauce over the fish and fold the tortilla over it. Serve the tacos with lime wedges and Guacamole. Serves 4.

Enchiladas

Enchiladas, sometimes called envueltos *in Nuevo León, refers to a type of dish rather than a single recipe. It is a generic term, like cake or pie or tacos, which includes many different recipes and an almost unlimited potential for variation. An enchilada is a corn tortilla filled with meat or cheese, topped with a sauce, cheese, and garnish, and then heated (except for the Sonora enchilada, which is somewhat different). In one common variation, the tortillas are folded without any filling and topped with sauce and cheese. A basic enchilada recipe and several variations follow.*

Basic Enchiladas

Place ½ to 1 inch (1.3 to 2.54 centimeters) cooking oil in a small skillet and heat it over medium to medium-high heat until a drop of water on the surface immediately sputters. Using kitchen tongs, immerse each tortilla for just a few seconds; then remove it to drain on paper towels. If the tortilla is left in the oil too long, it will become hard and rubbery, and difficult to fold (and chew). A little experience will prevent this problem. In addition to softening the tortilla, the immersion will coat it, preventing the filling and sauce from making it soggy. **NOTE:** At this point many cooks place the softened tortilla in the enchilada sauce before adding the filling and rolling. In fact, in some cases this is all the sauce that will be used in the dish.

Next, place the desired amount of filling a little to one side of each tortilla's center, roll it up, and place it on an ovenproof serving plate. Make the remaining enchiladas in the same way.

When all the enchiladas have been rolled up, top them with the desired sauce and garnish and place them in a preheated 375-degree F (190-degree C) oven. Bake until the sauce is bubbly, about 10 minutes.

Oil for softening tortillas
Corn tortillas
Sauce for filling
Garnish: usually cheese, onion, and, sometimes, sour cream

Enchiladas de queso

CHEESE ENCHILADAS

◈◈◈◈◈◈

ENCHILADAS

Oil for softening the tortillas

1 **dozen corn tortillas**

1 **pound (450 grams) mild cheddar cheese, grated**

¾ **cup (107 grams) onion minced**

SAUCE

2 *ancho* **chiles**

2–3 *de árbol* **chiles or** *japonés* **chiles, or to taste**

2 **cloves garlic**

1 **teaspoon (.6 gram) oregano**

½ **teaspoon cumin**

4 **tablespoons (60 grams) butter**

4 **tablespoons (35 grams) flour**

3¼ **cups (731 milliliters) mild beef broth**

¼ **cup (42 milliliters) tomato sauce (optional)**

Heat the oil in a small heavy skillet until very hot but not smoking. Using kitchen tongs, soften each tortilla by immersing it in the oil for just a few seconds; then remove it to drain on paper towels. Next, place about 1 ounce (28 grams) of the cheese and 1 tablespoon (8.8 grams) of the onion just off the center of each tortilla and wrap them tightly. Put 3 tortillas on each of 4 ovenproof serving plates and set aside while you make the sauce.

Toast the chiles over very low heat, being careful to avoid burning. Then remove their stems and seeds and soak them in hot water for about 20 minutes. Next, place the chiles in a blender with ½ cup (110 milliliters) of the soaking water and the garlic, oregano, and cumin. Blend into a smooth paste (about 1 minute) and strain the sauce.

Next, melt the butter in a saucepan over medium heat, whisk in the flour, and cook until the roux is lightly browned and gives off a nutty fragrance. Remove the pan from the heat and add about ½ cup (110 milliliters) of the broth, a little at a time, whisking constantly to prevent lumps from forming. Return the pan to the burner and continue to add the broth a little at a time, until it is fully incorporated. Then add the strained chile mixture and tomato sauce, if used. Bring the sauce to a boil, reduce the heat, and simmer, uncovered, stirring from time to time until the sauce is thickened, about ½ hour.

Top the enchiladas with equal portions of the sauce and the remaining cheese and onion. Put the plates in a preheated 375-degree F (190-degree C) oven for about 10 minutes, or until the cheese is melted and the sauce is bubbling.

Serve with Mexican Rice (pp. 101, 102) and/or Refried Beans (p. 107). Serves 4.

Enchiladas estilo Sonora

ENCHILADAS SONORA STYLE

I have never seen enchiladas prepared this way except in Sonora. Instead of wrapping cheese in several thin corn tortillas, the cheese, sauce, and garnishes are placed on a single thick tortilla. These are easy to make by following the directions on a package of Masa Harina.

Prepare 1 recipe of corn tortilla dough according to the directions on the Masa Harina package. Make 4 tortillas about ½ inch (1.27 centimeters) thick and 5 inches (12.7 centimeters) in diameter. The easiest way to do this is to roll the dough between sheets of waxed paper.

Cook the tortillas on an ungreased *comal* or griddle at low to medium heat for about 5 minutes on each side, or until they are cooked through. Place 1 cooked tortilla on each of 4 ovenproof serving plates. In the following order, top each tortilla with equal amounts of the cheese, sauce, sour cream, green chiles, onion, and olives.

Place the plates in an oven preheated to 375 degrees F (190 degrees C) and bake for 10 minutes, or until the cheese is melted and the sauce begins to bubble.

NOTE: Some Sonoran cooks fry the tortillas until they are cooked rather than using a griddle. Serves 4.

Masa Harina, packaged

8 ounces (225 grams) **Monterey Jack cheese, grated**

1 recipe **sauce for** *Enchiladas de queso* **(p. 208), or another sauce of your choice**

½ cup (113 grams) **sour cream**

½ cup (68 grams) **green chiles, peeled, seeded, and diced**

⅓ cup (48 grams) **onion, minced**

¾ cup **black olives, pitted and sliced**

Enchiladas familiares

ORDINARY ENCHILADAS

◆◇◆◇◆

**Oil for softening
tortillas (see
general directions
for "Enchiladas," p.
207)**

12 **corn tortillas
Hot sauce**

1 **pound (450 grams)
mozzarella cheese,
grated**

**Shredded lettuce or
cabbage and
chopped tomatoes
for garnish**

These enchiladas do not really have a name. However, I keep running into them in restaurants called "restaurantes familiares," or ordinary restaurants, which specialize in common or simple food at reasonable prices. They are easy to prepare and very satisfying, either served alone or with broiled meat. Use any salsa you wish. Salsa de jalapeño o serrano asado *(p. 39),* Salsa jalapeño cocido *(p. 38), or* Salsa de chile ancho *(p. 44) are good choices.*

Heat ½ to 1 inch (1.3 to 2.54 centimeters) of oil in a small heavy skillet until it just begins to smoke, and using kitchen tongs soften the tortillas for a second or two. Remove them to drain on paper towels.

Next, pass the tortillas through the sauce to coat them lightly, or rub about 1 tablespoon (15 milliliters) of the sauce on each side. Place about 1 ounce (28 grams) of cheese on each tortilla, wrap loosely, and place 3 on each of 4 ovenproof serving plates. Top the enchiladas with more cheese and bake at 375 degrees F (190 degrees C) for 10 minutes, or until the cheese is melted.

Serve with Refried Beans (p. 107), rice, and a garnish of shredded lettuce or cabbage and chopped tomatoes. Serves 4.

Enchiladas de chile ancho

ANCHO CHILE ENCHILADAS

These enchiladas use a mild, flavorful sauce found commonly in northern Mexico. Make them as for Cheese Enchiladas (p. 208), using mild cheddar cheese, and top with this sauce.

Soak the chiles in hot water for 20 minutes. Then place the chiles, garlic, oregano, and onion in a blender, add 1 cup (225 milliliters) water and blend for 1 minute or until the sauce is completely smooth. Add 1 more cup (225 milliliters) water and blend briefly.

Heat a saucepan over medium-low heat, add the oil or lard, and then the blended sauce. Add the bay leaves, tomato purée, salt, and vinegar. Allow the mixture to simmer, uncovered, for 15 or 20 minutes or until thickened. Add the flour and water mixture and cook an additional 5 minutes. If, at any point, the sauce becomes too thick, add a little more water. Serves 4.

8 *ancho* chiles, seeded and deveined

4 cloves garlic

1 teaspoon (.6 gram) oregano

¼ cup (35 grams) onion, chopped

Water

2 tablespoons (28 milliliters) olive oil, peanut oil, or lard (28 grams)

2 bay leaves

⅓ cup (79 grams) tomato purée

1 teaspoon (6.2 grams) salt

1 teaspoon (5 milliliters) mild vinegar

2 teaspoons (5.8 grams) flour, mixed with 2 tablespoons (28 milliliters) water

Enchiladas en salsa chipotle

ENCHILADAS IN CHIPOTLE SAUCE

❖❖❖❖❖

SAUCE

2 canned *chipotle* chiles, seeded and chopped

3 garlic cloves, minced

1 teaspoon (.6 gram) oregano

1 teaspoon (2 grams) cumin

4 tablespoons (60 grams) butter

4 tablespoons (35 grams) flour

1 cup (225 milliliters) Campbell's beef broth

2½ cups (560 milliliters) water

2–4 tablespoons (28–55 grams) *adobo* sauce from the chile can

ENCHILADAS

Cooking oil

12 corn tortillas

1 pound (450 grams) mild cheddar cheese, grated

½ medium onion, minced

Sauce

I came upon this enchilada recipe by chance, and it is by far my favorite.

I was visiting friends in northern Coahuila and accepted an invitation to fly to a ranch some 150 miles distant. The purpose of the trip was to deliver food and other supplies for an upcoming roundup. After a smooth flight over flat desert, we climbed high over the Sierra Oriental range until we reached our destination. The ranch rests in a high valley surrounded by acre upon acre of apple and pear orchards. The main house is constructed completely of wood and stone from the ranch, except for the floor tiles, which are from Saltillo. The serenity and beauty there make this one of the most wonderful places I have ever visited.

After seeing to the unloading of the provisions, we took a siesta. Upon arising, we realized that, to return before nightfall, we needed to leave very soon. In delightfully Mexican fashion, my host had not thought to worry, until just before we were to leave, that his plane was not equipped for night navigation. We strapped ourselves into the plane, only to discover that the engine was missing badly. The problem apparently was solved after an hour of tinkering, but by that time it was too late to beat the sun, which was just about to disappear over the mountains to the west. Accepting defeat, my host gave orders to ready the guest quarters and prepare dinner.

Dinner was magnificent, tenderloin steak sliced as for Carne asada *(p. 117), accompanied by the enchiladas in this recipe. When asked the name of the dish, the cook thought for a few moments, shrugged, and said, "Enchiladas de queso," or Cheese Enchiladas. His recipe was even less precise because, like many Mexican cooks, he cooks by feel and inspiration and, in any case, probably could not read or write. Fortunately, I was able to obtain a list of the ingredients. (Yes, Campbell's beef broth was one. We had brought a case of it that morning.) From this list I was able to re-create the recipe almost exactly.*

The key ingredient of these enchiladas is the chiles for which I have named them. The chipotle *chile is really the ordinary* jalapeño *which has been dried and smoked. They are sold dried and also canned in* adobo sauce, *which is how they are used here. Their smoky flavor wonderfully enhances the charbroiled foods of northern Mexico.*

Rinse, seed, and chop the chiles. In a *molcajete* or mortar and pestle grind together the garlic, oregano, cumin, and chiles.

Melt the butter in a medium saucepan over low heat and add the flour. Cook the roux over medium to low heat until it begins to brown and gives off a nutty fragrance. Remove the pan from the heat and add the broth a little at a time, stirring after each addition to make sure it is well incorporated. Return the pan to the heat and add the water in a slow stream, stirring constantly.

Add the garlic mixture and *adobo* sauce and bring to a boil. Then reduce the heat and simmer, uncovered, stirring often until the sauce is thickened, about 30 minutes.

Heat about ½ inch (1.27 centimeters) cooking oil in a small skillet until it just begins to smoke. Using kitchen tongs, immerse each tortilla in the oil for a few seconds or just until it becomes soft and pliable. Remove to drain on paper towels.

Place about 1 ounce (28 grams) of the cheese and a sprinkling of onion on each tortilla and wrap into a cylinder. Place 3 enchiladas on each of 4 ovenproof dinner plates. Divide the sauce over each serving of enchiladas and add the remaining cheese and onion to taste.

Preheat the oven to 375 degrees F (190 degrees C). Set the plates in the oven and heat until the cheese is melted and the sauce is bubbling, about 8 to 10 minutes.

Serve with rice and/or Refried Beans (p. 107), or with thin charbroiled tenderloin steak (as I had them originally). Serves 4.

Enchiladas de carne de res

BEEF ENCHILADAS

❖❖❖❖❖

1 pound (450 grams)
   lean stew meat, cut
   in 1-inch (2.54-
   centimeter) chunks

1½ teaspoons (9.3 grams)
   salt

5 cups (1,125 milliliters)
   water or mild beef
   broth

4 *ancho* chiles or 4
   tablespoons (36
   grams) mild chile
   powder

4 medium cloves garlic,
   minced

½ teaspoon cumin

½ teaspoon oregano

2 teaspoons (6.6 grams)
   black pepper

1 cup (167 milliliters)
   tomato sauce

4 tablespoons (60
   grams) butter

4 tablespoons (35
   grams) flour
   Oil for softening
   tortillas

1 dozen corn tortillas

½ cup (71grams) onion,
   minced

6 ounces (168 grams)
   mild cheddar
   cheese, grated

These enchiladas are delicious when made with inexpensive stew meat, but be sure to remove all the fat and gristle.

Place the meat, 1 teaspoon (6.2 grams) of the salt, and water or broth in a large heavy kettle or Dutch oven. Bring to a boil and simmer, covered, for 1½ hours or until the meat is very tender. Allow the meat to cool in the broth. Then remove it, reserving the broth, and shred the meat by hand or with the plastic blade in a food processor.

SAUCE

To make the sauce soak the chiles in hot water (unless using chile powder) for 10 to 15 minutes; then remove the seeds and stems and place in a blender. Add to the blender the garlic, cumin, oregano, the remaining ½ teaspoon salt, pepper, and 1 cup (225 milliliters) of the reserved broth, and the tomato sauce (there should be about 4 cups [900 millimeters] in all). Blend the mixture for 1 minute. If you are using chile powder, add it to the blender with the other ingredients.

Next, melt 4 tablespoons (60 grams) butter in a large heavy sauce-pan, add 4 tablespoons (35 grams) flour, and cook over medium heat, stirring constantly, until the mixture begins to brown and gives off a nutty fragrance. Remove the pan from the heat and add 1 cup (225 milliliters) of the remaining broth a little at a time, stirring constantly with a spoon or wire whisk. (Make sure each addition is completely incorporated into the sauce before adding more. This ensures that the sauce does not become lumpy.) Now return the pan to the heat, set at low, and add the remaining 2 cups (450 milliliters) broth. (If you run out of broth, use water.) When the broth is well incorporated, add the contents of the blender jar. Next add $^1/_3$ cup (49 grams) of the shredded beef, bring the sauce to a boil, turn the heat to low, and simmer, uncovered, until it is thickened, stirring often (about 30 minutes).

ENCHILADAS

Preheat the oven to 400 degrees F (205 degrees C). Next heat ½ to ¾ inch (1.27 to 1.91 centimeters) of oil in a small frying pan until it just begins to smoke and turn the heat to low.

Using kitchen tongs, soften each tortilla by immersing it for a few seconds in the hot oil. Remove and drain on paper towels. Divide the shredded beef into 12 equal portions, put 1 portion on each tortilla, and sprinkle some onion onto the meat. Wrap the enchilada tightly, placing 3 enchiladas on each of 4 serving plates.

Top the enchiladas with a generous portion of the sauce and sprinkle the cheese and remaining onion over them. Place the plates in the preheated oven and bake for 8 to 10 minutes, until the cheese is completely melted and the sauce is bubbling. Serves 4.

Enchiladas de puerco

PORK ENCHILADAS

◇◇◇◇◇

1 **pound (450 grams)
pork, diced in ½-inch
(1.3-centimeter)
pieces**

3¾ **cups (840 milliliters)
water**

6 *ancho* **chiles,
stemmed and seeded**

6 **medium cloves garlic**

2 **teaspoons (1.2 grams)
oregano**

2 **teaspoons (4 grams)
cumin**

¼ **cup (28 grams) onion,
diced**

2 **teaspoons (7
milliliters) cider
vinegar**

1 **cup (167 grams)
tomato sauce**

1 **teaspoon (6.2 grams)
salt**

**Oil for softening the
tortillas**

1 **dozen corn tortillas**

1 **cup (226 grams) sour
cream**

½ **cup (43 grams) green
onion, chopped**

*This is a colorful, hearty, and truly satisfying dish. The sauce is
thickened naturally by cooking down the ingredients.*

Place the pork and water in a saucepan and bring to a boil. Skim off
the scum which rises to the top, cover, and simmer briskly for ½
hour. Remove the top from the pan and continue simmering for 10
minutes, or until only 3 cups (675 milliliters) of liquid remain. Strain
half the broth into a blender and reserve the remaining half. Place
the cooked pork in a bowl.

Put the chiles, garlic, oregano, cumin, and onion into the blender
and blend for 1 minute. Pour the chile mixture into the saucepan and
add the reserved broth, vinegar, tomato sauce, and salt. Bring the
sauce to a boil, reduce the heat, and simmer for 10 minutes or until
the mixture begins to thicken.

Heat the oil until it begins to smoke and soften the tortillas for a
second or two, using kitchen tongs. Remove them to drain on paper
towels.

Toss the reserved pork with ½ cup (110 milliliters) of the sauce.
Divide into 12 equal portions. Next, make the enchiladas by wrapping 1 portion of pork blended with sauce in each of the softened
tortillas, placing 3 on each of 4 ovenproof plates.

Top the enchiladas with the sauce, then sour cream, and garnish
with the chopped green onions. Place the completed enchiladas in a
375-degree F (190-degree C) oven for about 8 minutes, or until they
are very hot and the sauce is bubbling. Serves 4.

Enchiladas suizas

SWISS ENCHILADAS

These enchiladas are a northern version of a popular central Mexican favorite. Use heavy Mexican-style cream or crème fraîche or make your own as described in the section on "Basic Ingredients."

Heat the oil until almost smoking. Using kitchen tongs, soften the tortillas by immersing them in the oil for just a few seconds. Remove the tortillas to drain on paper towels.

Place about 1 ounce (28 grams) of chicken on each tortilla and roll up into enchiladas.

Place 3 enchiladas on each of 4 ovenproof serving plates and pour ¼ cup (56 milliliters) of the cream over each one. Next, pour equal amounts of the *Tomatillo* Sauce over each plate of enchiladas and top with the cheese.

Place the enchiladas in a preheated 375-degree F (190-degree C) oven for 10 minutes, or until the cheese is completely melted and the sauce is bubbling.

Serve with Mexican Rice (pp. 101, 102) or white rice. Serves 4.

Oil for softening tortillas
12 corn tortillas
¾ pound (340 grams) chicken breast, boiled and coarsely shredded
1 cup (225 milliliters) cream
4 ounces (112 grams) Monterey Jack cheese
Double recipe *Tomatillo* Sauce (p. 46)

Entomatadas

CHICKEN ENCHILADAS WITH TOMATILLO SAUCE

These enchiladas are made exactly like the Enchiladas suizas *(p. 217) except that cream is not used. I call them "Queen's Enchiladas," for reasons that will become clear.*

In northern Mexican villages, it is the custom that for the yearly fiesta a queen is chosen. The contestants are often selected according to the amount of money they raise for the event. At that time of year you will often be stopped, as you drive through town, by a group of young girls asking for donations "para la reina." (It is difficult to refuse.)

One evening at the beginning of fiesta, I stopped to have dinner in a small restaurant in a village in Nuevo León. Not having tried them before, I ordered Entomatadas. *I noticed that the rather attractive waitress was quite plainly dressed, with her hair pulled back under a scarf. When the plate arrived, about 20 minutes later, I almost fell off my chair. There she was, wearing a dress that might have belonged to Marie Antoinette, heels that must have been 5 inches (12.7 centimeters) high, and a crown made of real silver, inset with multicolored stones. Her elaborately styled hair was thick and hung below her waist.*

After regaining my composure, I found out that she had been chosen fiesta queen. The restaurant was owned by her parents, and she did not seem to think it odd that she was waiting tables until literally minutes before she was due to be installed.

The Entomatadas *were great! Serves 4.*

Enchiladas de mole

ENCHILADAS IN MOLE SAUCE

These enchiladas often accompany Steak Tampiqueña.

Make the sauce according to the recipe for Turkey or Chicken Mole (p. 170). After adding the broth, simmer the sauce, uncovered, until it is thick enough that it will not run all over the place.

Using either shredded turkey or chicken, make enchiladas according to the general instructions at the beginning of this section (p. 207). You can also use Monterey Jack or mozzarella cheese, or a combination of both. Top the enchiladas with the sauce and bake on ovenproof serving plates at 350 degrees F (177 degrees C) for 10 minutes.

Serve with Mexican Rice (pp. 101, 102) or white rice. Serves 4.

Enchiladas de pipián rojo o verde

ENCHILADAS IN RED OR GREEN PIPIÁN SAUCE

These enchiladas are rarely seen on restaurant menus, but they are not to be missed.

Make the sauce by following the recipe for either *Pollo en pipián rojo* (p. 168) or *Pollo en pipián verde* (p. 169), omitting the chicken. Next, using boiled and shredded chicken meat, make enchiladas according to the general instructions at the beginning of this section (p. 207). Top them with the sauce and bake on ovenproof serving plates for approximately 10 minutes at 350 degrees F (177 degrees C).

Serve with Mexican Rice (pp. 101, 102) or white rice. Serves 4.

Torta Montezuma

MONTEZUMA'S SANDWICH

❖❖❖❖❖

6 tablespoons (84 milliliters) olive oil

1 pound (450 grams) boneless, skinless chicken breast

¼ cup (56 milliliters) dry white wine

1 large onion, chopped, about 1½ cups (214 grams)

2 cloves garlic, minced

3 *poblano* chiles, peeled, seeded, and thinly sliced or coarsely chopped

1 pound (450 grams) tomatoes, peeled, seeded, and finely chopped

½ teaspoon salt, or to taste
   Cooking oil to fry tortillas

12 corn tortillas

3 eggs, beaten

¾ pound (340 grams) *asadero* or mozzarella cheese, grated
   Shredded lettuce and chopped tomato for garnish

More like stacked enchiladas than a sandwich, this recipe from Marcella Widdoes, who lives in Saltillo, is one of the most interesting northern recipes I have found. Marcy, who has written a fine cookbook of her own, once ran a restaurant on the premises of the elegant and historical home in which she and her husband now live. This recipe is just one reason why many locals wish the restaurant was still open.

Preheat the oven to 425 degrees F (220 degrees C). Heat a skillet over medium-high to high heat, add 3 tablespoons (42 milliliters) of the olive oil, and sauté the chicken until it is turning golden brown on both sides. Turn the heat to low, add the wine, cover, and simmer until the chicken is cooked through, about 3 to 5 minutes or more, depending on the thickness of the chicken. Remove the pan from the heat and when the chicken is cool enough to handle, shred it, reserving the pan juices.

Heat a saucepan over medium heat, add the remaining 3 tablespoons (42 milliliters) olive oil, and sauté the onions until they are just golden brown, being careful not to scorch them. Add the garlic and continue cooking for 1 minute. Add the chiles, reserved pan juices from the chicken, and the tomatoes. Cook until the chiles are soft and the sauce has begun to thicken, about 5 minutes or more depending on the water content of the tomatoes. Then, add the salt, remove the pan from the heat, and stir in the shredded chicken.

Pour ½ inch (1.3 centimeters) cooking oil into a skillet just large enough to accommodate the tortillas. Heat the oil until a drop of water sputters immediately. One at a time, using kitchen tongs, dip the tortillas into the beaten egg, drain well, and fry to soften the tortillas and cook the egg, turning once. This should take just a few seconds on each side. The tortillas will be very soft so be careful not to tear them. Drain the fried tortillas on absorbent towels.

To assemble the *tortas,* place one cooked tortilla on each of 4 ovenproof serving plates. Top each tortilla with a little of the chicken/vegetable filling, then sprinkle on some cheese. Add the second and third tortillas and fillings in the same manner so that the third tortilla is topped with the remaining chicken/vegetable filling and cheese. Bake the *tortas* until the cheese is melted and turning golden on the top, about 8 minutes. Serve garnished with shredded lettuce and chopped tomato. Serves 4.

Burritos and Chimichangas

RED CHILE BURRITOS

2 **pounds (900 grams) beef stew meat or lean pork, cut in ½–¾-inch (1.27–1.9-centimeter) cubes**

Water

6 *ancho* **chiles**

3 *japonés* **chiles or** *de árbol* **chiles**

3 **tablespoons (42 milliliters) cider vinegar**

1 **teaspoon (.6 gram) oregano**

1 **teaspoon (2 grams) cumin**

3 **cloves garlic**

1 **teaspoon (6.2 grams) salt**

Although they are enjoyed throughout the north, burritos are most often found in the state of Sonora, and chimichangas, *their fried cousins, are found almost nowhere else. Burritos are made by wrapping a filling of green or red chile, or sometimes* machaca *(dried beef), in a large flour tortilla. Often the chiles are mixed with refried beans and a little cheese. For a really economical meal, just beans and cheese are used.* Chimichangas *are burritos that have been deep-fried, which gives them a crisp, flakey texture resembling a thin pie crust.*

In Sonora, burritos and chimichangas *are made with huge, paper-thin flour tortillas that I have also seen in Baja California but nowhere else in Mexico. In Arizona, across the border from Sonora,* chimichangas *are popular restaurant offerings. There they are usually topped either with an enchilada sauce or a sauce made with guacamole and sour cream, as is used for* flautas *in other areas.*

Cover the beef or pork with water in a heavy skillet and bring to a boil. Reduce the heat and simmer until the meat is tender and all the liquid has evaporated. If you are using beef, you may need to add additional water to achieve the desired tenderness.

Remove the seeds and stems from the chiles and soak them in hot water for 10 minutes. Remove the chiles to a blender jar, adding ½ cup (110 milliliters) of the "chile water." Add the remaining ingredients to the blender and blend for 1 minute.

When the meat is tender and all the liquid has evaporated, add the blended sauce and simmer for 10 minutes, stirring often over low heat.

Make 8 to 10 large tortillas, about 10 inches (25.4 centimeters) in diameter. Spoon ½ cup (110 milliliters) chile on each one and fold as shown in the diagram on page 223. If leftover meat is used for the filling, it is often shredded or finely chopped, fried in lard or cooking oil until crisp, and then mixed with a favorite sauce before being wrapped in the tortillas.

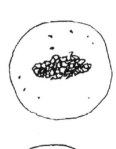

To make *chimichangas,* deep-fry the completed burritos until brown and crispy. A good way to do this is to "sandwich" the burrito between two fryer baskets to prevent it from unwrapping during cooking. Serves 4.

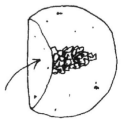

NOTE: *Machaca* Burritos are also made without the sauce. For this simpler version, minced onions, tomatoes, and peeled, seeded green chiles are fried in lard or oil until soft. The dried beef is then added and fried until crisp before being used to fill the burrito or *chimichanga.*

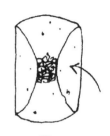

GREEN CHILE BURRITOS

These are burritos filled with Green Chile I (p. 224) or Green Chile II (p. 225). These are perhaps the best of all the burrito fillings, especially if you use the charbroiled version (Green Chile II). Use these filling for burritos or *chimichangas* as made in the preceding recipes.

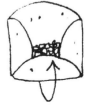

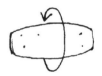

Green Chile I

2 pounds (900 grams) lean meat, either chile (coarse) grind or cut into small pieces
1 medium onion, chopped
8 green chiles, peeled, seeded, and chopped
2 tablespoons (28 milliliters) cooking oil
4 cloves garlic
½ teaspoon cumin, whole
1 teaspoon (.6 gram) oregano, whole
½ teaspoon salt, or to taste
1 tablespoon (9.5 grams) flour
Water

In a heavy pot, cook the meat, onion, and chiles in the oil over medium-high heat until the meat is browned. Add enough water to cover.

Grind together the garlic, cumin, and oregano in a *molcajete* or mortar and pestle and add to the chile. Add the salt and simmer the chile, covered, until the meat is tender, about 1¾ hours. Add additional water if necessary.

Mix the flour with 3 tablespoons (42 milliliters) water and add this to the pot, stirring rapidly. Continue to cook, uncovered, until the chile is thickened. Serve in burritos, *chimichangas*, or tacos, or over rice garnished with grated cheese. Serves 4.

Green Chile II

This longer process for preparing chile, using about the same ingredients as for Green Chile I (p. 224), achieves superior results.

A day or two ahead, broil the meat (use chuck, about ½ to ¾ inch [1.27 to 1.9 centimeters] thick) very slowly over mesquite until well done. (I usually use coals after I have cooked something else.) Allow the meat to cool and refrigerate until ready to cook.

Cut the meat into small pieces; then whirl it a few times in a food processor, using a steel blade, until the pieces are no more than ¼ inch (.64 centimeter) in size.

Soften the onion and chiles, in 1 tablespoon (15 milliliters) oil over moderate heat. Add the meat and proceed as in the recipe for Green Chile I, but use a little less water and cook for only 30 to 45 minutes.

Both recipes are better if prepared a day ahead and refrigerated overnight, which allows them to thicken and absorb flavors. Serves 4.

Machaca Burritos

This excellent filling may be used for burritos or chimichangas, *and is also good with tacos.*

Tear the chiles in small pieces and cover them with hot water for 20 minutes. Place the chiles in the jar of a blender and add the garlic, cumin, oregano, salt, and ½ cup (110 milliliters) water. Blend for 1 minute. Add 1 more cup (225 milliliters) of water and blend for 30 seconds.

Heat the lard or oil over medium-low heat and add a cup of sauce. Cook, stirring constantly, for 3 minutes.

Add the *Machaca* and cook for 2 minutes, stirring constantly. The mixture should be just moist but not soupy. If it is too thin, continue cooking until the proper consistency is reached. If it is too dry, add more sauce. Fill and roll the burritos as on p. 222 and serve, or deep-fry and serve as *chimichangas*. Serves 4.

2 *ancho* chiles, seeded
   and deveined
2 cloves garlic
¼ teaspoon cumin
½ teaspoon oregano
¼ teaspoon salt
   Water
2 tablespoons (30
   grams) lard or
   peanut oil (28
   milliliters)
2½ cups (235 grams)
   Machaca (p. 140)

Tamales

Tamales are made by combining corn masa, *lard, water or broth, and spices into a dough. This is placed on a softened corn husk, wrapped around a filling, tied, and steamed. While, as with other recipes in this book, shortening may be substituted for lard, the reader is advised that it will produce less successful results for tamales since the flavor of lard is very important. Tamales come in all sizes, shapes, and types. They range from more than a foot long (31 centimeters) to finger size. They usually are wrapped in corn husks, but in southern Mexico, particularly in the state of Chiapas, they are often wrapped in banana leaves.*

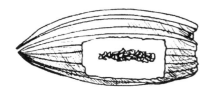

The masa *for tamales, like that for corn tortillas, is made by soaking and cooking dried corn in water to which a small amount of dolomitic lime has been added to soften it and loosen the skin on the kernels. It is then ground to a paste and combined with broth or water, whipped lard, and spices. In the south great care is taken to remove all the skin from the corn kernels, which produces a lovely white tamale with a wonderful, spongy texture. This is often done in the north as well, but there the preparation is a little more casual, and the tamales often have a darker color, similar to those found in this country. Using packaged Masa Harina provides a reasonably good alternative to the longer soaking and grinding method.*

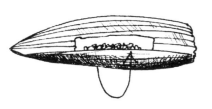

Tamales come in two basic varieties. Entrée or snack tamales are made with meat or cheese and vegetable fillings; dessert tamales use sweet fruit fillings.

The preparation of tamales is not something to be undertaken lightly. In Mexico the whole family becomes involved in the process, often at Christmas time, when they are traditionally made and served. While it is time-consuming, it can be a lot of fun to do, particularly on a rainy weekend day. Once you get the hang of it, it goes fairly quickly, as the fillings can be prepared the night before.

Tamales are often served several days (or months, if they have been frozen) after being cooked. Most Mexican cooks reheat tamales by steaming them, but for a much shorter period than was required during the initial cooking process. However, in the north of Mexico they are often reheated in a skillet over low heat, or placed on a grill far enough from the coals to keep them from burning. These methods of reheating, doubtless improvised on long trail drives, produce a wonderful smoky flavor and crunchy texture.

Tamales de chile colorado

RED CHILE TAMALES

This recipe uses pork, but tamales also are made with beef, chicken, or turkey. A particularly delicious choice is venison.

Place the pork in a heavy pot, cover with water, and simmer, covered, for 1 hour, or until the pork is tender enough to be shredded. Remove the pork from the pot, reserving the pork broth. When the pork is cool enough, shred it by hand, or whirl it a few times in a food processor, using a steel blade.

While the pork is cooling, remove the seeds and stems from the chiles, place them in a small bowl, and cover them with boiling water. Let the chiles soak for 20 minutes.

Toast the cumin and garlic in a small ungreased skillet until the contents are fragrant. Avoid burning. Reserve the chile water and, using a *molcajete* or mortar and pestle, grind the chiles, garlic, cumin, salt, and pepper into a paste. Mix the paste thoroughly with the shredded pork and refrigerate overnight to season.

Stir the broth and chile water gradually into the Masa Harina to prevent lumping. Add the remaining ingredients except the corn husks. The mixture should have the consistency of a paste, spreadable but not runny. Add more liquid or *masa* as required to adjust the texture.

Soak the corn husks for 1 hour in hot water, or until they are pliable. If corn husks are not available, substitute a piece of white cotton cloth, as from a sheet, about 7 by 5 inches (17.8 by 12.7 centimeters).

To assemble the tamales, lay a husk out flat on the work surface and cover a portion of it with the *masa*. Next, place a heaping tablespoon (14 grams) of the filling in the middle of the *masa* and roll the tamale as shown in the diagram on page 226. Tie the ends with short lengths of string or, if the husk is long enough, fold the ends over to seal in the filling, and place in a steamer.

When all the tamales have been rolled, bring the water in the steamer to a boil, cover, and steam the tamales for 1½ to 2 hours, or until they no longer stick to the husks when unrolled.

Tamales keep well and can be refrigerated or frozen and then reheated very successfully. Serves 4.

FILLING

1 **pound (450 grams) lean pork, chopped or whole**

4 *ancho* **chiles, stems and seeds removed**

1 **teaspoon (2 grams) cumin**

4 **cloves garlic, minced**

1 **teaspoon (6.2 grams) salt**

½ **teaspoon pepper**

MASA

1 **pound (450 grams) Masa Harina**

1½ **cups (240 milliliters) pork broth**

½ **cup (110 milliliters) chile soaking water**

1 **cup (225 milliliters) melted lard**

½ **teaspoon mild chile powder**

2 **teaspoons (5 grams) paprika**

1½ **teaspoons (9.3 grams) salt**

1 **pound (450 grams) dried corn husks**

Tamales de elote verde

GREEN CORN TAMALES

❖❖❖❖❖

2 cups (274 grams)
    frozen corn
1 pound (450 grams)
    Masa Harina
1 cup (225 milliliters)
    melted lard
1⅓ cups (308 milliliters)
    hot water
4 green or *poblano*
    chiles, peeled,
    seeded, and cut in
    thin strips
8 ounces (225 grams)
    Monterey Jack
    cheese
    Corn husks, soaked
    for at least 1 hour

This dish is usually made completely with specially ground fresh white corn, of just the right age and starch content. As this is often difficult to duplicate, I have modified the recipe to include a combination of corn and Masa Harina.

Thaw the corn and mash it. The easiest way to do this is to give it a few whirls in a food processor fitted with a steel blade. Mix the corn into the Masa Harina and add the lard. Next, add the water to make a paste that is easy to spread but not liquid or runny.

Lay a corn husk out flat on your work surface and cover the lower right ⅓ with *masa* about ⅛ to ¼ inch (.32 to .64 centimeter) thick. Put a strip of chile down the center and add a strip of cheese, about ⅛ inch thick by ¼ inch (.32 by .64 centimeter) wide, on top of the chile. Roll the tamale and tie the ends with string or fold them over to seal in the filling.

Steam the tamales for 1½ hours, or until they no longer stick to the husks when unrolled.

NOTE: The substitution of shortening for lard is not recommended for tamales. Serves 4.

Quesadillas

Quesadillas *make a delicious snack or appetizer and are very easy to prepare. They are made either with flour or corn tortillas but most often with flour in the north, and with the rich, stringy* queso de Chihuahua *made by the Mennonites. A good mozzarella cheese may be substituted.*

8 **flour tortillas or corn tortillas, or 4 of each**
2²/₃ **cups (290 grams) mozzarella cheese, grated**

Using an ungreased *comal* or heavy skillet, heat the tortillas, 1 or 2 at a time, on one side over medium heat. Turn the tortillas and sprinkle about ⅓ cup (34 grams) cheese on each one.

Continue to heat the tortillas until the cheese begins to melt. Then fold them (so they resemble tacos) and continue cooking on one side and then the other, until the cheese is melted and the tortillas begin to get crisp on the outside.

Remove the cooked *Quesadillas* to a warming oven, prepare the rest in the same way, and serve with your favorite sauce. Serves 4.

Quesadillas de flor de calabaza

SQUASH BLOSSOM QUESADILLAS

2½ tablespoons (37 grams) butter

¼ cup (36 grams) onions, minced

16 squash blossoms

¼ cup (56 milliliters) whipping cream

Salt, to taste

8 thin flour tortillas

¼ cup (56 milliliters) melted butter

8 slices of *asadero* cheese, each a little smaller than ½ a tortilla, or use ½ mozzarella and ½ Monterey Jack cheese

Guacamole (p. 83)

This is one of the most delicious and elegant northern Mexican recipes. Squash blossoms are now available in gourmet markets, but since they are nearly always a bit over-the-hill it is preferable to grow your own. The flowers produced by zucchini are perfect.

Melt the butter in a skillet over medium heat. Add the onions and the squash blossoms and stir the ingredients together. Cook for 1 minute, turning frequently. Stir in the cream and cook just until it begins to thicken. Add salt, to taste, and remove the pan from the heat.

Brush one side of a tortilla with butter and place (buttered side down) on a *comal* or griddle over medium to low heat. Place a slice of cheese on one side of the tortilla and then put 2 blossoms on it. Fold the tortilla in half and cook for 1 or 2 minutes, turning once, until the cheese is melted and the outside of the *quesadilla* is golden. Prepare the remaining *quesadillas* in the same fashion and serve with the Guacamole. Serves 8 as an appetizer or 4 as a light meal.

Flautas y Taquitos

FLUTES AND LITTLE TACOS

Flautas, *and their smaller cousins* taquitos, *are very popular snacks in northern Mexico and are frequently offered as main courses in Mexican-American restaurants.* Flautas *look like the flutes indicated by their name. They are made by tightly rolling 1 large or 2 small corn tortillas around a shredded meat filling, securing with a toothpick, and frying in oil.* Taquitos *are made in the same way, except that a small, very thin tortilla is used.*

In Mexico, flautas *and* taquitos *are sold by street vendors, often cooked in advance and arranged in crispy piles on the serving counters next to bowls of sauce and condiments. In this country, they are usually served 2 or 3 to an order, often covered with a sauce made from guacamole and sour cream.*

Heat the oil to 350 to 375 degrees F (177 to 190 degrees C). Dip the tortillas in the heated oil for just a few seconds each to soften them. Remove to paper towels to drain.

To make the sauce, mash the avocados with the other sauce ingredients and beat to a creamy consistency.

Put approximately 3 tablespoons (42 grams) filling on each large tortilla and roll as tightly as possible, securing in the center with a toothpick as shown in the diagram. If using small tortillas, arrange them in overlapping fashion so that the top of the lower one is in the center of the upper one.

To cook, place 2 or 3 at a time in the hot oil with tongs and fry until crispy, about 1 minute.

Drain on paper towels and serve covered with the sauce, or serve the sauce on the side. Serves 4.

Oil for deep-frying
12 large or 24 small corn
   tortillas
2½ cups (368 grams)
   shredded chicken,
   beef, pork, or turkey
   filling (p. 194)
   Toothpicks

SAUCE
2 medium avocados
2 teaspoons (8 grams)
   pickled *jalapeños*,
   chopped
1 tablespoon (15
   milliliters) liquid
   from the *jalapeño*
   jar
½ cup (113 grams) sour
   cream

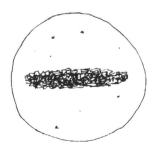
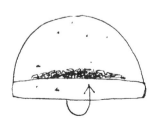

Flautas del norte

NORTHERN FLAUTAS

❖❖❖❖❖

- 2 tablespoons (30 grams) lard or olive oil (28 milliliters)
- ¾ cup (96 grams) onions, minced
- ¾ pound (340 grams) lean pork, finely ground
- ⅔ pound (300 grams) tomatoes, broiled and blended
- 1½ ounces (42 grams) raisins
- ⅓ cup (30 grams) blanched and slivered almonds
- ⅛ teaspoon ground cloves
- ⅛ teaspoon ground cinnamon
- ½ teaspoon salt
- ¼ teaspoon ground black pepper
- 12 corn or flour tortillas or a combination of both
  Cooking oil for frying

These flautas *utilize a filling that is similar to that used in some* chiles rellenos *and in Puebla's famous* Chiles en nogada. *Found most often in Nuevo León and Coahuila where they are often accompanied by french fries and guacamole,* Flautas del norte *can be made with either flour or corn tortillas, which produce very different results. Flour tortillas create the effect of a small* chimichanga, *and corn tortillas produce a more traditional result. As with other types of* flautas, *corn tortillas can be softened to permit them to be tightly rolled on a hot* comal *or wrapped in a towel in a microwave oven if they are fresh. If not, they must first be dipped in hot oil to keep them from cracking when they are rolled. However, because they contain fat, flour tortillas do not present this problem and should never be softened in oil.*

Heat a skillet over medium heat, add the oil, and sauté the onions until just browned. Add the pork and continue to cook, stirring constantly, until the meat is broken into bits and cooked through. Add the remaining ingredients except the tortillas and cook until the mixture is as dry as possible. This elimination of moisture is important because excess liquid will cause the oil to spatter dangerously when the *flautas* are fried. As the mixture thickens you will have to turn the heat to very low to keep it from scorching.

When the filling has cooled, heat about ¾ inch (1.9 centimeters) of oil in a skillet just big enough to hold 2 to 3 *flautas* until a small drop of water spatters instantly but not so hot that it smokes.

Meanwhile, roll the *flautas*. Soften the tortillas as described above. Place 2 to 2½ tablespoons (28 to 35 grams) on each tortilla, roll it as tightly as possible, and secure it with a toothpick.

Fry the *flautas* in the oil, 2 or 3 at a time, turning once or twice until they are just golden brown and crisp. Using kitchen tongs, drain any excess oil from each end of the *flautas* and place them on absorbent towels. Serve the *flautas* with Guacamole (p. 83) and french fries. Makes 12.

Tortilla azteca

AZTEC "TORTILLA"

This breakfast or brunch dish is yet another variation on the Torta azteca, *or stacked enchilada, theme. It is easy to prepare, once you have all the ingredients, and delicious. You can make these in one large baking dish or on individual ovenproof serving plates. (The directions call for the use of individual plates.)*

Heat about ¾ inch (1.9 centimeters) of cooking oil in a small skillet until a drop of water sputters. Using kitchen tongs, immerse the tortillas, 1 at a time, in the oil for a few seconds to soften them; then remove them to drain on paper towels.

Place 1 tortilla on each of 4 ovenproof serving plates and spread a thin layer of Refried Beans on it. Place another tortilla on top of the beans. Top this tortilla with a slice of ham and put another tortilla on top of it. Arrange some shredded chicken on top of this tortilla and place the final tortilla on top of the chicken. Spoon some *Tomatillo* Sauce on top of the stack, sprinkle some cheese on top of it, and garnish with some avocado slices and about 2 tablespoons (28 milliliters) cream. Bake for 10 minutes or until they are heated through and the cheese has melted. Serves 4.

Cooking oil
16 corn tortillas
⅔ cup (166 grams) **Refried Beans (p. 107)**
4 **thin slices of ham**
1½ cups (221 grams) **shredded chicken breast**
2 cups (450 milliliters) *Tomatillo* Sauce (p. 46)
1 cup (109 grams) *asadero* cheese, grated; or substitute Monterey Jack cheese
1 avocado, seeded, peeled, and sliced
½ cup (110 milliliters) heavy cream; or substitute sour cream

Empanadas

TURNOVERS

Empanadas *are a favorite in the north. I know of one restaurant in Piedras Negras, across from Eagle Pass, Texas, that serves nothing else.*

Empanadas *are turnovers filled with meats and served as appetizers or entrées. They also can be filled with fruits or pumpkin pie filling and served for dessert. The following recipe is for an appetizer or entrée* empanada. *To prepare dessert* empanadas, *see the recipe for* Coyotas *(p. 259), which are similar, or use this recipe and fill with any combination of fruits and nuts or pie fillings.*

DOUGH

This dough is easy to make in a food processor, using a steel blade. Put the dry ingredients in the bowl and whirl a few times. Add the shortening, lard, and butter. Process until well mixed with the flour, when a grainy consistency is achieved. Then, with the motor still running, add the eggs and just enough water to allow the dough to bind. The texture and consistency should be the same as for pie dough. If you do not have a food processor, proceed as above but cut and mix in the shortening by hand. Then add the liquids and knead for a few minutes.

Allow the dough to chill in the refrigerator for at least ½ hour. To form the *Empanadas,* cut the dough into 6 pieces and shape them into balls. Roll the balls into circles of 6 to 7 inches (15.2 to 17.8 centimeters) in diameter. Place about 3 to 4 tablespoons (42 to 56 grams) of the filling in the center of each circle, moisten the edges, fold over, and seal.

Prick the tops of the *Empanadas* to allow steam to escape. Bake at 350 degrees F (177 degrees C) for 25 minutes, or until lightly browned.

FILLING

Heat a medium-sized frying pan over moderate heat. Sauté the onion in just enough oil to coat the bottom of the pan, for 5 minutes or until soft but not browned. Add the garlic and cook for 1 minute.

DOUGH

- 2 cups (280 grams) all-purpose flour
- ½ teaspoon salt
- 1 teaspoon (3.3 grams) baking powder
- ½ cup (100 grams) shortening
- 1 tablespoon (15 grams) lard or vegetable shortening
- 1 tablespoon (15 grams) butter
- 2 eggs, beaten
  Water

FILLING

Cooking oil
- ½ cup (56 grams) onion, minced
- 2 cloves garlic, minced
- 8 ounces (225 grams) lean ground beef
- 1 teaspoon (2.3 grams) mild chile powder
- 1 teaspoon (3.3 grams) pepper
- 1 teaspoon (6.2 grams) salt
- 1 cup (131 grams) raisins
- 1 cup (92 grams) almonds, blanched and slivered

Add the ground beef in small pieces, breaking it up with a spoon to mix it well with the onion and garlic. Cook until well browned. Add the chile powder, pepper, and salt; turn the heat very low and cover. Simmer for 10 minutes.

Add the raisins and almonds and continue to simmer, covered, for an additional 5 minutes.

Allow the filling to cool before making the *Empanadas.* Makes 6.

Tostadas norteñas

OPEN-FACED CRISP TORTILLAS WITH TOPPING

A tostada *is usually a flat, crisp-fried tortilla topped with a ground meat* picadillo *(filling), shredded lettuce, tomato, and grated cheddar cheese; it is one of the mainstays of Mexican-American cooking.* Tostadas *are found less often in Mexico than in the United States, but this one from Sonora is one of the best I have ever eaten and bears no resemblance to those on this side of the border.*

Remove the stems, seeds, and veins from the chiles, break them into small pieces, and place them in a bowl. Pour boiling water over the chiles and soak them for 20 minutes. Drain the chiles and place them in a *molcajete* or mortar and pestle with the cumin. Grind the chiles and cumin into a paste and reserve.

Heat the oil in a deep fryer to 265 degrees F (128 degrees C) and fry the tortillas until they are crisp and golden, keeping them as flat as possible. Drain and reserve.

Separately, cook the potatoes and carrots in boiling water until they are just tender and reserve.

Heat the 3 tablespoons (42 milliliters) oil in a skillet over medium heat. Add the *chorizo* and fry it until it begins to brown. Add the chile paste and stir until it is well mixed into the oil and *chorizo.* Add the reserved potatoes and carrots and cook until heated through and beginning to brown. Add the salt and remove the skillet from the heat. Top each crisp tortilla with about ⅓ cup (83 grams) of the mixture and sprinkle on a couple tablespoons (about 15 grams) of the grated cheese. Serves 4.

4 *pasilla* chiles
¼ teaspoon cumin
8 5½-inch (14-centimeter) corn tortillas
Oil for deep-frying
2 cups (340 grams) white boiling potatoes, peeled and cut into ¼–⅓-inch (.64–.85-centimeter) pieces
1⅓ cups (171 grams) carrots, peeled and cut into ¼–⅓-inch (.64–.85-centimeter) pieces
3 tablespoons (42 milliliters) cooking oil
½ cup (112 grams) *chorizo* (preferably homemade, p. 154)
½ teaspoon salt
1 cup (109 grams) *queso panela;* or substitute ½ cup (54.5 grams) grated feta cheese mixed with ½ cup (54.5 grams) Monterey Jack cheese

2 cups (256 grams)
   Masa Harina
1½ cups (240 milliliters)
   water
3 cups (759 grams)
   Refried Beans
   (p. 107)
3 cups (327 grams)
   queso panela,
   grated; or substitute
   Monterey Jack
   cheese
2 cups (300 grams)
   Chilorio (p. 152),
   Mochomos (p. 141),
   or another filling
   (optional)
2 avocados, seeded and
   thinly sliced

Memelas

Memelas, *a regional specialty of Oaxaca, are a sort of unfried* tostada, *in that corn* masa *is pressed into an oblong shape a little thicker than for tortillas, baked on a griddle, and/or fried, then topped with various fillings and served open-faced. At their simplest* Memelas *are topped with just beans and cheese. This delicious northern version from Saltillo is easy to make using Masa Harina and makes a terrific snack or light meal.*

Place the Masa Harina in a bowl and slowly mix in the water until you have a workable dough. Knead the dough slightly and divide it into 8 pieces of roughly 2½ ounces (84 grams) each. Instead of forming each piece into a ball as you would to make tortillas, roll each one into a cylinder about 3½ inches (8.9 centimeters) long. This will give you the correct oblong shape when you press them. Place a piece of plastic wrap or plastic garbage bag on the bottom of a tortilla press. Put one of the dough cylinders on the plastic just back from the center of the press toward the hinge. Then place another piece of plastic on top of the dough and press it into an oblong measuring approximately 5 inches by 6 inches (12.7 by 15.2 centimeters).

Cook the dough as you would tortillas on a *comal* or griddle over medium heat. As the tortillas are cooked through, remove them from the griddle and cover them with a towel. To prepare the *Memelas* spread some Refried Beans on one side of each tortilla, sprinkle on some cheese and other filling, if used, plus the avocado, and replace them on the hot griddle until the cheese begins to melt. Serves 4 for a light meal or 8 as an appetizer.

Chiles anchos rellenos

STUFFED ANCHO CHILES

This delicious recipe illustrates another variation on the chiles rellenos *theme. This time the pepper used is the* ancho, *which is usually used for making sauces. The* ancho *is the* poblano *(the chile most often used in* chiles rellenos*) in its dried form. This special dish makes a terrific luncheon or light supper, or it can be used as a first course.*

Combine the water, vinegar, thyme, garlic, salt, and bay leaves in a large pot, bring to a boil, and simmer for 10 minutes. Place the chiles in a bowl, pour the hot water mixture over them, and allow them to soak for 20 to 30 minutes or until they are very soft. Remove the chiles and replace the soaking liquid in the pot. When the chiles are cool enough to handle, cut a slit down one side of each and carefully remove as many of the seeds as possible. Reserve the seeded chiles.

Bring the liquid in which the chiles were soaked to a boil, add the potatoes, and simmer until they are just tender. Remove the potatoes to a strainer and simmer the carrots until they are just tender; then add them to the strainer. Return the liquid to a boil and submerge the zucchini for 15 seconds and add it to the strainer.

Heat a large skillet over medium heat, add the oil, and sauté the onions until they are soft. Add the *chorizo* and continue cooking until it is golden brown. Turn the heat to medium high, add the strained vegetables, and cook, turning constantly, for about 3 minutes. Place the contents of the skillet in a large bowl and allow to cool nearly to room temperature.

Stir all but ½ cup (55 grams) of the cheese into the vegetable/*chorizo* mixture, then use it to fill each of the reserved chiles. (There should be quite a bit of stuffing left over.) Place the chiles on serving plates, spoon the remaining filling around them, and garnish with the remaining ½ cup (55 grams) cheese. Place the plates in the oven and bake until the cheese is melted and the chiles heated through, about 7 minutes. Alternately, the dish may be heated in a microwave. Serves 4.

1 **quart (900 milliliters) water**
¼ **cup (56 milliliters) white vinegar**
½ **tablespoon (.9 gram) thyme**
2 **cloves garlic, peeled**
½ **tablespoon (9.3 grams) salt**
2 **bay leaves**
4 **large (4–5 inches [10–12.7 centimeters]) or 8 small (about 2½ inches [6.4 centimeters]) *ancho* chiles**
3 **cups (510 grams) potatoes, cut into ¼-inch (.64-centimeter) pieces**
1 **cup (113 grams) carrots, cut into ¼-inch (.64-centimeter) pieces**
1½ **cups (212 grams) zucchini, cut into ¼-inch (.64-centimeter) pieces**
1 **tablespoon (15 milliliters) olive oil**
1 **cup (142.7 grams) onions, minced**
1 **cup (225 grams) *chorizo***
1⅓ **cups (136 grams) *queso panela;* or substitute ⅔ cup (68 grams) feta cheese and ⅔ cup (68 grams) mozzarella cheese**

Chiles rellenos con frijoles maneados

CHILES STUFFED WITH BEANS AND CHEESE

4 medium to large
poblano chiles,
skinned
½ recipe *Frijoles
maneados* (p. 108)

Some dishes that are really quite interesting do not sound much like it in the translation, and this is one of those. This recipe has a fresh, natural quality and is especially good for a light lunch or supper. Unlike the more common chiles rellenos, *these are not fried. So the dish can be quite light and even low in fat if one of the low-fat alternatives for making the beans (see p. 274) is combined with a low- or nonfat cheese.*

The best way to skin the chiles for this dish is to hold them over an open flame, preferably one produced by burning mesquite because of the flavor it imparts, until the skin is thoroughly charred. Otherwise use a long fork or hinged barbecue basket to hold the chiles over a gas or propane burner. If you have no gas appliances, deep-fry the chiles until the skins blister. No matter how you blister the skins, place the hot chiles in a plastic bag and enclose them so they will "sweat" for about 20 minutes.

Cut a slit on the bottom side of each chile and carefully remove the seeds. This can be done a day or so in advance.

Prepare the *Frijoles maneados* and bring the chiles to room temperature if they have been refrigerated.

Stuff the chiles with the bean and cheese mixture and serve with rice and squash for a complete meal or with a salad or pickled vegetables for a light lunch or supper. Another interesting accompaniment is Stuffed Jalapeños (p. 88)—deep-fried *jalapeño* chiles stuffed with cheese. Serves 4.

Chiles rellenos con arroz verde

STUFFED CHILES WITH GREEN RICE

This is perhaps the most elegant northern Mexican recipe I have found. The roasted chiles are stuffed with cheese and steamed with the rice during its final stage of cooking to produce a beautiful and succulent dish. It is suitable for a formal banquet and easy enough to prepare for dinner at home. This version of chiles rellenos *can also be prepared ahead and heated at the last minute. Another advantage is that, unlike the more common calorie-laden* chiles rellenos, *these are not fried in batter—or fried at all!*

Preheat your oven to 350 degrees F (190 degrees C).

If possible, roast the chiles over mesquite because the flavor will add considerably to the dish. If this is not feasible, use any of the other methods suggested in the section on chiles (see "Basic Ingredients"). After you have removed the skins, cut a slit in the side of each chile and remove the seeds (this is best done under running water), but leave the stems attached. Stuff the chiles with the cheese and reserve them.

Prepare the *Arroz verde* up to the point where it has cooked, covered for the initial 20 minutes, and you have carefully stirred it. At this point you can either place the stuffed chiles in the pot, pushing them slightly into the rice, or arrange the rice in an attractive casserole dish with the chiles. The latter method makes a much more dramatic presentation. In either case, cover the rice and chiles and place them in the preheated oven for 10 to 15 minutes or until the cheese is melted.

In the meantime, prepare the squash blossoms by sautéeing them in a covered skillet with the butter over medium heat for about 3 minutes or until they begin to soften. Remove the top of the skillet, stir in the cream, and continue cooking until it begins to thicken; then add the salt.

To serve, you can either place the rice and chiles on individual serving plates and surround them with the squash blossoms, or you can arrange the squash blossoms in the casserole dish with the chiles and present the entire dish to your guests. Serves 4.

4 large or 8 small *poblano* chiles, roasted and peeled

1 pound (450 grams) *manchego* cheese, grated, or substitute ½ pound (225 grams) gouda, grated, mixed with ½ pound (225 grams) Monterey Jack, grated

1 recipe *Arroz verde* (p. 103)

¼ cup (60 grams) butter

24 squash blossoms

½ cup (110 milliliters) heavy cream or crème fraîche

Salt, to taste

Spaghetti arriero

MULE DRIVER'S PASTA

◈◇◈◇◈◇◈

- 3 tablespoons (42 milliliters) olive oil
- 2 tablespoons (30 grams) butter
- 6 cloves garlic, minced
- 2 green onions, white and green parts minced separately
- 4 *serrano* chiles, seeded and minced
- 1 *ancho* chile, seeded and minced
- ½ teaspoon oregano
- ½ teaspoon thyme
  Heaping ¼ teaspoon salt, or to taste
- ½ teaspoon ground pepper
- ½ cup (30 grams) sun-dried tomatoes, chopped (optional)
- 1 pound (450 grams) spaghetti
- 2 tablespoons (6.2 grams) cilantro, minced
- 2 tablespoons (8 grams) parsley, minced
- ½ cup (23 grams) Parmesan cheese, grated
- ½ cup (54.4 grams) *asadero* cheese, grated; or substitute provolone cheese
- ½ cup (54.4 grams) *panela* cheese, grated; or substitute feta cheese

This dish, which I adapted from one served at Ciudad Juárez's Casa del Sol restaurant is one of the best pasta dishes I have ever had, inside or outside of Italy. While the optional sun-dried tomatoes are not traditional (or even Mexican), they blend so well with the other ingredients, especially the ancho *chiles, that it is worth risking the wrath of traditionalists.*

Place a saucepan over low heat, add the olive oil and butter, and sauté the garlic, the white part of the green onions, and the *serrano* chiles until the garlic is soft but not browned. Remove the pan from the heat and add the *ancho* chile, oregano, thyme, salt, pepper, and sun-dried tomatoes, if used. Allow the contents of the pan to sit for at least 15 minutes.

Bring a large pot of water to a boil, add the spaghetti, and simmer until it is al dente, about 11 or 12 minutes for dried pasta. Pour the spaghetti into a strainer and strain, being careful not to shake off quite all the moisture; then return it to the now empty but still hot pot in which it was cooked. Quickly heat the reserved sauce over the stove, or, better yet, in a microwave and pour it over the spaghetti. Add the cilantro, parsley, and cheeses, toss, and serve with a green salad. Serves 4.

Huevos rancheros

EGGS RANCHERO

While Huevos rancheros *do not fit into any category in this book, they are such a common breakfast or brunch item in northern Mexico that they should be included.*

Huevos rancheros are eggs which are fried, placed on heated corn tortillas, and topped with the *ranchero* sauce for Steak with *Ranchero* Sauce (p. 123). First make the sauce and keep it warm. Next, heat the tortillas (usually 2 per person) on a *comal* or griddle until they have softened and begin to get crispy on the outside. Place them on serving plates.

Fry 1 egg, any style, for each tortilla. When the eggs are cooked, place them on the tortillas. Spoon sauce, to taste, over the eggs. Serve with Refried Beans (p. 107), the traditional accompaniment to this dish.

Machacado

SCRAMBLED EGGS WITH DRIED BEEF

This delicious recipe for a classic northern dish produces fairly small, but very rich, portions that are particularly adequate when served, as they traditionally are, with Refried Beans and flour tortillas.

Heat a skillet over medium heat, add the lard or olive oil, and cook the onion, green onions, chiles, tomatoes, and garlic until they are softened, about 3 to 5 minutes. Add the dried beef and cook 2 minutes more. Stir in the eggs and continue to cook, stirring constantly, until the eggs are done the way you like them. Add salt to taste. Serve the *Machacado* with Refried Beans (p. 107), a tomato-based salsa, and flour tortillas. Serves 4.

3 tablespoons (45 grams) lard or olive oil (42 milliliters)

²/₃ cup (95 grams) onion, minced

2 green onions, minced

2–3 *serrano* chiles, seeded and minced

1 cup (167 grams) tomatoes, minced

2 cloves garlic minced

¹/₃ cup (32 grams) finely chopped dried beef

6 eggs, beaten as for scrambled eggs

Salt, to taste

Huevos con cilantro y cebollas

SCRAMBLED EGGS WITH CILANTRO AND ONIONS

This breakfast or brunch dish allows 2 eggs per portion. If you desire more, simply increase the ingredients proportionately.

In a mixing bowl, beat the eggs with the cilantro until well incorporated. Next, melt the butter in a large skillet over medium heat, add the onions, and fry them for about 30 seconds. Pour in the eggs and cook, stirring nearly constantly, until they are scrambled as you like them. Salt and pepper the eggs and serve with bacon or sausage. Serves 4.

8 eggs

½ cup (30 grams) cilantro, chopped and tightly packed

2 tablespoons (30 grams) butter

6 tablespoons (32.4 grams) green onions, minced

Salt and pepper to taste

Huevos al albañil

MASON'S EGGS

This recipe from Coahuila produces some of the best scrambled eggs I have ever tried. Because chipotle *chiles, which are* jalapeño *chiles that have been smoked and, in this case, canned with* adobo *sauce are extremely hot, add a little at a time to avoid surprising yourself and your guests.*

To make the sauce, simmer the *tomatillos* in enough water to cover them until they are tender, about 5 minutes; then place them in a blender with the onion, vinegar, sugar, *chipotle* chiles, and salt. Blend until the ingredients are puréed and reserve. You should have about 2 cups (450 milliliters) sauce.

Next, place the eggs in a bowl and beat them well. Melt the butter in a large skillet over medium heat and add the eggs. Cook, stirring constantly, until the eggs are nearly set. Then stir 1 cup (225 milliliters) of the sauce into the eggs and continue cooking until the eggs are the consistency you desire. Divide the scrambled eggs among 4 plates, top each portion with a little more of the sauce, and serve. Serves 4.

20 ounces (560 grams) *tomatillos*

½ cup (57 grams) onion, coarsely chopped

1½ tablespoons (21 milliliters) vinegar

1½ tablespoons (6 grams) sugar

1 tablespoon (12 grams) chopped canned *chipotle* chiles with some of the sauce from the can

Heaping ½ teaspoon salt, or to taste

8 eggs

2 tablespoons (30 grams) butter

Gorditas del norte

NORTHERN-STYLE GORDITAS

Gorditas, literally "little fat ones," are favorite evening snacks. They are usually prepared and sold by street vendors and are rarely available in restaurants except by special order.

Making a good gordita *takes some practice. Because* gorditas *are shaped like small, very thick tortillas, the dough must be thoroughly cooked if they are to be light and puffy. If it is not, the result will resemble a half-baked cookie. The critical steps are to use a fairly dry dough, to bake the* gorditas *on a* comal *until they are cooked through, then to fry them in about* 1/3 *inch (.85 centimeter) of oil which is at just the right temperature. Unfortunately, describing things like "the right consistency" and "the right temperature" at which to fry them are difficult to do with precision. Because of this, some trial and error is inevitable, but they are worth the effort.*

2	cups (256 grams) Masa Harina
½	cup plus 2 tablespoons (99 grams) cornstarch
	Approximately 1¾ cups (296 milliliters) water
	Oil for frying
	Filling, such as *Chilorio* (p. 152) or *Mochomos* (p. 141)

Heat a *comal* or griddle over medium heat. Mix the Masa Harina and cornstarch. Stir the water in until you have added just enough to make a dough that sticks together well without crumbling. Roll the dough out until it is ¼ inch(.6 centimeter) thick. You may want to do this in 2 batches. Cut the dough into 3¼-inch (8.3-centimeter) circles with a cookie cutter or glass.

Place the pieces of dough on the *comal* and bake them until they are just cooked through. Adjust the heat so that they are a light golden color at the end of the process.

Meanwhile, place about ⅓ inch (.85 centimeter) of cooking oil in a heavy skillet and heat it over medium heat until a drop of water just sputters. To test the temperature, put in 1 *gordita*. Within 1½ minutes it should begin to puff. After this happens, continue to cook the *gorditas* until they are a dark golden color and well puffed. Using kitchen tongs, remove them from the oil and allow them to drain and cool on paper towels.

To prepare the *Gorditas del norte* for serving, place them flat on a cutting board and slice them about ¾ of the way through so that they can be opened like clam shells. Place 1 or 2 tablespoons (15 or 30 grams) of filling inside each *gordita* and serve. Makes about 10.

Tortas

❖❖❖

Sandwiches

Tortas are one of the undiscovered culinary treasures of Mexico. In the United States we seldom think of Mexico as a sandwich-eating country, but the truth is that they are very popular and Mexican cooks have brought the same creativity to the genre as they have to other aspects of the cuisine. *Tortas* are traditionally served either on *Bolillos*, the bobbin-shaped, French-style rolls (p. 96), or *teleras*, made with a similar dough but oval-shaped with three ridges on top so that they resemble a trilobite. For the following recipes any crusty French roll will do.

Tortas y Sincronizadas

SANDWICHES

Sincronizadas are a sort of fried tortilla sandwich. They are made by placing sliced ham and cheese between two flat corn tortillas. The "sandwich" is then secured with toothpicks and fried in ½ to 1 inch (1.3 to 2.5 centimeters) of oil. They are usually served with guacamole and salsa.

4 *Bolillos* (p. 96) or French-style sandwich rolls, split lengthwise

1 pound (450 grams) *Fajitas*, marinated (or heat already cooked *Fajitas* [p. 120])

4 thick slices bacon

2 tablespoons (28 milliliters) olive oil or cooking oil

2 medium onions, sliced

½ cup (113 grams) mayonnaise

½ cup (116 milliliters) tomato-based salsa

2 tomatoes, sliced thin

4 pickled *jalapeños*, sliced

2 medium avocados, seeded, peeled, and thinly sliced

4 slices *asadero* cheese; or substitute provolone cheese

Tortas de fajitas

FAJITA TORTAS

This is one of the best sandwiches I have ever tried, and it is ideal for leftover Fajitas *(warmed in the oven or a microwave).*

Preheat your oven to 450 degrees F (232 degrees C). To hollow out the rolls, carefully pull as many of the crumbs from the inside of the rolls as you can while still leaving a layer of bread on top of the crust about ½ inch (1.27 centimeters) thick.

Broil the *Fajitas* over slow coals. Cook the bacon over the coals until just crisp. Slice the *Fajitas* thinly and cut the bacon into small pieces.

Heat a skillet over medium heat, add the oil and onions and sauté, stirring often, until the onions are golden. Reserve the cooked onions.

When the above preparations have been completed, place the hollowed-out rolls on a baking sheet and bake in the preheated oven for 2 minutes. Remove the rolls and spread each side with mayonnaise. Spoon some salsa over the bottom half of each roll and place some sliced tomato on top. Add some of the sliced *jalapeños*, the sliced avocados, some sliced *Fajitas*, the bacon, the cheese, and the fried onion. Place the top of each roll over the ingredients and bake the finished *tortas* for 2 to 3 minutes or until the cheese is melted. Serves 4.

Molletes

CHEESE AND BEAN SANDWICHES

Molletes *are probably the simplest of the* tortas *served in northern Mexico. They consist of sliced* Bolillos *covered with a layer of Refried Beans and melted* asadero *cheese. Most often eaten at breakfast, these* tortas *are usually served open-faced accompanied by salsa.*

Toast the *Bolillos* on the cut side until they are crisp but not browned. Spread on a layer of Refried Beans, top with some cheese, and place them under the broiler until the cheese is just melted. Serves 4 for breakfast or a snack.

4 **_Bolillos_ (p. 96) or small French-style sandwich rolls, cut in half lengthwise**

1 **cup (253 grams) Refried (pinto) Beans (p. 107)**

1 **cup (109 grams) _asadero_ cheese, grated; or substitute mozzarella cheese**

Torta especial

SPECIAL SANDWICH

❖◈◈◈◈❖

This sandwich, which I found in Monterrey, is one of the most interesting combinations of all those I have tried.

4 French-style
   sandwich rolls
   Mayonnaise

½ cup (127 grams)
   Refried (pinto)
   Beans (p. 107), fried
   with 2 slices bacon

¼ cup (56 milliliters)
   heavy cream

2 large pickled *jalapeño*
   chiles, seeded and
   minced

4 thin slices of tomato

10 ounces (280 grams)
   roasted pork
   (preferably roasted
   over mesquite),
   thinly sliced

4 thin slices ham

4 ounces (112 grams)
   queso fresco; or
   substitute Monterey
   Jack cheese, thinly
   sliced or grated

1 avocado, seeded,
   skinned, and cut
   into thin slices
   Tomato-based salsa

Preheat your oven to 450 degrees F (230 degrees C). Split the rolls, remove some of the crumbs from each side to form hollows, place them on a baking sheet, toast them for 2 minutes, then remove them from the oven.

On the bottom slice of each roll, spread some mayonnaise, then some of the pinto bean/bacon mixture. Next, spoon a tablespoon (15 milliliters) of the cream over the beans; then add the chiles, tomato, roast pork, ham, and cheese in that order.

Replace the topped tolls in the oven and bake them until the cheese begins to melt, about 1 minute; then remove them. Place slices of avocado on top of the cheese and spoon some salsa on the top part of each roll to complete the sandwiches. Serves 4.

Sincronizadas

TORTILLA SANDWICHES

Sincronizadas are made by placing sliced ham and cheese between 2 tortillas. The "sandwich" is then fried in oil and often served with guacamole and salsa.

Sprinkle half the cheese, equally, on each of 8 tortillas. Place a piece of ham on each tortilla, sprinkle on the remaining cheese, and top with the remaining tortillas. Pin each "sandwich" together with 2 toothpicks.

    Meanwhile, heat about ½ inch (1.3 centimeters) oil in a skillet until a drop of water sputters instantly. Fry the *Sincronizadas,* 1 or 2 at a time, turning once, until the tortillas are just semicrisp. They should not be crisp like tortilla chips, but just chewy. Serve the *Sincronizadas* with Guacamole (p. 83) and salsa for breakfast, a light lunch, or a snack. Makes 8.

16 **corn tortillas**
12 **ounces (336 grams)**
      ***asadero* cheese; or**
      substitute
      mozzarella cheese
 8 **slices ham**
     Toothpicks
     Cooking oil

Desserts & Sweets

❖❖❖

*Postres y
Dulces*

Dessert in northern Mexico usually consists of a small portion of flan, or some candy or fruit. Occasionally, sweet or dessert tamales are served. The recipes included here are both typical and tasty.

Flan

CARAMEL CUSTARD

◈◈◈◈◈

CARAMEL SAUCE
⅔ cup (130 grams) sugar
¼ cup (56.3 milliliters) water

CUSTARD
4 eggs and 2 additional yolks
½ cup (100 grams) sugar
2 cups (450 milliliters) heavy or whipping cream
½ teaspoon vanilla

Flan is probably the most popular dessert in Mexico. While this recipe is very good when made with factory-raised supermarket eggs, it is exquisite when eggs from chickens on natural feed are used.

Melt the sugar in a heavy medium-sized skillet over moderate heat. Then add the water a little at a time, stirring constantly. Use caution, as the water will spatter when it hits the sugar. Cook the mixture for a few minutes until it is a deep caramel color. Pour the mixture into a Flan pan, or a pie or loaf pan, and swirl to coat the pan until it begins to set, about 2 minutes.

To make the Flan, beat the eggs and sugar until well combined. Meanwhile, heat the cream until it is hot but not quite boiling. Allow it to cool for a few minutes; then beat it into the eggs and sugar, adding just a little at a time. Also stir in the vanilla at this time.

Pour the Flan mixture into the caramelized pan and place it in a larger pan filled with enough warm water to come halfway up the side. Place the 2 pans in an oven preheated to 350 degrees F (177 degrees C).

Bake the Flan for 45 minutes or until the custard is set, lightly browned, and a knife, when inserted, comes away clean. Remove from the oven and allow to cool. Refrigerate for at least 4 hours, or overnight.

To unmold, loosen the custard by passing a knife around the edges of the pan. Then invert it onto a serving plate. Serves 4.

Budín de leche o Cajeta o Leche quemada

MILK PUDDING OR BURNED MILK

Cajeta, *or* Leche quemada, *literally "burned milk," is sold in jars throughout Mexico. It consists of milk that has been mixed with sugar and cooked into a brown paste. It is delicious, but I prefer its cousin, Milk Pudding, which is the same milk and sugar mixture that is not cooked as long. The texture is smoother, and I also prefer the flavor. Both variations make a simple but rich dessert that should be served in very small portions.*

Mix the milk and sugar in a medium-sized pot, bring to a boil over medium-high heat, then turn the heat very low. The mixture should just barely simmer.

For *Budín de leche*, cook, uncovered, stirring often until it has the consistency of light syrup and is still white. For *Leche quemada*, continue to cook until medium brown. The milk usually begins to brown and develop a grainy texture after it has simmered for between 1 and 1½ hours. If the pudding begins to brown, remove the pot from the heat and place it in a larger one filled with cold water to stop the cooking process.

For both, add the vanilla and pecans and serve in demitasse or other very small cups.

NOTE: In Mexico this dessert is usually made with goat's milk, but cow's milk is an adequate substitute. Serves 4.

3 **cups (675 milliliters) milk**
1½ **cups (300 grams) sugar**
¼ **teaspoon vanilla**
¼ **cup (29 grams) pecans, diced**

Cajeta rápida

◈◈◈◈◈◈

QUICK CAJETA OR LECHE QUEMADA

1 14-ounce (396-gram)
  can sweetened
  condensed milk
¼ teaspoon vanilla

Cajeta is milk that has been mixed with sugar and cooked into a brown paste. This recipe uses sweetened condensed milk, which has already been partially reduced, allowing you to prepare this dessert in very little time.

Place the milk and vanilla in a saucepan and bring to barely a simmer very slowly. You must be very careful since the milk will easily scorch and ruin the dish. Cook the milk at a simmer until it becomes a golden brown and thickens into a paste, about 25 to 30 minutes. Serves 4.

Capirotada

◈◈◈◈◈◈

BREAD PUDDING

12 slices French bread
⅓ cup (83 milliliters)
  butter, melted
1½ cups (324 grams)
  brown sugar
4 cups (900 milliliters)
  water
1 stick cinnamon
5 cloves
1 cup (131 grams) raisins
½ pound (225 grams)
  Monterey Jack
  cheese, grated
⅔ cup (76 grams)
  pecans, chopped
¾ cup (170 grams) sour
  cream

This is primarily a Lenten and Easter dish in Mexico. It is eaten hot, but is also good cold the next day.

Brush the bread slices with melted butter. Bake them at 350 degrees F (177 degrees C) for 10 to 15 minutes, or until they are well dried but not browned. Dissolve the sugar in the water and add the cinnamon and cloves. Bring to a boil; then barely simmer, uncovered, for 20 minutes. Remove the cinnamon and cloves.

Place 4 of the bread slices, overlapping, in a baking dish. Top with ⅓ of the raisins, cheese, nuts, and sour cream. Add the next 2 layers in the same way. Pour the syrup over the top.

Place the dish in the oven and bake at 350 degrees F (177 degrees C) for 20 to 30 minutes, or until it is very hot and just beginning to brown on top. Serves 4.

Arroz con leche

RICE PUDDING

Preheat the oven to 350 degrees F (177 degrees C). Soak the rice in hot water for 10 minutes. Drain and place in a 2-quart (1,800-milliliter or 1 liter + 800 milliliter-) pan with a lid.

Add 2 cups (450 milliliters) of milk to the rice and stir. Bring to a boil, covered, over medium-high heat. As soon as the milk begins to boil, place the covered pan in the oven for 15 minutes, then remove. The milk should be completely absorbed and the rice cooked.

While the rice is in the oven, in another pan heat the remaining cup (225 milliliters) of whole milk, the evaporated milk, sugar, and the cinnamon stick. Allow to barely simmer for 5 minutes. Add the raisins, brandy, and vanilla and simmer for an additional 10 minutes. Add the rice and continue cooking, stirring often, for 5 minutes.

Serve in individual dishes and sprinkle with powdered cinnamon. Serves 4.

- **1 cup (192 grams) long grain rice**
- **3 cups (675 milliliters) whole milk**
- **1 cup (225 milliliters) evaporated milk**
- **½ cup (100 grams) sugar**
- **1 stick cinnamon**
- **½ cup (28 grams) raisins**
- **½ tablespoon (6 milliliters) brandy**
- **1 teaspoon (5 milliliters) vanilla**
- **Powdered cinnamon**

Dulce de frijoles

SWEET BEANS

²/₃ **cup (130 grams) pinto beans**

2 **cups (450 milliliters) milk**

2 **tablespoons (30 grams) butter**

³/₄ **cup (150 grams) sugar**

¹/₂ **teaspoon cinnamon**

2 **egg yolks, beaten**

¹/₄ **cup (29 grams) pecan halves**

This is a very simple, peasant-style dessert from Nuevo León made with leftover beans and other staples.

Cover the beans with water and cook until very soft, drain, and put them in a blender with the milk. Purée the beans and strain them through the finest blade of a food mill.

In a saucepan, melt the butter over medium heat, add the bean mixture, sugar, and half of the cinnamon and simmer until thick, about 25 minutes. Remove the pan from the heat, add the beaten egg yolks, then continue cooking over very low heat until quite thick. Pour the mixture onto a plate, top with the nuts, and sprinkle with the remaining cinnamon. Serve at room temperature. Serves 4.

Nopalitos en almíbar

CANDIED NOPALITOS

This simple confection is my favorite way of preparing nopalitos. *The cactus paddles are transformed into an unexpected delight. Chances are that if you get your* nopalitos *in a market that the spines will have been removed, but be very careful until you are sure. For this dish you must use very young, tender* nopalitos, *or the result will be tough and slimy.*

2 cups (400 grams) sugar
1 cup (225 milliliters) water
4 thin, young cactus paddles with all spines removed

Place the water and sugar in a pot and bring to a boil over medium to medium-high heat.

Meanwhile, make sure spines and imperfections have been removed from the *nopalitos* and cut them into pieces about 1 inch (2.54 centimeters) by 3 inches (7.6 centimeters) or into small shapes with a cookie cutter. Rinse the *nopalitos* under cold water until the mucous-like substance that appears along cut portions ceases to do so.

Add the *nopalitos* to the boiling syrup, turn the heat down until you can just maintain a simmer, and cook for 15 minutes. Using tongs, remove the *nopalitos* to a plate and spoon some syrup over them. Serve as snacks or with coffee and dessert after a meal. Serves 4.

Tamales dulces

SWEET TAMALES

◈◈◈◈◈

1 **pound (450 grams) Masa Harina**
1 **cup (225 milliliters) melted lard**
2 **tablespoons (28 milliliters) melted butter**
1½ **cups (340 grams) strawberry preserves**
Corn husks, soaked for at least 1 hour

This dessert is a treat. Any jam or jelly may be substituted for the strawberry preserves.

Beat together the Masa Harina, lard, butter, and 1 cup (226 grams) of the preserves. Lay a corn husk out flat on a work surface and cover the lower right with *masa*, about ⅛ to ¼ inch (.32 to .64 centimeter) thick.

Spread about ½ tablespoon (7 grams) of the remaining preserves down the center, roll the tamale, and tie the ends with string.

Steam the tamales for 1½ hours or until they no longer stick to the husks when unrolled.

NOTE: If shortening is substituted for lard in this recipe, the results will not be as successful. Serves 4.

Coyotas

APPLE-FILLED PASTRIES

Coyotas are similar to Empanadas *but made in a different shape. They are a specialty of Sonora.*

FILLING

Slice the apples as thinly as possible and then chop them into pieces about 1 inch (2.54 centimeters) square.

Add the lime juice, sugar, and cinnamon and mix well.

DOUGH

As with *Empanadas,* this dough is best made in a food processor. Put the dry ingredients in the bowl and, using a steel blade, whirl a few times. Next, add the shortening, lard, and butter and process until well mixed with the flour to a grainy consistency. Finally, with the motor running add just enough milk (about ¼ to ½ cup [56 to 110 milliliters]) to allow the dough to bind. The texture should be the same as for any pie dough. If you do not have a food processor, proceed as above but cut and mix the shortenings in by hand. Then add the milk and knead for a few minutes.

Allow the dough to chill in the refrigerator for at least ½ hour. Divide the dough into 12 equal pieces and shape them into balls. Roll the balls into circles, as thin as possible. They should be about 5 inches (12.7 centimeters) in diameter. Place enough of the filling to cover 1 of the circles to within 1 inch (2.54 centimeters) of the edge. Next, moisten the edges with water and place another dough circle on top of the covered one to make a sort of sandwich. Fold over and seal the edges. Prick the tops of the *Coyotas* to allow steam to escape and bake at 350 degrees F (177 degrees C) for 25 minutes or until lightly browned. Makes 6.

FILLING
2 **green cooking apples, such as Granny Smith, peeled**
Juice of 1 lime
2 **tablespoons (24 grams) sugar**
½ **teaspoon cinnamon**

DOUGH
2 **cups (280 grams) all-purpose flour**
1 **teaspoon (6.2 grams) salt**
½ **cup (113 grams) shortening**
1 **tablespoon (7.5 grams) lard**
1 **tablespoon (15 grams) butter**
¼–½ **cup (56–110 milliliters) milk**

Empanadas de cajeta

CAJETA TURNOVERS

❖❖❖❖❖

Dough for flour tortillas using 2 cups (280 grams) flour (p. 92)

¾ **cup (230 grams) *cajeta* (to make, see recipe for *Budín de leche o Cajeta o Leche quemada* [p. 253] or *Cajeta rapida* [p. 254]) or buy it in a jar**

½ **cup (50 grams) pecans, minced (optional)**

¾ **cup (180 grams) cream cheese**

Oil for deep-frying

¼ **cup (32 grams) powdered sugar**

This recipe, given to me by Cornelia Muzquiz, is one of the best desserts I have ever had; with a little practice, is easy to make.

Divide the tortilla dough into 12 pieces, roll them into balls, and allow them to rest, covered by a towel, for about 15 minutes. Meanwhile, thoroughly mix together the *cajeta*, pecans (if you are using them), and cream cheese. (This task will be simplified if the ingredients are at room temperature.)

Roll out 1 of the balls of dough as if you were making a tortilla about 7 inches (17.8 centimeters) in diameter, and wet its edges with a little water. Place about 2 tablespoons (28 grams) of the *cajeta* mixture just off center and fold the tortilla over it, pressing the edges together tightly. Fold about ½ inch (1.3 centimeter) of the turnover's rim over and press to thoroughly seal with the tines of a fork. Deep-fry the turnover at 350 degrees F (177 degrees C) until it is golden brown, remove it to drain, and dust it with powdered sugar. Make the remaining turnovers in the same way. Makes 12.

Piedras

MEXICAN "ROCK" COOKIES

Piedras are typical of the type of Mexican baked goods that are eaten as desserts, snacks, or for breakfast.

Preheat your oven to 350 degrees F (177 degrees C). Cream together the butter, sugar, and eggs. Sift together the flours, baking soda, and salt and add this to the butter-sugar-egg mixture. The dough should be just stiff enough to hold its shape. Stir in the pecans.

Oil a cookie sheet and spoon onto it pieces of dough about 2 inches (5.08 centimeters) in diameter. Bake the *Piedras* for 10 minutes, turn the heat down to 300 degrees F (148 degrees C), and bake 5 to 10 minutes more, or until they are done. Makes about 1 dozen.

1 cup (227 grams) butter

1¹⁄₃ cups (293 grams) dark brown sugar

4 eggs, beaten

3¹⁄₂ cups (438 grams) all-purpose flour

¹⁄₂ cup (63 grams) whole wheat flour

1 teaspoon (3.3 grams) baking soda

¹⁄₂ teaspoon salt

1 cup (116 grams) pecans, chopped fine

FILLING

1 **pound (450 grams) lean pork, cut into 1-inch (2.54-centimeter) pieces**
2 **tablespoons (30 grams) lard or cooking oil (28 milliliters)**
¼ **teaspoon salt**
4 **ounces (112 grams) *piloncillo* or dark brown sugar**
1 **cup (225 milliliters) water**
¼ **teaspoon aniseed**
⅛ **teaspoon powdered cloves**
⅛ **teaspoon powdered cinnamon**
2 **ounces (56 grams) raisins**
2 **ounces (56 grams) pecans, finely chopped**

DOUGH

1 **cup (225 milliliters) water**
½ **teaspoon aniseed**
7 **cups (980 grams) all-purpose flour**
1 **tablespoon (18.6 grams) salt**
2 **tablespoons (20 grams) baking powder**
¼ **cup (50 grams) sugar**
1⅓ **cups (300 grams) lard**
1⅓ **cups (300 grams) shortening**
2 **eggs, beaten**

Turcos

TURKS

In northern Mexico the word turcos, *or Turks, is sometimes used to refer to people from the Middle East in general. Certainly the sweet meat filling and general form of this traditional dish from Nuevo León shows definite Middle Eastern roots. Of course the dough, made with lard, and the use of pork and pecans gives the dish a true Mexican character.*

One of the ingredients called for in the filling is piloncillo, *which is raw sugar cooked with a little water and formed into hard cylinders of various sizes (see "Basic Ingredients"). Piloncillo is widely available in supermarkets in the Southwest and can usually be found in Hispanic groceries in other areas. If you cannot find it, substitute dark brown sugar. You will find that a disadvantage of piloncillo is that it is difficult to cut. I have found a hacksaw the best tool for this job.*

The dough recipe calls for one-half lard and one-half shortening. The lard creates a slightly flakier pastry and more authentic flavor than using all shortening, but for health reasons you may wish to forego these advantages. Although not traditional, Turcos are also delicious made with frozen puff pastry dough.

FILLING

Place the pork in a pot and cover with water by 2 inches (5 centimeters). Bring the water to a boil, skimming any scum off the surface, and simmer gently for 45 minutes or until the pork is very tender. Shred the pork by hand, in a *molcajete,* or with a plastic blade in a food processor.

Heat a large skillet over medium heat, add the lard or oil, and cook the meat on one side until it begins to brown. Turn the meat and brown again, then, stirring frequently, continue to cook until the meat is a light golden brown. Sprinkle on the salt.

Meanwhile, combine the *piloncillo* or brown sugar with the water, aniseed, cloves, and cinnamon in a small saucepan. Simmer the mixture until it thickens to the consistency of a light pancake syrup. This will take 20 to 30 minutes, and there should be about ¼ cup (56 milliliters) left in the pan. Add the raisins and pecans and immediately toss the mixture with the pork. The dish can be prepared to this point and refrigerated overnight, but you will need to warm the filling since it will harden and be unmanageable in the cool temperature.

DOUGH AND BAKING

Preheat your oven to 375 degrees F (190 degrees C). Bring the water to a boil, add the aniseed, remove the pan from the heat, and allow it to steep for 15 minutes. Then strain and discard the seeds.

In a large bowl mix the flour, salt, baking powder, and sugar. Cut in the lard and shortening until it is fully incorporated; then add just enough of the aniseed water to make a dough that can be worked.

Divide the dough into separate balls of a size convenient for your work surface and roll each, in turn, out to between ⅛ and ¼ inch (.32 and .64 centimeter) thick. Cut the dough into circles 5 inches (12.7 centimeters) in diameter. Place 2 level tablespoons (28 grams) of the filling on each circle and fold in half the way you would for any turnover. Fold the edges over and press with the tines of a fork to seal.

Place the completed *Turcos* on baking sheets, brush with the beaten egg, and bake in the preheated oven for 20 to 25 minutes or until they are golden brown and cooked through. Makes 16.

Dulce de dátiles

DATE CANDY

½ cup (110 milliliters)
  milk

¼ cup (56 milliliters)
  honey

¼ cup (50 grams) sugar

⅛ teaspoon salt

1 cup (114 grams)
  chopped pecans

½ pound (225 grams)
  chopped, pitted
  dates

½ tablespoon (6
  milliliters) vanilla

2 tablespoons (30
  grams) butter

This is one of the most delicious confections I have ever eaten. Good by itself, it also makes a potentially award-winning filling for pecan pie. In addition, it is simple to prepare!

In a saucepan, mix the milk, honey, sugar, and salt, and bring to a boil; then simmer the mixture for 15 minutes. Add the chopped pecans and dates. Stir the mixture until it is thick. This should take less than 1 minute. Next, stir in the vanilla and butter and spoon the mixture into a greased mold or onto a plate and allow it to cool. To use as a filling for pecan pie, either double or increase the recipe by 50 percent, depending on the size of your pan, and pour the mixture into a prebaked crust. Makes 1 large candy.

Dulces con nueces

MEXICAN SOFT PRALINES

1 cup (216 grams)
  brown sugar

4 tablespoons (60
  grams) butter

1 cup (225 milliliters)
  half-and-half

2 tablespoons (28
  milliliters) corn
  syrup

2 tablespoons (28
  milliliters) dark
  rum

1 cup (114 grams)
  pecans, chopped

This is a candy that is enjoyed in several variations throughout northern Mexico.

Butter a cookie sheet. Place all the ingredients in a small ceramic or stainless steel pan and bring to a simmer over medium heat, stirring frequently to keep the candy from burning. Cook gently until the mixture thickens enough so that a spoonful dropped on the buttered sheet holds together, keeping its shape with the nuts intact, 30 to 40 minutes. Using a large spoon, drop spoon-sized amounts of the candy on the sheet and allow to cool. If the candy does not harden sufficiently, refrigerate it for 1 or 2 hours. Makes 8.

Conserva de ciruelas

PLUM CONSERVE

This simple confection is so good and so easy to make that you wonder why anybody pays a big price for premium jams.

Put the plums in a large saucepan and pour the sugar on top. Place the pan over medium heat and bring to a simmer. Do not stir the mixture until the sugar on top of the plums is nearly melted; then stir it frequently until the mixture is thickened, about 15 to 20 minutes. Remove it from the heat and allow it to cool. Remember that the mixture will continue to gel as it cools. The only tricky part of the recipe is to avoid overcooking it, which will make it very hard when cold. However, even if this happens all is not lost since the hardened conserve can be softened by microwaving it for about 30 seconds. Either keep the conserve in the refrigerator or place it in sterile jars according to the manufacturer's directions. Makes 2 cups (450 grams).

2 cups (285 grams)
   plums, seeded,
   peeled, and chopped
2 cups (400 grams)
   sugar

Appendixes

Appendix A

Entertaining with Northern Mexican Cuisine

Because of its simplicity, northern Mexican cooking lends itself marvelously to entertaining. The name of the most typical meal for a group, *carne asada,* denotes not only broiled beef but a picnic or party at which broiled meat is served. A meal I had recently at the Jardines de Xochimilco restaurant in Hermosillo exemplifies the fare for such occasions. The first course consisted of a plate of *quesadillas* and small *chimichangas.* Next there was a large salad with lettuce, tomatoes, and peeled green chile strips in a vinaigrette dressing. The main course was a plate that must have contained a kilo of mesquite-broiled tenderloin strips and another of beef ribs. Dessert was 4 *Coyotas.* (This is their standard dinner for 2, but it would adequately serve up to 6 diners here.)

You may make various combinations for several festive *carne asada* dinner parties by choosing from the following items.

APPETIZERS

 Cacahuates con chile (p. 57)

 Verduras en escabeche (p. 62)

 Roasted Pumpkin Seeds (p. 17)

 Tostadas with Salsas (two sauces or more) (p. 53)

 Pan de maíz (p. 59)

 Chicharrones (p. 56)

 Nachos (p. 54)

FIRST COURSE

> *Quesadillas* (p. 229)
>
> *Empanadas* (p. 234)
>
> *Taquitos de harina* (p. 197)

ENTRÉE

> *Carne asada* (p. 117)
>
> *Fajitas* (p. 120)
>
> *Costillas de res* (p. 127)
>
> *Cordero al pastor* (p. 143)
>
> *Costillas de puerco* (p. 151)

SIDE DISHES

> *Frijoles de olla* (p. 106), *Frijoles a la charra* (p. 106), *or*
>> *Frijoles borrachos* (p. 107)
>
> *Guacamole* (p. 83)
>
> *Pico de gallo* (p. 49)
>
> *Tortillas (flour and/or corn)* (pp. 92, 95)
>
> *Charbroiled Green Onions*

DESSERT

> *Any desserts in the chapter "Desserts & Sweets"*

This is an excellent menu for entertaining, with the cooked dishes set on platters in the middle of the table for guests to serve themselves according to individual preference. Prepare several sauces to be used with *Tostadas* as an appetizer, and place them on the dining table with the Guacamole, *Pico de gallo,* and tortillas. To keep the tortillas warm, use covered, plastic tortilla warmers or wrap them in towels and serve them in baskets. If necessary, tortillas may be heated at the last minute, in the warmer or wrapped in a towel in the microwave oven. Avoid overheating, which makes them tough and rubbery. Serve the beans in individual bowls.

Fajitas make a good scaled-down version of the *Carne asada* dinner. Bring them to the table sizzling in lime juice for a dramatic presentation. Serve everything else as for *Carne asada*, using sliced *Fajitas* as the only meat. Your guests may prepare their own tacos by placing the meat in tortillas and topping it with Guacamole, *Pico de gallo*, and sauces.

Another good dish for entertaining is enchiladas. They can be prepared ahead of time, up to the point where the sauce, cheese, and other toppings are added, then placed in the oven for 10 minutes. Since most ovens will not accommodate more than 4 dinner plates, cook the enchiladas on platters or baking sheets and then transfer them to individual plates, adding servings of Mexican Rice (pp. 101, 102) and Refried Beans (p. 107). Garnish the plates with shredded lettuce or cabbage tossed in a small amount of vinaigrette dressing, and stand a *tostada* upright in each serving of beans. Some *queso añejo* or feta cheese can be crumbled over the heated beans. To make an easy combination plate, add a steamed tamale. Guacamole served in fried *tostada* shells is a perfect prelude to enchiladas. Always provide heated tortillas and a hot sauce for making tacos with the rice, beans, and garnish.

If you want to make a big hit with guests, serve a Steak *Tampiqueña* (p. 126). But be warned that, even if you are only serving 4, some experience or an extra pair of hands is necessary to make everything come together at the same time.

Fish Steamed in Foil (p. 188) makes a tantalizing party dish that requires very little last-minute preparation. Place the fish on a platter in the middle of the table with bowls of Guacamole, Mexican Rice, *Pico de gallo*, hot sauce, *Bolillos* (p. 96), butter, and a plate of limes. The steam rises from the fish when it is unwrapped at the table for a mouthwatering presentation. Guests then help themselves to the fish, using serving forks and spoons. Fish soup makes a perfect first course for this meal.

Carnitas (p. 145) is another recipe that lends itself to entertaining large groups. For a big party you can rent (or buy if you intend to do it often) a huge iron pot or cauldron in which to cook the *Carnitas*. For small groups or large, begin with Nachos (p. 54) and then serve the *Carnitas* with flour and corn tortillas, several different sauces, sliced onion, and Guacamole (p. 83). Enchiladas are an excellent accompaniment to *Carnitas.* Place them to the side of the enchiladas in some of the sauce after the latter have been heated.

For a really elegant easy-to-prepare-ahead meal, the recipe for Stuffed Chiles with Green Rice (p. 239), served with soup and Flan (p. 252), is hard to beat.

Appendix B

Nutrition &
Northern Mexican Cuisine

There is increasing and authoritative evidence that what we eat has a great impact on our health. The medical profession and professional nutritionists are urging us to reduce consumption of foods high in fat, salt, sugar, and cholesterol, and recommending that we increase our intake of foods high in natural fiber and carbohydrates.

It will be obvious to the reader that some of the foods and recipes in this book are high in fat and cholesterol. T-bone steaks, rib eyes, and beef ribs certainly are excluded from many diet plans. However, if such foods are used only occasionally, and in moderate portions, they should pose no problem to those whose physicians have not suggested severe dietary restrictions.

With most of the dishes included here, this question will not arise. Also, by making some simple substitutions, even those on strict diets can enjoy northern Mexican cooking without compromising the essence of the cuisine. Some of the tips and information that follow should be helpful in this regard.

Corn tortillas made from ground corn and water are an ideal health food, high in fiber and carbohydrates. For flour tortillas, a cholesterol-free shortening may be substituted for lard and butter and the total amount of fat in the recipe cut from 4 tablespoons to 1 (15 grams), reducing it to only ¼ teaspoon in 1 tortilla.

You will notice that many dishes are served with both Mexican Rice (pp. 101, 102) and beans. Experts say that combining rice and beans creates a combination of amino acids that provides for all our protein needs. Mexican Rice contains less than 2 teaspoons (7 milliliters) of polyunsaturated oil per serving. Although it takes longer to cook and requires more water than white rice, brown rice makes a tasty and nutritious substitution in this recipe. Simmer the brown rice in a large quantity of water for 10 minutes, drain it, and then proceed with the recipe, as given, adding more water as needed. The quantity of water required may vary according to the type of brown rice you are using, but you will soon discover how much you need.

Frijoles de olla (p. 106) can be made without bacon or salt pork, and Refried Beans (p. 107) can be very tasty when prepared without frying. Put the cooked *Frijoles de olla* in a food processor, add 1 tablespoon (15 milliliters) of oil in which 2 cloves of minced garlic have been gently cooked but not browned, and process.

Perhaps the most typical of all northern dishes, *Carne asada* (p. 117), is made with tenderloin, which, when trimmed of all fat, has a much lower fat content than most meats. Steak with *Ranchero* Sauce (p. 123) also can be made with tenderloin and beef stew with a diet-lean stew meat.

Many of the *antojitos* are made with cheese, which is high in both fat and cholesterol. To minimize fat and cholesterol, substitute mozzarella, which is lower in fat, for cheddar and Monterey Jack, use half the quantity called for in the recipe, or use some of the new low-fat cheese.

Tacos made with either soft corn tortillas or the lard-free flour tortillas, stuffed with shredded chicken or turkey and topped with any of the sauces, should present no problem to those not on a stringent diet. *Tacos de pollo al carbón* (p. 195) is an excellent choice for those who do not want to lose the real flavor of northern Mexican cooking while maintaining a low-fat diet. *Entomatadas* (p. 218) are a fine enchilada option for the health conscious. Fill burritos with the low-fat version of Refried Beans (p. 107), lettuce, *Pico de gallo* (p. 49), and a hot sauce and add 1 or 2 teaspoons (2.56 or 5.13 grams) of feta cheese for an authentic and healthful "diet" dish.

INDEX

A